THE MAGNIFICENT
NAHANNI

THE MAGNIFICENT
NAHANNI

The Struggle to Protect a Wild Place

GORDON NELSON

With the research and editorial assistance of
SHIRLEY NELSON

foreword by **HARVEY LOCKE**

 University of Regina Press

Printed and bound in Canada at Marquis. The text of this book is printed on 100% post-consumer recycled paper with earth-friendly vegetable-based inks.

COVER AND TEXT DESIGN: Duncan Campbell, University of Regina Press
COPY EDITOR: Kirsten Craven
PROOFREADER: Kristine Douaud
INDEXER: Sergey Lobachev, Brookfield Indexing Services
COVER ART: Cirque of the Unclimbables Mt. Harrison. Photographer Fritz Mueller. *Courtesy of Parks Canada.*

All photographs courtesy of the author.

Library and Archives Canada Cataloguing in Publication

Nelson, J. G. (James Gordon), 1932-, author
    The magnificent Nahanni : the struggle to protect a wild place / Gordon Nelson ; with the research and editorial assistance of Shirley Nelson ; foreword by Harvey Locke.

Includes bibliographical references and index.
Issued in print and electronic formats.
ISBN 978-0-88977-460-5 (softcover).—ISBN 978-0-88977-464-3 (PDF).—
ISBN 978-0-88977-465-0 (HTML)

1. Nahanni National Park Reserve (N.W.T.)—History. 2. National parks and reserves—Northwest Territories—History. 3. Natural areas—Northwest Territories—History. I. Title.

FC4163.N34N44 2017   333.7809719'3   C2016-907588-5   C2016-907589-3w

10 9 8 7 6 5 4 3 2 1

University of Regina Press, University of Regina
Regina, Saskatchewan, Canada, S4S 0A2
TEL: (306) 585-4758 FAX: (306) 585-4699
WEB: www.uofrpress.ca
U OF R PRESS EMAIL: uofrpress@uregina.ca

We acknowledge the support of the Canada Council for the Arts for our publishing program. We acknowledge the financial support of the Government of Canada. / Nous reconnaissons l'appui financier du gouvernement du Canada. This publication was made possible through Creative Saskatchewan's Creative Industries Production Grant Program.

 Canada Council Conseil des Arts
for the Arts du Canada   Canada   creative
SASKATCHEWAN

Dedicated to:
Dehcho First Nations,
Parks Canada,
The Canadian Parks and Wilderness Society,
The Canadian Wildlife Service,
Nahanni River Adventures,
The Royal Canadian Geographical Society,
The Wildlife Conservation Society, and
The leaders in research: George Scotter, Derek Ford, and John Weaver

CONTENTS

ILLUSTRATIONS

Tables

Foreword

The Nahanni is a place touched by magic. The river enchants as it meanders past hot springs, through deep canyons, plunges over an enormous waterfall, and braids out into boreal forest. The landscape includes the stunning granite spires of the Cirque of the Unclimbables, vast karst features, and the extraordinary Ram Plateau. There are only a few places with such power on Earth. The Nahanni's magic touched me so deeply that I willingly devoted a good part of ten years to its protection. And I was far from alone.

In the first decade of this century, Canadians packed auditoriums in Whitehorse, Halifax, Victoria, and many cities in between to hear about the glories and stories of the Nahanni. By the thousands they responded to the urgings of a collaboration of the Dehcho First Nations and the Canadian Parks and Wilderness Society (CPAWS) to join the chorus of musicians, scientists, public figures, canoe guides, businesses, and conservationists calling for its protection. It became so important to so many varied people that Parks Canada was able to successfully drive a park expansion through the labyrinth of mining interests inside government almost unscathed.

The social movement we generated achieved that rarest of things: political consensus. The 2009 legislation to expand the park sped through a contentious minority Parliament by all-party agreement and I was told it was the fastest bill any senator could remember passing through the Senate. The Governor General rushed to the Senate floor to give it royal assent. The sixfold expansion of the park meant Canadians had accomplished something great together while honouring the Dehcho First Peoples' deep connection to the land. For twenty-first-century conservationists, it represented a scenic national park expanded to a scale that matters to large mammals and the large landscape conservation initiatives of Yellowstone to Yukon and the Canadian Boreal Forest.

The massive expansion of Nahanni National Park Reserve became an international conservation cause célèbre. Feted at WILD 9, the Ninth World Wilderness Congress, in Mérida, Mexico, the host country even issued a postage stamp to celebrate it. The excitement also led to partial protection of the river's headwaters in a new Nááts'ihch'oh National Park Reserve created with the support of the Sahtu Dene in 2014. These two parks of the Nahanni together constitute one of the world's largest national park complexes. However, as great as they are, they suffer from problematic boundary anomalies. It remains for an enlightened government to do the obvious and remove the mining threats to the Nahanni.

Just as the Nahanni is an exceptional place, this is no ordinary book. It contains reflections on this remarkable national park landscape by one of the keenest students of parks and protected areas this country has ever produced. For fifty years Gordon Nelson has been thinking about and influencing how the rest of us see national parks in Canada. He brings his unique perspective to the Nahanni and places the conservation story in the context of evolving ideas about conservation. It will be a valuable reference for years to come.

I am honoured to have been asked to provide my photographs and this foreword to support Dr. Nelson's fine consideration of the magnificent Nahanni. I am glad he was touched by its magic, too.

—Harvey Locke, co-founder of the Yellowstone Yukon Conservation Initiative and Nature Needs Half Movement, and past president of the Canadian Parks and Wilderness Society
Banff National Park, July 2016

Acknowledgements

This book grows from decades of personal observations on the development of Nahanni National Park Reserve. I was president of the National and Provincial Parks Association of Canada at the time the federal government made the original proposal in the early 1970s. The book is highly dependent on interviews with Alison Woodley, Canadian Parks and Wilderness Society; David Murray, Park Establishment Branch, Parks Canada; Stephen Woodley, formerly chief ecosystem scientist, Parks Canada, and former senior advisor, protected areas and climate change for the International Union for the Conservation of Nature; Herb Norwegian, grand chief of the Dehcho First Nations; Chuck Blyth, retired superintendent of the Nahanni National Park Reserve;[1] and Neil Hartling, president of Nahanni River Adventures.

These people spent hours in conversation with me and often supplied numerous references. I am grateful to them, as well as Derek Ford and George Scotter, for reviewing earlier drafts of this book, making many useful suggestions based on years of research in the valley, and helping with photographs. Ford and Scotter arranged for me to see early and difficult-to-obtain personal and government reports on the Nahanni. George Scotter sent me a copy of E.G. Oldham's important 1948 letter on Nahanni National Park. I also owe thanks to Warren Wulff, librarian, Environment Canada, in Saskatoon, for making it possible to review the now rare 1971 report by Scotter and his colleagues on *Ecology of the South Nahanni and Flat River Areas.* Librarians at the Hudson's Bay Archives in Winnipeg and the National Archives in Ottawa were also of great assistance.

Thanks to Tom Andrews, archaeologist, Prince of Wales Northern Heritage Centre, in Yellowknife, for our discussions and a copy of the Arctic special issue on snow-patch work in the upper Keele River area. I am very grateful to the staff at the University of Waterloo Library for their continuing support, especially Laurie Strome, circulation, as well as Joan Mitchell and Cindy Preece at the Wilfrid Laurier Archives.

I am profoundly in debt to Neil Hartling of Nahanni River Adventures for a great river trip. In August 2013, I travelled with my energetic and supportive friend, Bill Graham, to the Nahanni for a raft trip downriver with Nahanni River Adventures. En route, in Yellowknife and Fort Simpson, we had some revealing discussions. I thank the participants, including Erica Janes, Kevin O'Reilly, Bertha Norwegian, and David Britton. I also had the opportunity to learn from participants on the raft trip as well as the staff. I thank all my raft trip companions, including Kristin Morch, Al Pace, Bob Kelly, Chris and Noah Henderson, Andrea and Isaac Prazmowske, and, most particularly, Bill Graham, all from Ontario; Bob Warner and Sean Hommersen from British Columbia; and John Hommersen from Alberta. The staff was outstanding: Jamie VanDrunen of British Columbia, and Dylan Bajer and Mitch McCambly of Alberta, as well as enthusiastic Natalie Haltrich, trip planner, and Neil Hartling, owner and master guide of Nahanni River Adventures, both of Whitehorse, Yukon. I spent much of the trip talking with Neil. He also provided valuable advice on early drafts of this book, assisted with contacts and observations from his long Nahanni experience, and helped with photographs. I owe thanks to Chuck Blyth, former Nahanni National Park Reserve superintendent, and Herb Norwegian, grand chief of the Dehcho First Nations, for the valuable conversations we had when I was preparing the manuscript. Kevin O'Reilly and Gordon Hamre carefully reviewed and commented on earlier versions of the manuscript, offering advice from their long experience in parks and environmental issues in the Northwest Territories. Kevin O'Reilly offered an additional helpful review of a late version of the manuscript. Alison Woodley also made a special contribution by reviewing both an early and a late version of the manuscript. Ann Baggio provided information on CPAWS work in northern Ontario and Manitoba. Barry Levely did his usual fine job on the figures.

Many people with deep experience of the Nahanni helped me in trying to secure suitable photos for this book. This was not easy, with the University of Regina Press having high standards for photos in line with current digital photography. Older historic photos taken in black and white or as slides in the 1970s, 1980s, and 1990s had difficulty meeting these standards. George Scotter, in particular, located many black-and-white and slide photos, only some of which could be used, including some by his colleague, Norman Simmons. George was helpful in many other ways. I am greatly in debt to him. Others were very helpful in finding more recent photos for consideration. Some of these are included in *The Magnificent Nahanni*. I owe special thanks to Alison Woodley, Wendy Francis, Derek Ford, and Neil Hartling. John Weaver also offered photos and was very helpful at a later stage, reading and suggesting improvements to Chapter 3. Finally, I am deeply grateful to Harvey Locke for offering photos, being kind and experienced enough to write a foreword quickly just before the manuscript was submitted to the press, and finally for his ideas, commitment, organization, and sustained leadership in expanding the Nahanni National Park Reserve in 2009 and for his ongoing efforts to conserve wild places in Canada, the United States, and the world.

I learned much from research and conservation colleagues over the years, including the late Jim Cragg, Steve Herrero, the late Larry Cordes, John and Mary Theberge, Harvey Buckmaster, Chad Day, Ellsworth LeDrew, and the late Len Gertler, as well, in the mid-1970s, as the people at the Inuit Tapirisat of Canada, where my appreciation of Indigenous culture was enriched by service as a renewable resources consultant. I have had many years of lengthy and rewarding contacts with Parks Canada and am especially grateful to Al Davidson and Stephen Woodley. I have also benefitted greatly from my membership on the Carolinian Canada Coalition, the Bruce Peninsula National Park Advisory Committee, and the Bruce Peninsula Sources of Knowledge Forum. I owe much to Canadian Parks and Wilderness Society colleagues such as the late Gavin Henderson, John Marsh, Bob Peart, Phil Deardon, and Mary Granskou. We are all in debt to Harvey Locke, long-time president and vice-president conservation, as well as Alison Woodley, now national director, parks program, and Eric Hebert-Daly, currently executive director. My understanding of provincial parks and the human dimensions of park planning has also been enriched by long service on the Ontario Parks Board of Directors.

I also owe much to Roger Byrne, Bob Scace, John Marsh, Jack Glenn, Jim Masyk, Sabina Jessen, Scott Slocombe, Amer Rghei, the late Terry Fenge, Judy Harris, Caron Olive, Lucy Sportza, Patrick Lawrence, Ken Van Osch, Kerrie and Steve Wilcox, Chris Lemieux, Heather Black, and other students and friends too numerous to mention, but each has my thanks. Of fundamental importance over the years has been the financial, logistical, and other support by the University of Waterloo, notably the Faculty of Environment. My debt to the anonymous reviewers of the manuscript for the University of Regina Press is very considerable as their observations made for substantial improvements in the book. I owe thanks to the individuals and organizations giving me permission to use their maps. And, as always, I owe enormous thanks to Shirley Nelson for her research, editorial and typing skills, memory, and strong overall support. Stacy Cooper, of Cooper Admin, was very helpful in working with the citations and references in completing the book. My sons, Jim and David, were supportive, as was my daughter, Kathryn, who referred me to newly published work on Fenley Hunter's Nahanni journals. The style and general quality of this book owe much to the guidance, hard work, and dedication of my editors, Karen Clark and Donna Grant, and copy editor Kirsten Craven; the technical and artistic skills of Duncan Campbell; the commitment to marketing of Morgan Tunzelmann; and the encouragement of U of R Press director and publisher Bruce Walsh. I am very grateful to all of them. The ultimate responsibility for this work remains with me.

Introduction

The *Magnificent Nahanni* is written for researchers, planners, conservationists, teachers, students, ecotourists, and citizens generally concerned about great wild environments and the North. The book focuses on the natural wonders of the Nahanni River and the long, more than forty-year struggle to protect it from pollution, habitat disturbance, and wildlife losses arising from mining or other development. Unlike the Yukon, Mackenzie, and other northern rivers, the Nahanni is not remarkable for its size. It begins in the mountains of the Northwest Territories near the Yukon border and flows about five hundred kilometres to the small Indigenous village of Nahanni Butte. Here it joins the Liard River, which runs on for about 150 kilometres, to join the mighty Arctic-bound Mackenzie River at the old fur trade settlement of Fort Simpson.

What is unique and remarkable about the Nahanni is the richness and diversity of its caribou, wolf, grizzly, Dall's sheep, and other wildlife; its old-growth forests; upland tundra; seemingly endless surrounding mountains; deep long canyons; swift waters; towering Virginia Falls; and majestic scenery. It was these natural wonders that motivated the federal national park agency, scientists, and nongovernment conservation organizations to begin publicly planning for a national park in the early 1970s. The initial result was the creation of a small national park reserve around the great canyons and Virginia Falls in 1976. It was not until 2009, with the vital co-operation of the Indigenous people, that the long struggle resulted in approximately thirty-five thousand square kilometres being protected in a watershed-scale national park reserve. But two private enclaves within its boundaries remain open to mining and other development. And the struggle continues.

The intriguing story of the natural and human history of the Nahanni, and its escape from the effects of the fur trade, the late nineteenth-century Yukon Gold Rush, prospecting, sports hunting, and other European, American, and Canadian activities remains untold, as does the tale of how the current national park reserve came to be. Like other past conservation struggles in Canada, the ideas, policies, and practices that eventually led to the establishment and expansion of the Nahanni National Park Reserve are at risk of being forgotten. We will be the poorer for this, destined to begin the process anew somewhere else. This risk was prominent in my mind when I decided it would be valuable to prepare this conservation history of the Nahanni.

I have built the book on more than fifty years of research, planning, and personal and professional involvement in national parks and conservation in Canada and other parts of the world. This lengthy experience has made me aware of many important changes in thinking, policy, and practice that are relevant to the story of *The Magnificent Nahanni*.

I first became involved with the river in the early 1970s, when the federal government first announced the proposal for a national park. I have followed the story ever since, reading widely on the natural and human history of the Nahanni region, as well as other parts of the North. My research for this book has included archival and documentary studies, interviews and general discussion with knowledgeable people, and extensive travel in the North, including a monumental raft trip down the Nahanni in August 2013.

The Magnificent Nahanni is organized into nine chapters. Chapter 1 extols the natural wonders of the Nahanni, the cause of so much sustained interest in its protection as a national park. The descriptions are built on my impressions from the August 2013 raft trip and more detailed observations made by two 1920s travellers and adventurers: the Englishman, Raymond Patterson, and the American, Fenley Hunter. Patterson's observations became widely known through his writings, particularly his book, *The Dangerous River*, published in 1954. The writings were interpreted by government officials, nongovernment conservation organizations, and many citizens as describing a valley that was pristine, essentially undisturbed by past or present human activity—the vision of ideal wilderness that came to Canada from the United States.

Chapter 2 analyzes the ideas, policies, and practices behind the creation of the first small Nahanni National Park Reserve in 1976. A larger park was wanted, especially by nongovernment conservation organizations, but was not achieved mainly because of opposition from mining interests and the Indigenous people of the area. The national park agency and conservation organizations generally were committed to the guiding concept of pristine or ideal wilderness, as well as the federal policy requiring that all the lands and waters in a national park be publicly owned or Crown land. These conditions led to the Indigenous opposition to a larger national park, since they meant that the people would lose the opportunity to pursue hunting and traditional activities within its boundaries. The Crown ownership question was put in abeyance by labelling the protected area as a national park reserve, the ownership decision postponed until there was agreement on a comprehensive land claim settlement. The overall result was the small initial reserve shaped in a narrow belt around the lower river valley and Virginia Falls.

Chapter 3 describes the growing commitment to biological, landform, and other research begun in planning for the initial 1976 reserve. The chapter also describes the introduction of landscape ecology, conservation biology, and other innovative concepts in ecological theory, as well as new and more effective research and mapping methods, including remote sensing and geographical information systems (GIS). These theoretical and methodological advances were applied to the Nahanni and demonstrated that the initial reserve was too small to provide for the food and survival needs of the wide-ranging nomadic caribou, wolf, grizzly, and other animals within it, supporting reserve expansion to near watershed scale in 2009. This expansion was also built on the introduction of the science-based concept of ecological integrity, which involved thinking about and managing the Nahanni as a diverse, dynamic, self-generating ecosystem rather than an essentially static wilderness. The ecological integrity concept was more amenable to Indigenous hunting, fishing, and other long-time traditional uses and ultimately contributed to agreement by conservationists to accept these activities as part of the historic and current Nahanni ecosystem.

Another important change was the shift from relatively exclusive top-down corporate planning by the federal government to a more inclusive, interactive, and co-operative approach with and among nongovernment conservation organizations and Indigenous people. This also facilitated acceptance of the idea of "inhabited wilderness" and the negotiations and compromises that led to the expansion of the reserve in 2009.

Chapter 4 addresses the Parks Canada claim that the ecological integrity or dynamic state of the Nahanni ecosystem is similar today as in the past. This means that while forests, wildlife, and landscape conditions can change through space and time—due to fires, floods, earthquakes, and other processes—they are still the product of the same underlying self-generating ecosystem. This contention seems reasonable in scientific terms. However, it is not supported by historical analysis of any landscape changes. I thus undertook a study to determine if historical evidence supported the claim.

This investigation was organized in terms of a series of historical eras, characterized by distinct sets of economic, technical, and ideological features and processes considered likely to produce different effects on the Nahanni ecosystem. Wildlife and natural observations recorded in the journals and other writings of early traders and travellers are drawn on to determine what changes occurred in each era. It begins with a focus on the early fur trade era from circa 1800 to 1840. Knowledge of wildlife and the state of the system at that time rests largely on the observations of John McLeod, a Hudson's Bay Company (HBC) trader, who appears to be the first person of European origin to travel into and describe forests, upland tundra, caribou, beaver, and other wildlife in the lower valley of the Nahanni, principally near the Jackfish River.

Chapter 5 then discusses the fur trade and its effects in the middle and later years of the eighteenth century when the previously isolated Mackenzie–Liard River region was opened up by free traders arriving on recently introduced steamboats from the Pacific coast. They set up shop at Hudson's Bay posts such as Fort Simpson, attracting Indigenous peoples to trade, taking a rising toll on marten, fox, and other fur bearers, as well as moose, caribou, and game animals. One of the trade items was alcohol, and it unfortunately brought more Indigenous peoples in from outlying areas and created dislocations and social disturbances additional to the distress previously caused by smallpox and other new Old World diseases introduced early on by traders from Montreal. I did not have access to any traveller's accounts of the state of the ecosystem at this time, although it may well be that further research in the post records at Fort Simpson or Fort Liard could fill this gap. Indigenous oral history does indicate that the ecosystem remained remote, diverse, wild, and apparently fundamentally unchanged.

Chapter 6 describes the prospecting, mining, and mixed economy that developed after the great Yukon Gold Rush of 1896–1899. The hunt for the precious metal spread into the Nahanni, although apparently only to a limited extent. The 1930s wildlife and natural observations of the adventurers Raymond Patterson and Fenley Hunter reveal a system still rich in wolf and other predators, as well as caribou and other wildlife. Dick Turner, a long-time resident of the nearby Liard Valley, wrote of numerous moose, caribou, Dall's sheep, and other game he saw in the 1930s while searching for gold along the Flat, the big west bank tributary of the Nahanni. E.G. Oldham, a wildlife officer, inspected the Nahanni in 1948 and reported it was rich in game, devoid of fires, essentially "unspoiled," and worthy of study as a possible Nahanni national park.

In contrast, Raymond Patterson despaired of heavy wildlife losses, notably Dall's sheep, in the country around the First Canyon and Tlogotsho Plateau during his return to the lower valley in 1951. The observations of other long-time prospectors, trappers, and travellers such as the Klondiker, Poole Field, and the American "mountain man," Albert Faille, are lost in time, although further research may turn up records of what they saw.

Chapter 7 briefly summarizes the findings in Chapters 4, 5, and 6. It concludes that the Nahanni did essentially retain its natural diversity, resilience, and high ecological integrity up to the beginning of national park conservation efforts in the 1970s, although reports by Patterson, sports hunters, and government officials indicate declines, notably of Dall's sheep in the lower valley. The establishment of the first phase of the Nahanni National Park Reserve in 1976 and its expansion in 2009 were timely in limiting prospecting, mining, sports hunting, and other economic activities, and stemming wildlife losses. The rest of Chapter 7 is a search for reasons why the Nahanni escaped the fur trade, mining, and other activities that caused extensive wildlife and ecosystem changes in surrounding lands and waters. The answer seems to lie in difficult access, remoteness, frequently ineffective company or government conservation efforts, and particularly strong stewardship of wildlife and habitat for centuries by Indigenous people. The anthropologists Hugh Brody and Richard Nelson, who lived with Indigenous people for months in the 1970s, describe these stewardship measures in detail. The hunting regulations posted by the Dene people of Nahanni Butte after the expansion of the reserve are vivid testimony to the strength of their stewardship today.

Chapter 8 describes the major challenges and opportunities now facing the Nahanni National Park Reserve. These include mining, notably threats from the Prairie Creek development in a private enclave within the boundaries of the reserve. Other challenges or opportunities include the need to adjust boundaries in the upper Nahanni Valley if wildlife is to be well protected against mining and the threats it poses to wild animals, habitat, and water quality. More archaeological work is generally needed to promote greater understanding of the early activities and effects of Indigenous people in the Nahanni in the centuries before the arrival of Europeans. Government commitments to the Dehcho First Nations for offering ancestral lands and waters to the expansion of the reserve remain to be fulfilled, along with opportunities to work with them in securing greater benefits and a richer yet still diverse and traditional way of life through the Nahanni National Park Reserve.

Chapter 9 concludes the study and does so by drawing analogies between what has been done in the Nahanni and other places in Canada, the United States, and other parts of the world. The stress is on the idea of inhabited wilderness and the significance of co-operation in research, planning, and management of national parks and protected areas by government, conservation nongovernmental organizations (NGOs), and Indigenous people. Examples are given from the historic experience of conservation leaders in the United States, such as the legendary Aldo Leopold. Reference is also made to recent relevant experience along the U.S.–Mexico border, as well as elsewhere on the international scene. In the end, considerable emphasis is placed on the opportunities national parks offer to provide economic, environmental, and lifestyle choices for Indigenous people. Opportunities are available for Indigenous people to maintain an essentially traditional lifestyle while participating in tourism, research, and other national park activities in co-operation with responsible government officials, NGOs, and citizens generally. The recent report of the Truth and Reconciliation Commission of Canada underlines the need to rectify colonial injustices of the past. National parks and other protected areas offer relatively direct ways of doing so.

The book then ends with "A Note on Sources" that explains the cross-disciplinary fields of study and schools of thought that were drawn upon in preparing this book, as these may interest students, researchers, and citizens concerned about its origins.

A set of plates can be found between pages 128 and 129. These photographs are organized to show major features of the Nahanni Valley from the Ragged Range in the upper watershed through towering Virginia Falls, the long, deep canyons of the lower river and the braided channels, or Splits, leading to the Liard, the major west bank tributary of the mighty Mackenzie River. Readers may find it helpful to look over these photographs before reading the text.

A Note on Terminology

Long-time residents of the land have been called "Indians," "Savages," "Red Men," and other terms that are historically derived and often less than accurate. "Aboriginals" or "First Nations" are terms used frequently now, often for legal or political reasons. "Native" is also widely used. "Indigenous" is a current favoured appellation. It is generally used in this book, except where another name may be more appropriate in suggesting historic views or attitudes applicable at the time under consideration.

Old World newcomers also bear various names, such as English, Scottish, French, white man, Canadian, and American. Use of such specific names is generally neither possible nor especially desirable in this book. People intermingled; for example, Canadian can embrace people of French, Quebec, Metis, or American background. I have been guided in my usage by simplicity and circumstances, tending to describe people according to their enterprise or origin—for instance, Montreal or Hudson's Bay Company traders. I write in a time of intense interest in identity, but such an approach is not necessary to this book. Here the focus is on interactions of Old World and Indigenous North American peoples and how their markedly different cultural, social, economic, technical, and natural values and characteristics influenced land use, landscape, and environmental changes, and the conservation of the great Nahanni wildlands.

Parks Canada is now the name of the federal agency for Canadian national and historic parks. Its name changed often in the period under study. Constant shifts in terminology in the text are avoided by using general terms, such as national park service. A similar path is followed with other agency and government names. Measurement is given in kilometres or miles, depending on the circumstances, treating one metre as about three feet and a kilometre as about 0.62 miles.

Part I

THE WONDERS OF THE NAHANNI:

Planning for a National Park Reserve

Chapter 1

Envisioning the Magnificent Nahanni

Despite centuries of pressure from trapping, prospecting, mining, big game hunting, and other exploitive activities, the magnificent Nahanni River still runs wild and free in Canada's Far North. More correctly known as the South Nahanni, the river is the stuff of legend and awe-inspiring reality. River rafters see and feel the ghosts of the past: rare cabins left by long-gone prospectors and trappers, with Indigenous people still travelling the lower river. Yet the wild predominates: the river's rush; colourful flowers, butterflies, and birds; caribou and wolf; vast green and yellow spruce, pine, and aspen forests; upland prairie and tundra; waterfalls, cliffs, clefts, canyons, caves, and uneven limestone karst terrain. These unique natural wonders are now protected in the Nahanni National Park Reserve. After decades of struggle, they have eluded "the paw of the ape," imagery evoked by Raymond Patterson, the adventurous traveller who trapped and prospected in the lower valley in the 1920s.[1]

The Nahanni stands out among northern rivers, not because of its size but because of its unique grandeur and rich natural diversity. It begins in the Mackenzie Mountains in Canada's Northwest Territories (Figure 1.1) and flows southeast for about five hundred kilometres before emptying into the Liard River near its junction with the great

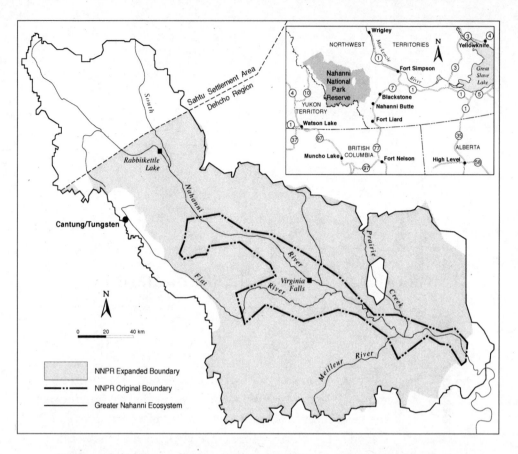

Figure 1.1. Initial Phase of Nahanni National Park Reserve, General Borders of 2009 Expansion and Greater Park Ecosystem Boundaries. Adapted from Weaver (2006).

Arctic-bound Mackenzie. Along its course, the Nahanni passes from steep mountain slopes into a wide gently inclined basin fringed on the south side by the jagged towering glaciated peaks of the Ragged Range. It plunges over the precipitous 130-metre-high Virginia Falls and races through four great canyons before running into a maze of branching channels—the Splits—flowing to the Liard near the small Indigenous village of Nahanni Butte.[2]

Along the way, the Nahanni passes extensive forests, wetlands, and high alpine tundra housing caribou, moose, black and grizzly bears, Dall's sheep, lynx, wolf, and many other animals and plants in a wild ecosystem increasingly rare in much of the North. These natural wonders have been described and briefly explained in books and guides such as Neil Hartling's *Nahanni: River of Gold . . . River of*

Dreams (1998), Peter Jowett's *Nahanni: The River Guide* (1998), Pat and Rosemarie Keough's vividly illustrated *The Nahanni Portfolio* (1988), Richard Davis's *Nahanni Journals: R.M. Patterson's 1927–1929 Journals* (2008), and Chuck Blyth's *Nahanni Nah? ą Dehé: A Selection of Photographic Images of the South Nahanni Watershed (2007–2010)* (2011).[3] *The Magnificent Nahanni* expands on these publications by giving more recent explanations of its outstanding landforms, wildlife, scenery, and human activities. But this book is unique in its focus on the long struggle to conserve the river and its watershed in a national park reserve.

I first became interested in the Nahanni in the early 1970s when the long struggle to protect the river really got underway. But I was not able to actually visit the Nahanni until August 2013, when my good friend, Bill Graham, and I took a raft trip down the river. We flew from Toronto to the long-time mining centre of Yellowknife, staying for two days talking to experienced northerners. We went on to Fort Simpson, the old fur trade settlement at the junction of the Mackenzie and its west branch tributary, the Liard. Just 150 kilometres upstream, the Nahanni enters the Liard at Nahanni Butte. We stayed in Fort Simpson for two days, walking the dusty streets, visiting the small, intriguing museum, the local pub, and the big general store, getting our gear together for the raft trip.

A small float plane took us over a vast panorama of mountains, forests, lakes, bogs, and muskeg to an arcing landing on a pool of relatively quiet water above the steep cliffs of Virginia Falls. We stayed overnight in a small Parks Canada campground, then portaged down to the river. Canoes and rafts rested on the bank amid thin mist, the roar of falling waters, and trembling ground. Our party of about ten was broken into groups of two or three, placed on rafts, and we were on our way.

The run was like a dream, the wide Nahanni flowing at times through turbulent rapids, at times through comparatively gentle reaches where we basked in the sun. Eagle nests, caribou, wolf, and black bear appeared here and there. Mountains loomed large on the horizon. We surged through the four great canyons. The last—or First Canyon upstream from the Laird—is virtually vertical, scarred with caves sometimes leading to long tunnels dissolved in limestone bedrock underlying pitted karst terrain on the bordering Nahanni Plateau. We saw only one other party in the six days before our rendezvous with a big powerboat. It took us swiftly through the Splits, shifting channels carved relentlessly by the river as it erodes its way across the broad lowland sediments leading to the Liard, Nahanni Butte, and the end of a remarkable journey.

We can dig much deeper into the wonders of the Nahanni by turning to the writings of Raymond Patterson, who spent months prospecting and trapping in the lower valley in 1927 and 1928–1929. Patterson was an Englishman in his late twenties at the time of his sojourns in the Nahanni. He had enjoyed natural beauty, hunting, and outdoor life since boyhood. He served in the British Army during the First World War (1914–1918) and was captured and imprisoned by the Germans. Upon his release, he returned to England, worked for awhile for a bank, then left for Canada, seeking new experiences and adventure. He spent several years on ranches, mainly in British Columbia. He homesteaded in Peace River Country, living off the land, before undertaking his adventurous trip to the little-known Nahanni Valley in 1927.

Patterson's interest in the Nahanni seems to have been activated when he encountered stories of the river in the book, *The Arctic Forests*, by Michael H. Mason.[4] Patterson found this book at Harrod's, the well-known department store in London, while on a trip home from Western Canada in the winter of 1927. The book had physical and ethnographical maps of Alaska, Yukon, and the Mackenzie Valley, then a little-known region that had intrigued Patterson since he was a boy. One map had a large, beige-coloured area, labelled "Nahanni" after the poorly understood people of the region.

According to Patterson, Mason described the Nahanni as "a hearty, virile people, but have suffered much from white influences. They are hostile to strangers and many white pioneers have been done to death by them. The tribe was for many years under the complete domination of one woman, supposed to be partly of European descent."[5] Patterson had had a run of luck lately. He could afford to satisfy his curiosity and visit this exotic place. He proceeded to do so on his return to Western

Canada in the spring of 1927. Patterson described his journey in his classic book, *The Dangerous River*. It was not originally published until 1954 and has been republished numerous times since. *The Dangerous River* is a somewhat romanticized story written sometime after the fact for popular audiences. Fortunately, in 2008, Richard Davis edited and published Patterson's daily Nahanni River journals prepared while he was on the river in 1927 and 1928–1929. The journals give much more direct observations of his actual experiences and will be relied upon heavily in the following account.

In spring 1927, Patterson travelled about three hundred miles by rail to Waterways, now the oil sands town of Fort McMurray on the Athabasca River.[6] He then went about eight hundred miles downstream by canoe and steamer to Lake Athabasca, then down the Great Slave River, across Great Slave Lake, and on to the mighty Mackenzie River. Patterson ascended this great river to the mouth of its first major west bank tributary, the Liard. He moved by steamer and canoe up this stream to the South Nahanni River, where it enters the Liard after the long run from its source in the Mackenzie Mountains and the Yukon border country to the northwest.

After months of arduous travel, Patterson reached the South Nahanni in late July 1927. A major reason for coming to the valley was to face the challenges of a hostile yet beautiful wildland. He wanted to learn to survive through his own skill and labour in the bush tradition. Patterson poled, dragged, and sometimes paddled his canoe through the snyes and canyons of the lower South Nahanni up to the Flat River, a large tributary from the west. While in Nahanni Butte, he encountered the wildlands traveller, Albert Faille, originally from Minnesota. Faille was a veteran of the U.S. Army in the Great War. After his return home, he eventually found his way to the Lake Athabasca area, where he trapped for a couple of years before going to the Nahanni to trap and prospect.[7] Faille helped Patterson learn the ways of the canoe and the bush. He accompanied Patterson upstream on a very challenging canoe trip through the Nahanni canyons to the vicinity of the towering and majestic Virginia Falls.

Patterson did not go beyond the falls into the middle or upper Nahanni Valley on this or his later 1928–1929 journey to the valley. For the most part, he and Faille travelled separately as Patterson acquired the skills and experience he needed to live on the land. Patterson spent several weeks exploring the Flat River. He found traces of gold and resolved to come back the following year to seek his fortune in the precious metal. He saw this wealth as a means to marry and support a young woman he had left behind in England.

Patterson returned to the Nahanni by another route in March 1928, going by train to Peace River Country. He and an English friend, Gordon Matthews, then journeyed by horse wagon, sled, and boat north along the Rockies and then down the Nelson River to the Liard. They were on the Nahanni by May 1928 and stayed until the end of January 1929. Patterson built a log cabin at Wheat Sheaf Creek in Deadmen Valley,[8] not far downstream from the junction of the Nahanni and the Flat. He used it as a base to explore and trap in the surrounding country. For the most part, the two men spent the winter very much alone. Among rare visitors was a group of Indigenous people who apparently had come over the mountains from the Liard Valley. Patterson gave them hot tea with lots of sugar. When they left, they dumped chunks of moose meat on his cabin roof.

In both his 1927 and 1928–1929 journals, Patterson's descriptions focus on two things: his own experiences and challenges; and the stunning natural qualities of the lower Nahanni and the Flat rivers. He describes the poplar, willow, and other trees, gold, red, and vividly beautiful in the late summer and fall. While on a reach of the Nahanni Valley between the Flat River and Virginia Falls on August 21, 1927, he says he is in an area where no one has stayed for seven years. He implies that this hiatus was due to tales of murder, suicide, and starvation.[9] Patterson later used such stories to dramatize *The Dangerous River*. Patterson writes often of feasting on blueberries and other wild fruit. He describes struggling up through spruce, tamarack, and alpine fir forests to the treeless tundra of the uplands, hundreds of feet above the Nahanni and the Flat. He sees Dall's sheep on high ground and kills one, saving the horns to ship south as a trophy of his northern hunts and adventures.

His observations of wildlife are numerous and paint a vivid picture of the natural wonders that eventually led to strong interest in creating a national park. For example, while in the Nahanni Valley near "Murder Creek" on August 25, 1927, he was awakened at three a.m. by wolves. Later, he saw tracks of wolf, fisher, marten, and lynx in the sands where he had lunch.[10] Patterson saw, or saw signs of beaver and frequently of moose, especially in the late summer and fall in the favourable habitat along the lower slopes and floodplains of the Nahanni and the Flat.

Moose were a major source of food for Patterson, as well as for Indigenous hunters who seemed to concentrate their efforts in the lower Nahanni closer to the village of Nahanni Butte. Moose and other animals were less common and harder to get in the cold, snow, and quiet of winter. Patterson and Matthews found it difficult to live off the land. Flour, cereal, and other supplies had to be packed in from their downriver caches or Nahanni Butte. Their trapping in the winter of 1928–1929 seems to have been quite successful. They sold marten they had trapped for nearly $2,000, not including what was received for pelts of weasel, fox, mink, coyote, and at least one wolverine.[11] They saw wolf, or signs or sounds of wolf, fairly frequently but do not seem to have trapped or killed many. These animals seemed to fascinate and disturb Patterson, who was impressed with their size. Two timber wolves "about the size of calves" were seen not far from his cabin on November 14, 1928.

On August 21, 1927, while travelling up the Flat, Patterson portrayed the valley as "a dream of peace and beauty." It had its rapids, but there were long and lovely reaches where the trout jumped and little brown waterfowl nested "and always the splendid chocolate, black and golden butterfly and the one of pure gold."[12] At supper he saw a great black bear, possibly a grizzly, and heard the plunging of an otter or beaver in the night. A cow moose appeared at midday on August 22. At 5:30 p.m., as he was poling up a riffle, Patterson heard sounds on the river shingle and saw a great bull moose about two hundred yards away, going to the river to drink. "The moose was not the least afraid and stood looking at me. I took his photo twice . . . I said Good-bye and went on my way but he stayed stock still in the water looking after me for a long while." Patterson concluded that these animals do "not seem to know men" and that the river came "out of Eden." At supper that day, he heard marmots "piping amongst the rocks over the river—otherwise no sound but that of water."[13]

Patterson continued up the Flat and was awakened early on the morning of the twenty-third by a squirrel running across his face. He later saw a pair of "whisky jacks" and watched a woodland caribou leave the woods about five hundred yards away. It apparently was the first caribou he had seen: "A very pretty animal—smaller, more graceful and lighter than a moose."[14] This could suggest that caribou were generally rarer than moose and other animals. But we need to be careful about drawing firm conclusions, because today caribou mainly spend summers in the upper Nahanni and its cooler, less mosquito-rich highlands, moving downstream in winter.[15]

Patterson's observations give the impression of a diverse fauna and flora in the lower Nahanni and Flat valleys in the mid- to late 1920s. Overall, animals appear to have been relatively numerous. Patterson's observations were concentrated largely in the lower valley of the Nahanni and along the Flat, where the slopes and floodplains offer favourable habitat for wildlife. His observations also suggest that the animals may have been recovering from heavier hunting, trapping, and prospecting in the late nineteenth and early twentieth centuries.

His allusions to murder along the valley reflect long-held tales and legends of the river. They suggest that in earlier days, prospectors and trappers may have been numerous enough to come into conflict with one another over gold or the fur-bearers of the country. However, their numbers and effects remain elusive because a few people can range widely in the search for fur or precious metal. Their activities may have been sufficient to threaten yield and create hostilities over territory. Some of the conflict may also have been due to struggles among Indigenous people and newcomers to the valley. Patterson does refer to an old path near Virginia Falls said to have been used by prospectors in the Yukon Gold Rush some twenty to thirty years earlier, around the turn of the twentieth century. He also records finding, in various parts of the valley, abandoned campsites, old cabins, old river scows, and other equipment.

Patterson stresses the endurance and persistence needed to survive on the land. He faced dangers and risks in swinging his canoe across surging currents when going upriver, yet enjoyed the pleasure and swiftness of the return journey. He revels in his surroundings, in baking bannock, hunting, and preparing wild foods. He is proud of his craftsmanship and of the log cabin he built—his friend Matthews not being so good with his hands. It was stories similar to, but older than, his own that helped attract Patterson to the Nahanni. During his years in British Columbia, he undoubtedly heard tales of the northern wilds and Yukon from former trappers and prospectors he encountered not long after their return from the Yukon Gold Rush or trapping in the North. Stories may have spread in these informal as well as more formal ways.

It is difficult to grasp the speed, vast extent, duration, and effects of the great Yukon Gold Rush on the land and the people. In 1896, major discoveries were made along the Klondike and other streams in Yukon. Thousands of people from all over the world quickly set out to find their bonanza. A few big discoveries were made. But the rush was essentially over by 1899.

In his *Klondike: The Last Great Gold Rush*, Pierre Berton describes the diverse routes the gold seekers took into what were then very isolated wildlands, the home of a few thousand Indigenous people, as well as the successors of a thin band of eighteenth- and nineteenth-century Euro-American fur traders.[16] Trails were rudimentary. Travel was mostly by river and canoe. Indian villages and camps were small and often migratory. Scattered trading posts rose and declined with fluctuations in the opportunity for fur.

The gold seekers came with supplies, horses, livestock, and equipment from all directions. Most came by boat and over the mountains from the Pacific coast or via the British Columbia interior. Those of greatest interest to us came from the south and Edmonton, through bush and muskeg to the Peace and the Mackenzie rivers, along the general route used by Raymond Patterson three decades later in 1927.[17] The Klondikers then went west along the Liard or north up the Mackenzie. Along the way, some turned off at tributaries, intending to go west over the mountains into the Porcupine and other watersheds leading to Yukon gold.

Figure 1.2. Sketch Map of Gold Rush Trails from the East

Figure 1.2 outlines routes from Edmonton and the east to the gold-fields. The South Nahanni apparently was not used much by gold seekers en route to the Klondike. This contrasted with more accessible tributaries such as the Gravel (Keele) and Porcupine rivers further north along the Mackenzie. Many travellers used the Liard or Mackenzie routes. Some succeeded in reaching the Klondike. Some turned back, and some stayed along the way, talking of their experiences or those of others, eventually building a kind of gold rush mythology about places such as the South Nahanni that became a beacon for adventurers in later years.

Stories of places like the Nahanni spread around campfires and on hunting trips that adventurous southerners from cities such as New York, Chicago, Toronto, or Vancouver made to remote and alluring parts of the world, including Canada's North. Travellers were attracted through clubs and societies such as the Royal Geographical Society, the Hudson's Bay Record Society, the Boone and Crockett Club, and the Explorers Club in the United States. For example, in early August 1928, Patterson met Fenley Hunter, an American who was on his way up the Nahanni to the falls, which he named Virginia after his young daughter.[18] Hunter was a well-to-do businessman from Flushing, New York, who had made several challenging journeys north into the great boreal forest. In 1923, he and two Indigenous companions made a long journey from the North Pacific coast up the Stikine River, overland by pack horse through northern British Columbia and on to the upper Liard River. Here he came upon an old trail pioneered for the Hudson's Bay Company in the 1840s by the trader, Robert Campbell, who will be discussed more fully later in this book. The trail took Hunter north to Frances Lake and the Pelly and Yukon rivers, west of the Nahanni.

In 1928, when he met Patterson, Hunter was involved in a long arduous journey up the Peace, along the Athabasca and Slave rivers, and across Great Slave Lake to the Mackenzie, the Liard, and the Nahanni. With the aid of an early-model outboard motor, he and two Indigenous companions canoed up the powerful river to the falls. Hunter's plan was to continue up the Nahanni and cross the bordering northern mountains to the Gravel River. He then intended to go down this river to its junction with the Mackenzie and turn downstream as far

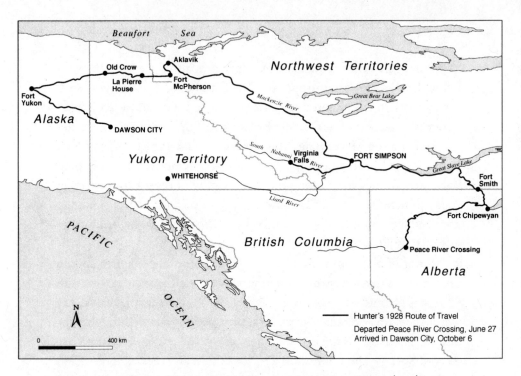

Figure 1.3. 1928 Route of Travel of Fenley Hunter. Adapted from Hunter (2015).

as the Rat, or another of the old fur trade routes across the western mountains to the Porcupine and Yukon rivers. A steamer would then be boarded to begin the long trip home (Figure 1.3).

Amazingly, Hunter did complete this arduous journey. He travelled by foot, pack horse, steamer, and canoe from Peace River Country all the way to Yukon City. He made the trip between June 28 and September 28, covering the remarkable distance of about three thousand miles in ninety days. But Hunter did not go beyond the falls and complete the upper Nahanni–Gravel Creek portion of his great trip. He believed time was too short for him to do this and still connect with a Yukon River steamer before freeze-up and a long winter in the North. So he returned down the Nahanni and followed the Mackenzie north, going over the mountains to the Yukon River and home.

Hunter kept good notes in his daily journal about his Nahanni trip. His observations generally parallel, or go beyond, those recorded by Raymond Patterson in *The Dangerous River* or his journals. Hunter was more gregarious than Patterson, showing greater interest in people and their activities, learning much from them along the way. One was the old

Klondiker and early Nahanni prospector, Poole Field. He told Hunter of going beyond the falls after the Klondike rush in 1905 and described a forty-mile route north across the mountains to Gravel Creek.

Hunter frequently refers to game animals and other wildlife. For instance, while at camps near the border of First Canyon and Deadmen Valley, he writes of numerous game animals. Lots of moose, bear, wolf, and sheep tracks were "close at hand." He had never seen "so many black bear and bear signs, there are great raspberry bushes there for them."[19] He and his crew came upon and tried to kill six bears and a moose. They shot rather freely, yet apparently only wounded two bears. They followed one blood trail for more than a mile without success. The next day, they killed a big, 350-pound black bear. On the third day they went south about seven miles up the south bank tributary known as Sheep Creek and killed three or four of these animals, taking the heads and one complete hide that Hunter intended to donate to "the Ottawa Museum."[20] Hunter also successfully fished along the Nahanni and Prairie creeks, catching some fish in the two-pound range, likely grayling.

Hunter was quite unusual among early travellers in making a map of the Nahanni (Figure 1.4). He seems to have had some surveying gear but gives few details on this. In preparing his Nahanni map, he consulted with Patterson and Matthews about place names, using some that appear to have originated before they appeared on the scene. Others were introduced by them—for example, Wheat Sheaf Creek. This was Patterson's name for the small stream where he and Matthews built their cabin in 1928. Hunter's map is invaluable in showing details on animal, vegetation, and landform patterns in the lower valley. His map portrays the state of the valley at the end of the fur trade era and the threshold of large-scale mineral exploration and other economic activities.

Unlike Patterson, Hunter's observations had little impact on the thinking and planning for the Nahanni National Park Reserve. He did not call for the conservation of wildlife or the valley itself. More to the point, his journals were generally unavailable in the 1960s and 1970s when interest in a national park was growing. Only fifty copies of the journals apparently were privately printed, and these largely

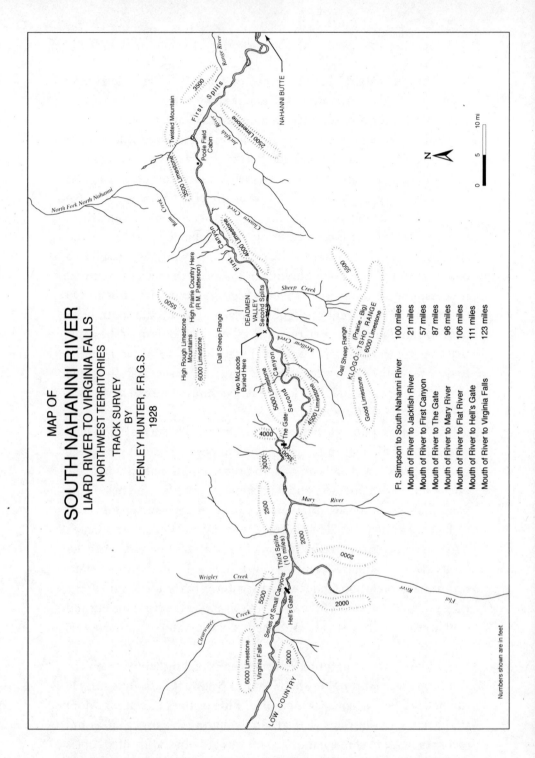

Figure 1.4. Map of South Nahanni River, Fenley Hunter, 1928. Adapted from Hunter (2015).

disappeared. Finally, in 2015, a typescript was edited and published as *That Summer on the Nahanni 1928*, along with other maps and photographs. Hunter's journals were, consequently, unknown to conservationists and other concerned parties when the initial phase of the Nahanni National Park Reserve was established in 1976 and expanded in 2009.

In contrast, Raymond Patterson's *The Dangerous River* was widely available. It was republished several times during the course of the long struggle to establish a national park in the Nahanni and sold well for decades. It helped induce an image of the Nahanni as a remote wilderness little disturbed by past or recent human activity. This ideal view of wilderness can be traced to the United States in the early 1900s. It gained prominence through a national struggle against the eventually successful early-nineteenth-century construction of the Hetch Hetchy Dam in renowned Yosemite National Park, California.[21] The dam was to supply water to the growing city of San Francisco. Over the years, this classical or ideal view of wilderness was reinforced by the Wilderness Society and the Sierra Club and spread through Canada, especially in the "environmental decade" of the 1960s.[22]

Influential conservation leaders in the United States, such as David Brower and Justice William O. Douglas of the Supreme Court, worked hard to pass the Wilderness Act in 1964. Its definition of wilderness took centre stage and has served as a banner in both the United States and Canada ever since. Thinking of national parks and other protected areas as dynamic working ecosystems was not in the air at the time, although the late Ian McTaggart Cowan, a pioneer Canadian ecologist, made an early plea for more science and ecology in park planning and management at the first Canadian National Parks Today and Tomorrow Conference in 1968.[23]

As Justice Douglas put it, the Wilderness Act was unusually poetic for government legislation. "A wilderness, in contrast to those areas where man and his works dominate the landscape, is hereby recognized as an area where the earth and its community of life are untrammeled by man, where man himself is a visitor who does not remain." Wilderness is "land retaining its primeval character and influences, without permanent impacts or human habitation," protected and managed so as to preserve its natural conditions, which "generally appear to have been affected primarily by forces of nature" with "the imprint of man's works substantially unnoticeable."[24]

Wilderness lands were to offer "outstanding opportunities for solitude or a primitive and unconfined type of recreation." They were to be at least five thousand acres, or big enough to make practicable their "preservation and use in an unimpaired condition." Wilderness lands could also "contain ecological and geological, or other features of scientific, scenic or historic value." Justice Douglas thought of wilderness as "a roadless area where only a trail makes passage through a forest or over a range, unpolluted, unbroken, the earth before any of its wildness has been reduced or subtracted."[25]

In contrast to this image of the wilderness ideal, it should be recognized that, in the 1960s, land use history and landscape change studies were revealing that Banff and other national parks were actually better seen as protected wildlands in the process of restoration to a "wilderness state," rather than as little disturbed remnants of "original or undisturbed wilderness."[26] These early 1960s studies focused on written historic evidence of lumbering, mining, hunting, and other effects of Euro-American invasion on the Rocky Mountain National Parks region prior to and during the early first phase of national park establishment in Canada in the late nineteenth and early twentieth centuries.

Historic studies have continued since the 1960s and been paralleled by archaeological research revealing activities of Indigenous peoples—the First Nations—since about ten thousand years ago. Over the years, this research has demonstrated that few areas in North America were not used by Indigenous people long before the arrival of Europeans in the sixteenth, seventeenth, and eighteenth centuries.[27] Indigenous people should, therefore, be seen as having been an integral part of North American and national park ecosystems for millennia. And their as yet incompletely understood activities and effects have to be considered in planning for these systems, as does their Aboriginal right to engage in the planning of these ancient homelands.

Since the 1980s, studies in various parts of the world have reached conclusions similar to the early studies in Banff National Park.[28]

Somewhat surprisingly, even apparently remote areas such as the wild forests and coasts of Indonesia and Malaysia have been influenced by cultural or human practices: "few, if any, of the 'natural' habitats viewed as 'pristine' by global environmental organizations are actually what they seem to be."[29] Rather, they are seen as landscapes and seascapes whose features have been shaped over time by complex and varied interactions with human societies. Thus, we read about the Bentium Dayak of Borneo "transforming large regions of 'wild' forest with a patchwork of partly cultivated forest gardens,"[30] or the Tamian horticulturalists of the Macassar Strait region who shaped nature "as landscape and ecosystem for centuries."[31] Witness, also, the nurturing in wild forests of durian or other fruit trees by the Salako Dayak of West Kalimantan.[32]

In the 1970s and earlier, decisions on differences between historic uses and practices of Indigenous people and the ideas and plans of newcomers were overwhelmingly made in Canada and elsewhere by national governments and agencies such as the national park service, a conservation story with a long history.[33] Today, however, the focus is on reconciliation through co-operative planning, guided, on the one hand, by the interactions of Western concepts of science, conservation, and tourism and, on the other hand, by Indigenous ideas of land, traditional practices, and ways of life. Western and Indigenous approaches are underpinned by different ways of knowing. The Indigenous people call for careful consideration of their historical experience and learning, or traditional knowledge. The newcomers rely heavily on science, especially ecological or ecosystem science, which has advanced greatly since the 1980s. The unfolding of the foregoing interacting principles and approaches is a fundamental part of the story of the long struggle to establish Nahanni National Park Reserve, which is described in the following chapters.

Chapter 2

Creating the Initial Nahanni National Park Reserve: Ideal Wilderness and Top-Down Planning

The next two chapters analyze the ideas, processes, and events leading to the establishment of the Nahanni National Park Reserve. Chapter 2 describes how these influences worked to create the small initial reserve in the lower valley in 1976. Chapter 3 goes on to discuss changes that culminated in reserve expansion to watershed scale in 2009.

The establishment of the first phase of the Nahanni National Park Reserve was a contentious issue. Many interests inside and outside of government opposed the large park proposed and persistently advocated by nongovernmental organizations such as the National and Provincial Parks Association of Canada, later the Canadian Parks and Wilderness Society (Table 2.1). Without a large national park, mining and other activities outside the highly valued lower valley could easily result in pollution there and elsewhere in the system. In the end, however, the first phase of the national park reserve consisted only of the narrow corridor along the middle and lower stem of the Nahanni and lower Flat rivers, including Virginia Falls (see Figure 1.1). Arguing for a large park on watershed and wilderness grounds was sound but ahead of its time. It did not carry the scientific or ecosystem understanding for a large park provided later by 1980s advances in ecology and the introduction of ecological integrity as the fundamental mandate for national parks.

The earliest known reference to the Nahanni as a possible national park was made on February 6, 1948, by E. G. Oldham, superintendent of forests and wildlife in the Northwest Territories. In a letter to his director, federal Deputy Minister of Mines and Resources R.A. Gibson, Oldham raised the national park possibility after a trip north to inspect a Laplander-inspired reindeer herding project underway in the Anderson River–Eskimo Lakes area east of the Mackenzie Delta.[1] During his return, Oldham decided to investigate reports of very large wolf numbers in the South Nahanni country.

After a flight over the Mackenzie Mountains, he arrived at the junction of the Flat and South Nahanni rivers and went upstream above the falls, staying later in or near the lower valley. Oldham and his party saw no wolves or wolf tracks, nor did they hear howls at night. It is not entirely clear whether he was in the upper or the lower valley when he made these observations. Oldham did suggest that the reports of numerous wolves might be trappers' tales to blame these animals for any scarcity of game or fur, the implication being that this might cause the government to allow them to participate in a cull. In his flights over the valley and beyond the falls, Oldham did find that the Nahanni Valley was rich in wildlife, with little sign of hunting or trapping. He found the valley to be "unspoiled by man." Moose and caribou abounded and there was no sign of forest fires. He was told that the valley contained at least four species of sheep, including Dall's, as well as mountain goat and "black and brown bear."[2] This somewhat misleading information on the differentiation of sheep and bears may have come from V.L. Shattuck, a member of Oldham's party and a game warden admired for his hardiness and bush skills in winter patrols in the region.

Oldham recommended research on a possible national park with the precocious name of Nahanni National Park. What the government did with his proposal is unknown. Numerous articles on the valley, its hot springs, supposed tropical climate, and travellers' mysterious

Table 2.1 Canadian Parks and Wilderness Society's Public Communications for the Nahanni

"Move on the Nahanni," *Park News*, October 1970.

"Needed—A New Home for the National Parks," *Park News*, July 1971.

"Park or Power," *Park News*, January 1972.

"Well Done, Mr. Chretien," *Park News*, April 1972.

"Canoeing the Little Nahanni," *Park News*, March 1973.

"The Upside of Nahanni," *Park News*, Fall 1979.

"The South Nahanni River, Nahanni National Park," *Park News*, Fall 1984.

Deh Cho Gathering on Protected Lands: A Summary of the Interim Report by Canadian Parks and Wilderness Society (CPAWS) on Deh Cho Gathering on Protected Lands, March 23–26, 1998, and Elder's Council, May 12–14, 1998.

"The Fight to Save the Nahanni," *Taiga News*, no. 40, Summer 2002.

"Nahanni Activists Score Victory—but the battle is not yet won," Paddling Briefs, *Kanawa*, Summer 2002.

"Nahanni Momentum Builds, but Mining Application Looms, *Wilderness Activist*, Fall 2003.

"True North Wild and Free?" *Canadian Wilderness*, Spring 2006.

"10 Year Report," CPAWS, Northwest Territories Chapter, 2006.

"Nahanni Forever: A CPAWS National Tour," CPAWS, 2009.

"Nahanni Forever, Your Voice Counts," *Yellowknife News*, October 26, 2007.

Recommendations for Federal Action on Wilderness Conservation, prepared for meeting with the Honourable Jim Prentice, Minister of Environment, November 21, 2008.

"Naha Dehé Nahanni Protected Forever," CPAWS, 2009.

This table was compiled from various CPAWS documents.

deaths appeared in the press in the 1940s and 1950s.[3] Pierre Berton, an aspiring author and later prolific northern historian, made a midwinter, light-plane, Vancouver-to-Nahanni trip in 1947 to investigate these claims. He landed in Deadmen Valley amid bitter cold and much snow.[4] He prepared vivid articles for the *Vancouver Sun* and newspapers across Canada.[5] In 1959, an intergovernmental panel apparently recommended a national park for the Nahanni. But we do not have details on any relevant research until the Canadian Wildlife Service (CWS) began to do biological surveys in the 1960s and 1970s.

Some major economic developments in the 1960s propelled the growing interest in a Nahanni national park. Of fundamental importance was the 1950s discovery of oil offshore the north slope of Alaska, the subsequent development of processing facilities at Prudhoe Bay, and the construction of a trans-Alaska pipeline to carry the oil toward southern markets in the United States. These developments spurred the search for oil and gas in the Beaufort Sea and the Mackenzie Delta. Long seismic lines and hard rock mineral exploration were widely carried out in the Northwest Territories and Yukon. These activities contributed to growing concerns about impacts on caribou, grizzly bear, polar bear, musk-ox, and other wildlife, as well as the way of life and land rights of Indigenous people.

Various steps were taken by the Canadian government to counter these problems. One was the creation of a commission led by Justice Thomas Berger to investigate the impacts of a proposed pipeline down the Mackenzie Valley on Indigenous people and make relevant recommendations. Berger recommended a ten-year delay in any construction to allow the Indigenous people to prepare adequately for its economic, social, and environmental impacts.[6] The process that Berger employed in his study included extensive communication and consultation with the Indigenous people, as well as other Canadians. He reached out and held meetings in Indigenous villages throughout the region.[7] These consultative processes represented a major departure from the top-down approach typically used by the federal government in making decisions in the North. As we shall see later, Berger's outreach activities set the stage for a move from predominately top-down federal government planning to the more participatory and co-operative approach that was so important in easing the way for a major expansion of the Nahanni National Park Reserve in 2009.

The federal government and its national parks agency also moved to lessen the impact of oil and gas and hard rock mining development in the North by going beyond the cloak of government and publicly announcing its intentions to protect outstanding landscapes such as the Nahanni, Kluane in southwest Yukon, and Auyuittuq in southern Baffin Island as national parks. But the announcement of these new parks was made by the federal government without significant consultations with Indigenous people or nongovernment conservation organizations in Canada generally. At the time of the announcement, in the early 1970s, the federal government had two fundamental policies in regard to national parks. The first was that the Crown should ultimately own all land in such a park. The second was that the park should be planned and managed as pristine or ideal wilderness, devoid of past or present human activity. This meant the exclusion of hunting, fishing, collecting, and other traditional activities from what Indigenous people generally regarded as their own ancestral lands. The combination of government ownership and the ideal wilderness policy, not surprisingly, led to Indigenous opposition to the creation of a national park in the Nahanni, as well indeed as Kluane and Auyuittuq. Mining, gas, and mineral development interests were also very much opposed to the national parks, although their plans were not welcomed by many Indigenous people because of fears about opening up of the country and disturbing wildlife habitat. On the other hand, some Indigenous people did see advantages in mining and other development as a probable source of employment and income.

At this time, the position of the National and Provincial Parks Association and other nongovernment conservation organizations was generally favourable to the federal government. The association saw the goal of ideal wilderness as a generally desirable guiding concept. However, total federal land ownership was more problematic. Some conservationists favoured this policy. Others were uncertain and wondered about a possible alternative involving Indigenous people. Informal discussions between association board members and senior national park agency personnel revealed a high level of concern about any concessions to Indigenous people, on the grounds that mining and development interests might then also claim them.

Moving ahead with Nahanni National Park Reserve plans was greatly strengthened by a late-1960s engineering proposal for a major dam and power project at Virginia Falls. The 1960s was an era of great interest in and concern about dam projects around the world. Big dams like those planned and built in the Colorado River Basin, on the Nile at Aswan, or the Volta River in Nigeria were recognized as causes of major sedimentation problems, habitat disturbance, reduction of fisheries, erosion of shorelines, and environmental, social, and economic impacts, often unanticipated by engineers and planners.[8] These effects were on the minds of those opposed to the Virginia Falls dam. They foresaw wide-ranging and potentially profound disturbances to water quality and flow, wildlife, wildness, and Indigenous people through road construction, habitat destruction, decline of plants and animals, and other effects over a large part of the Nahanni watershed.

In the midst of these threats and uncertainties, studies by the Canadian Wildlife Service, the national park agency, and university and other researchers continued into the 1970s. Canadian Wildlife Service work led to a major report outlining the plant and animal life, rare species, and other features of the Nahanni Valley and surrounding lands.[9] The report was requested by the national parks agency following early survey work in the early 1960s, more detailed studies in 1969, and the preparation of an initial draft park proposal in 1970. The CWS brought an ecological perspective to bear on this initial proposal and its focus on a narrow Northern Wilderness River National Park, with boundaries more or less parallel to the lower Nahanni Valley. The initial proposal included Virginia Falls and the great canyons of the river (see Figure 1.1).

In their report, Scotter and his colleagues put the Nahanni Valley into a wider natural setting, including surrounding habitat for woodland caribou, Dall's sheep, hot springs such as Rabbitkettle, floristically diverse wetlands, and other features of broader scientific, conservation, scenic, and planning interest. They also proposed an extension of the park boundaries to include a large part of the Nahanni watershed. In doing so, they were guided by more comprehensive understanding of the geology, landforms, glacial features, fauna, flora, human history, and beauty of the South Nahanni.

In their research, they went beyond the impressionistic descriptions of Raymond Patterson and provided a scientific analysis and description of the natural wonders of the Nahanni. They also took a major step toward the more dynamic ecological thinking of the 1980s and 1990s, as well as more explicit ecosystem thinking and innovative concepts such as ecological integrity. In this sense, Scotter's 1971 report is a park-planning milestone, unfortunately unpublished and rare today, when key reports along the conservation trail are at risk because of lack of government and public concern about their value to policy makers, researchers, public officials, and citizens in the future.

In the early 1970s, George Scotter gave citizens a better understanding of the riches of the Nahanni in a series of public lectures on some of the results of this early research. The lectures were organized by non-governmental organizations such as the National and Provincial Parks Association of Canada, through its vigorous executive director, Gavin Henderson, and the Royal Canadian Geographical Society. Thousands of members and concerned citizens attended Scotter's vividly illustrated talks in cities such as Toronto and Vancouver, making many Canadians much more aware of the significant wildland qualities of the Nahanni.

Ongoing Canadian Wildlife Service research in the 1970s was important in gaining a better scientific understanding of the state and distribution of the flora and fauna of key places along the river, such as the confluence of the Nahanni, the Flat, and Deadmen Valley where Patterson, Matthews, and Fenley Hunter were so successful with game in 1928 and 1929. The research revealed diverse types of forests, wetlands, plants, birds, and other animals, including grizzly and black bear, moose, woodland caribou, Dall's sheep, deer, beaver, muskrat, wolf and lynx, as well as butterflies and birds.[10] Observations were also made of signs of human activity, particularly near sites offering potential for camping and recreation. Remains include what was thought to be Patterson's 1928–1929 log cabin. Along with these were more recent and better-preserved cabin and tent sites of early trappers and sports hunting and fishing guides, who had, by that time, been using the Nahanni for years.

Overall, the ecological effects of human activity were found to be low. In this respect, one of the major aims of these studies was to locate suitable sites for park visitor campsites and trails that would have minimum impacts on natural systems and maintain "the wilderness experience." These goals ranked high on national park agency and conservation NGO agendas at a time of rising general interest in identifying the recreational carrying capacity of wildlands.[11]

A summary of the research of Scotter and others was published in the 1984 *Nahanni National Park Reserve Resource Description and Analysis*.[12] Some of the major features of the forests and plant life were presented in terms of the ecological concept of life zones. These are based on changes in elevation and relief, giving a general view of the varied vegetation in the Nahanni watershed. The zones fall eastward from the rugged northwestern Ragged Range Mountains, with their high subalpine fir forest and treeless tundra, to the more robust spruce, pine, white birch, and poplar forests of the lowlands along the Liard and Mackenzie valleys.

Five life zones are identified along an east-west transit of the Nahanni. The boundaries are only approximate and overlap at the margins.

1. The eastern lowland life zone extends from two hundred to 1200 metres above sea level (a.s.l.). It includes spruce, jackpine, birch, muskeg, and other vegetation covering about 7 per cent of the original wilderness river phase of the Nahanni National Park Reserve.

2. The montane life zone rises above the lowland forests along the lower and middle slopes of the valley, with spruce, pine, and other forest stands from about 250 to 1700 metres a.s.l. This zone covers about 50 per cent of the initial reserve.

3. The subalpine zone extends above the montane to about 2000 metres a.s.l. It consists of subalpine fir, larch, aspen, and other hardier species that cover about 25 per cent of the original

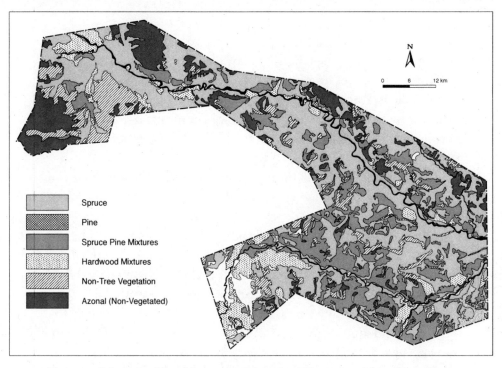

Figure 2.1. Schematic of Land Systems and Associated Vegetation. Adapted from Parks Canada (1984).

reserve. Stunted dense growth is common on the colder northern and upper slopes of the zone.

4. The harsh alpine zone rises to about 2700 metres a.s.l., and is composed of shrub birch, willow, Labrador tea, and other plants of alpine communities that cover less than 2 per cent of the initial reserve.

5. The cold nival zone of the higher mountains consists of perennial ice, snow, and windblown bare ground. This zone covers less than 1 per cent of the original reserve.

Figure 2.1 is a schematic of a 1980s land systems and associated vegetation map. This gives more detail on Nahanni Valley forests and plant life in the initial phase of the Nahanni National Park Reserve. The forest and land cover types on this map generally reflect life zone patterns and have the additional advantage of showing the distribution of vegetation along the length of the valley. Since the preparation of this map, forest fires have burned parts of the lower Nahanni and Flat River valleys. Patches of sun-loving, quick-growing, fire-successional species, such as aspen and pine, which we saw during our 2013 raft trip downriver from Virginia Falls, would likely show up more frequently if the map were done today.

Owing to its location at the intersection of several North American forest and wildlife habitat types, the flora and fauna of the Nahanni are quite diverse in comparison to the surrounding areas, where plant and animal life fit more completely into one forest type or another. In the case of animal life, for example, the Nahanni includes the northern range limits of southern species such as mule deer, white-tailed deer, woodchuck, porcupine, black bear, and possibly cougar. The watershed also includes the southern range limits of Arctic species such as the Arctic ground squirrel, the tundra vole, and Dall's sheep.[13] The Nahanni watershed is also rich in plant diversity. The numbers of vascular plants (683), bryophytes (352), and lichens are all, very likely, the greatest in the entire Northwest Territories.[14]

Mixing of Cordilleran, northern forest, and Great Plains species results in a diverse bird population.[15] As early as 1984, 170 bird species had been identified in the initial reserve area. This bird population was overwhelmingly seasonal, with most species being summer residents (126) and migrants (sixteen). Some were winter visitors and twenty-two were recorded as year-round residents. At least twelve more species were expected to turn up as migrants or summer residents because of their identification in similar habitats nearby.[16] A copy of the Northwest Territories Nahanni migrant bird checklist survey form, obtained while visiting the Nahanni in August 2013, suggested that additional bird species had been listed since the 1984 report, including hummingbirds.[17]

The Nahanni provides good opportunities for naturalists with its warblers, buntings, pipits, waterfowl, and other diverse Cordilleran and boreal species. Relatively uncommon iconic species include the trumpeter swan, peregrine falcon, gyrfalcon, bald eagle, and golden eagle. The trumpeter has been of special interest as a threatened species due to the profound impacts of historic hunting for skins and quills, loss of wetland habitat in southern wintering areas, and unregulated shooting.

Numbers have increased somewhat, however, because of conservation efforts and the discovery of new populations in Alaska. Yohin Lake in the lower Nahanni is a trumpeter swan nesting area given special zoning and protection by Nahanni National Park Reserve planners.

As a result of the biological surveys in the 1960s and 1970s, Nahanni fauna and flora were considered by Parks Canada to be similar to historic populations. Exceptions include the northern spread of mule deer in the 1920s and 1930s and white-tailed deer, coyote, and possibly cougar in the 1960s and later. The effects of hunting and other activities by local Indigenous people were considered to be low in relation to the long-term viability and resilience of the wildlife. A very general wildlife survey was conducted by park wardens from 1976–1977 to 1980–1981. Although not scientifically valid, the survey gave a total harvest of just fifty-nine beaver, thirteen lynx, four bears, twenty-three moose, and one caribou.[18] These figures were very likely an underestimate, yet seem low, even allowing for a substantial upward adjustment. The authors of the 1984 *Resource Description and Analysis* were far more concerned about growing air, road, and transport improvements and the opening up of the area to intense and extensive sport hunting, mining, and resource development, with attendant risks of habitat loss and a heavier toll on wildlife.

Another excellent example of the use of research in improving understanding and support of Nahanni's first phase and later 2009 expansion is the work of Derek Ford, a geographer and expert in caves and other features of karst terrain. Around 1970, Ford undertook research on the caves and karst in and bordering the lower Nahanni Valley at the request of national park planners. Initially, Ford was in the company of some Quebec adventurists led by Jean Poirel, who, in earlier years, had parachuted into the Nahanni and gone downstream on small floats, finding caves in the lower canyon walls.[19] They had reported these to national park personnel, who agreed to finance further exploratory work, with Ford along as a cave expert since he had worked previously on caves in Banff and other national parks in Western Canada.

Ford found extensive cave, sink hole, and other karst features at a scale and grandeur he considered to be unique globally. He made the earth science case for the protection of the karst in research reports,

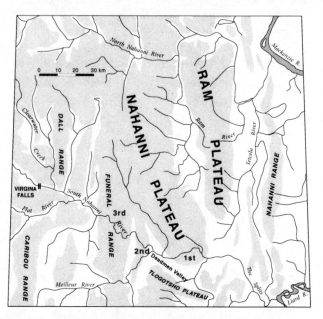

Figure 2.2. North and South Nahanni Region. Adapted from Ford (1991).

letters, and presentations to government and other concerned organizations in 1971–1975. Like many of the plant and animal features valued by the biologists, much of the karst lay outside the boundaries of what became the initial national park reserve and, in some cases, beyond the South Nahanni watershed itself, in terrain studied by Ford in 2006–2007 before being included in the 2009 expansion of the reserve.

Ford, McMaster University graduate students, and others undertook research in the lower Nahanni Valley area for many years.[20] This research revealed geology and landforms of extraordinary scenic, conservation, scientific, and educational value for numerous reasons other than the globally significant karst. Ford concluded that the Nahanni "displays perhaps a greater variety of landforms," or earth science diversity, "than any other area of comparable size in Canada."[21] Among the Nahanni's outstanding landforms are the Rabbitkettle travertine mounds in the upper valley, the great Virginia Falls, the canyons, and "splits" or braided channels unfolding toward its outlet into the Liard (Figure 2.2). The Nahanni also contains an array of alpine and continental glacial and proglacial landforms, along with frost-riven periglacial, fluvial, karst, and windblown or eolian features. Like Scotter and his ecological colleagues, Ford was an innovator in using the dynamic concept of "earth science integrity" in his research.

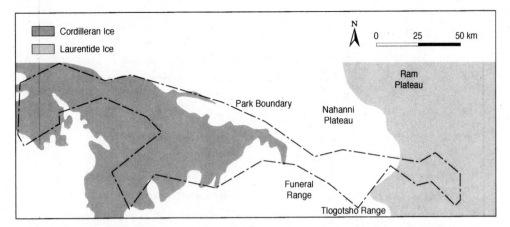

Figure 2.3. Glaciation of Nahanni. Adapted from Hartling (1998). Original map by Derek Ford.

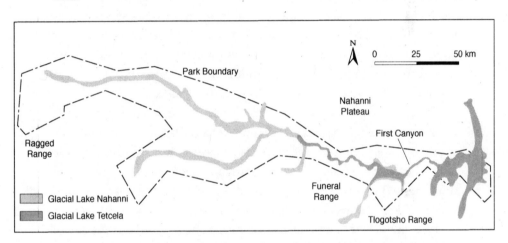

Figure 2.4. Ancient Glacial Lakes. Adapted from Hartling (1998). Original map by Derek Ford.

According to Ford, this exceptional geomorphic wealth is the consequence of two major factors. First is the unusual variety of rock types and geologic structures that occur in this comparatively small area, together with the fact that some of the structures continue to form today. Second, the landforms of the Mackenzie Mountains reveal a glacial history not found elsewhere. The northern highlands of the Ragged Range were occupied by eastward-flowing cirque and valley glaciers. The lower Nahanni Valley was invaded repeatedly by the westward-flowing Laurentide Continental Ice. The central valley includes areas glaciated only in older ice advances, as well as an ice-free core that was never glaciated. River canyons are the most striking features because "the absence of effective glacial erosion has permitted fluvial processes to dominate with little hindrance for long periods"[22] (Figure 2.3).

Ford was impressed with the remarkable Nahanni canyons stretching below Virginia Falls, the scene of many wild river and wilderness struggles by R.M. Patterson, who never fully realized the dimensions of the river he was tackling in his canoe. A discharge gauging station has been operating since 1961 at the Splits near the mouth of the first of three successive major canyons. The Nahanni watershed above this station is 33,700 km². The mean yearly discharge of the Nahanni is comparable to the Colorado River in the Grand Canyon.[23] The power of the Nahanni puts it well up on a global scale. In the main summer flow season, mean discharges have been recorded at five hundred to 1500 cubic metres per second (m^3s^{-1}) and maximum instantaneous discharge at 3600 m^3s^{-1}. At high river stages, boulders can be heard rumbling along the channel bed and the water is "very turbid indeed."[24]

Ford gives details on the size, character, and unusual origins of the canyons as an ongoing product of numerous geologic and geomorphic processes rarely found in one place elsewhere in Canada. These include ancient earth movements forming anticlines and synclines, proglacial flooding, sedimentation and downcutting, entrenchment and re-excavation. Using uranium series dating of stalactites in caves, and estimates of the influence of factors like those noted above, Ford put the age of the well-preserved fluvial structures in the First Canyon upstream of the Splits at between two and four million years ago, with the more westerly Second and Third canyons probably a little older.[25]

Ford's initial work on the unique Nahanni karst spoke strongly for the protection of the valley. His subsequent research on the long geological and fluvial history of the canyon country makes an even more compelling case. Every time a lobe of the Laurentide Ice Sheet advanced westward into the Nahanni Range, it blocked the South Nahanni flow to the Liard and the Mackenzie. According to Ford, the Nahanni then backed up in the canyons "like a giant Lake Mead, until high enough to overspill north or south along strike valleys within the Mountains" (Figure 2.4).[26] Sediments were found indicating at least three successive proglacial lakes. Most of these sediments have been eroded over time. Some are preserved in Deadmen Valley, as well as downstream of First Canyon. Two early phases of glacial Lake Nahanni rose more than six hundred metres above sea level, submerging the canyons and Virginia Falls.[27]

Ford and others summarized their research on the bedrock geology, structural history, hydrology, and landforms in the 1984 *Resource Description and Analysis*. In the northwest, the dark Ragged Ranges, with their grey-black granitic peaks, rise above 2700 metres, scarred with ice-scoured valleys, steep cliffs, and sharp jagged ridges by extensive ancient alpine glaciers whose remnants remain active today (See Figures 2.3 and 2.5). The Ragged Ranges originated from a great intrusion, or massive upthrust, of molten lava or magma—a batholith—into the earth's crust about 100 million years ago. The intrusion created a dome in the overlying sandstones, limestones, and other sedimentary rocks originally deposited in ancient oceans hundreds of millions of years previously. Over the millennia, the rocks atop the dome were eroded, exposing the granite core and leaving remaining flanking sedimentary rock dipping away to the east (Figure 2.6).

The interior or geothermal energy that produced the Ragged Ranges is still evident in the hot springs near the mountains. An excellent example can be seen at Rabbitkettle Creek in the upper Nahanni. The hot springs bring carbonates to the surface, building colourful terraces, porous and too fragile to withstand much walking yet very attractive to visitors. Over an estimated ten thousand years of flow, the Rabbitkettle Hot Springs have created a mound about twenty metres high and seventy in diameter, one of the largest of its kind in Canada.[28]

Beyond the Ragged Ranges, the Nahanni flows generally east in a wide valley eroded into the shales, sandstones, and limestones flanking the mountains. Exposed cliffs show rocks that have been warped, folded, faulted, and displaced by the upthrust of the molten lava. The valley has been sculpted by ancient great alpine glaciers that eroded its originally winding river slopes into a broad u-shaped basin. Today, the flow in this part of the Nahanni is relatively even, broken here and there by the entrance of tributaries draining interior highlands and lakes.

A truly spectacular change takes place when the Nahanni reaches Virginia Falls. Here it plunges through several channels from heights

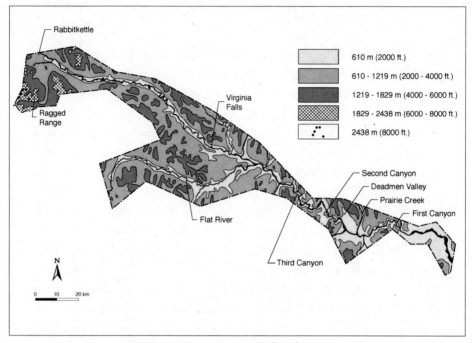

Figure 2.5. Elevations. Adapted from Parks Canada (1984).

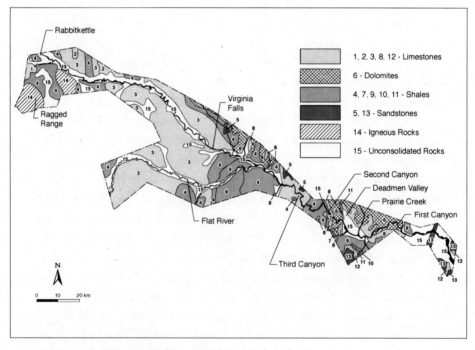

Figure 2.6. Geology. Adapted from Parks Canada (1984).

well above those at the more famous Niagara Falls. The Virginia Falls area was overridden by alpine glaciers several times, then buried by postglacial lake sediments now being eroded by the Nahanni. At the falls, the river has cut new channels into underlying bedrock, as well as exhuming old ones beneath the ancient lake sediments.

Below the falls, the river drops into Five Mile Gorge, or Fourth Canyon, the start of the largest river canyon system in Canada, mapped in his own way by Fenley Hunter in 1928 (Figure 1.4). These great canyons cut through the three main eastern ranges of the Mackenzie Mountains: the Funeral Range (Third Canyon); the Headless Range (Second Canyon); and the Nahanni Plateau (First Canyon).[29] In the canyons, the valley has cut deeply, yet meanderingly, not straight. The probable cause is that, through the ages, the Nahanni and its original meandering channel have been lowered onto and cut into the bedrock rising gently beneath the river, i.e., the meandering Nahanni channel pattern predates the river flowing through it today.

The long Third Canyon runs through high Funeral Range cliffs rising more than 1600 metres above the river. Near the ten-kilometre mark, the valley narrows sharply to about one hundred metres and turns ninety degrees, between two steep cliff faces, into "the Gate." This sharp turn is one of the places where the Nahanni left an old channel, now marked by an abandoned course or meander, to cut a more direct route downstream. Just below the Gate is the unusual sentinel, or Pulpit Rock, isolated midriver by erosion of the cliffs on either side.

At the Headless Mountains, the river flows through Second Canyon on unconsolidated silts and sands set out in places along the walls, a reminder that the deep valley was carved long before it was flooded by the postglacial lakes that deposited the silts and sands. The river flows here and elsewhere in the canyon system, on these relatively soft uniform lake sands and silts. The result is a relatively even channel profile lacking the sharp falls and breaks in slope that often occur where streams flow on bedrock of uneven hardness and resistance to erosion.

At George's Riffle, the Second Canyon opens into the wide Deadmen Valley, which has developed on less resistant shales, sandstones, and limestones at the gap between the Headless Range and the flat-lying, hard dolomite and limestone rocks of the ensuing Nahanni Plateau. The evocative names in this reach—Deadmen Valley and Headless Creek—are due to the nearby 1908 discovery of the apparently headless bodies of two post-Klondike prospectors, Frank and Willie McLeod (See Figure 1.4).

Here we enter the steeply incised First Canyon where the valley reaches its ultimate. The river runs in a narrow, spectacularly deep canyon in the shadow of the near-vertical limestone cliffs of the bordering Nahanni Plateau. This is the zone of the unique subarctic karst landscape where Ford and his colleagues did so much revealing research. Caves can be seen in the walls—entrances to underground water courses that have dissolved the surrounding limestone. Solution and collapse during the hundreds of thousands of years since this land was last covered with ice have created the solution basins, or dolines, collapse features, or poljes, and dry-walled valleys that mark terrain north of the canyon, one of the world's outstanding karst landscapes, making a strong case for northward expansion of the original reserve.

Toward the lower end of First Canyon are the Nahanni hot springs, where Gus Kraus, the long-time (1940–1980) intermittent Nahanni resident, built a family home in the early days. The hot springs have created a warmer local climate with unusually lush vegetation and floral species, sufficiently mild to allow for some early cultivation by Kraus.[30] Just north of the terminus of First Canyon is Yohin Lake with its valuable trumpeter swan habitat. On leaving First Canyon, the Nahanni escapes into the Splits and the wide lowland leading to Nahanni Butte and the Liard River. In this stretch, the Nahanni's velocity and erosive capacity diffuse into the interconnected series of braided or anastomosing channels through which Patterson struggled upriver for days in the late 1920s.

Discharge gauges above Virginia Falls, and at the mouth of First Canyon, measure the river's flow patterns or hydrology at the end of its long course from the Ragged Range and the upper valley (Figure 2.7).[31] Most of the flow occurs in spring and summer because of snow and ice melt and seasonal rains. The rise begins in May and falls off in September and October, peaking in June, July, and, to a lesser extent, August. Floods are more frequent in June and July but can happen at

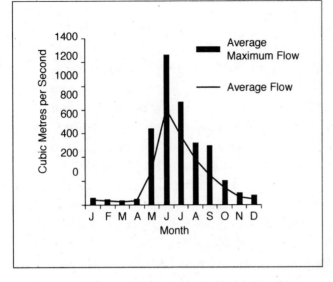

Figure 2.7. Discharge Record above Virginia Falls. Adapted from Parks Canada (2011).

any time in spring, summer, and fall depending on the vagaries of ice, snowmelt, and heavy rains. Floods can discomfort but do not seem generally to disrupt the raft and canoe expeditions that are a feature of current tourism in the Nahanni National Park Reserve. The great size and flow of the river in the warmer months makes it astonishing that Patterson was able to paddle and pole upriver alone, in a small canoe, testimony possibly to his lack of understanding of the power of the Nahanni and certainly to his great fortitude.

Few, if any, observations of ice retreat or behaviour seem to be available in the historic record for the glaciers of the Ragged Range. Some research began in 2007 as part of an overall research and monitoring program in the Nahanni.[32] It was carried out co-operatively by Parks Canada,[33] Brock University, and the Geological Survey of Canada.[34] The position of glaciers in 1949 was mapped from historic air photos. More detailed work included measurement of snow thickness, meltwater runoff, and other characteristics. The record of study is short. But considerable glacial retreat has occurred since 1949. Little evidence has been found, however, of changes in meltwater and downriver flow. Evidence of such changes is important to local Indigenous people, as well as tourists, scientists, and policy makers concerned about the effects of global warming and climate change on the environment and human activities in the Nahanni and the greater Mackenzie Mountain area.

Monitoring glacier behaviour and climate change is especially important in high northern latitudes where greater rates of warming and associated geological and ecological effects are anticipated: for example, widespread melting of ground ice, or permafrost, and increased instability of landforms. The Nahanni area is subject to earth tremors and quakes. One in 1985 ranked at 6.9 on the Richter scale and was felt in northern Washington state and southern British Columbia.[35] Today's traveller can hear and see rockfall, as well as older slides and slips, while floating down the river. Some undoubtedly would recognize the prospects for more movements given continued climate warming and the melting of permafrost, snow, and ice. Yet it is uncertain whether funding and support will be provided to continue important glacial history and climate change studies in the Nahanni. One scientist at the Northwest Territories Geological Survey reports a doubling of the amount of land scarred by slumping and debris in the Northwest Territories since the late 1980s. But no specific results seem available for the Nahanni watershed.[36]

Much research was available in 1976 when the initial Nahanni National Park Reserve was confined to the narrow corridor around the rapid waters, canyons, caves, and great falls of the lower valley. The early research was of high quality, but not enough to surmount the political pressure from Indigenous and mining interests outside and inside government. Lack of support from Indigenous people largely arose from national park and federal government commitment to Crown ownership of the park's land and the guiding concept of ideal wilderness. Both were detrimental to Indigenous interests. Some compromise was made by labelling the Nahanni as a national park reserve, the reserve terminology indicating postponement of the ownership question until the settlement of Indigenous claims for traditional lands not only for a national park but for pipelines, roads, and other purposes.

The proposed Nahanni National Park Reserve plans were presented to Pierre Trudeau, then prime minister of Canada and the principal decision maker, for his views. Trudeau had done some reading about the Nahanni before he took a trip there in 1970, in part apparently for greater understanding and in part for recreation. He may have read *The Dangerous River*, although Patterson's biographer, David Finch, is not convinced he did so.[37] But he could have heard or read of Patterson's work in other ways. Trudeau was a wild river enthusiast, a member of a group that regularly took canoe trips in the North. Some of these people may have read or talked about the Nahanni because they—or even Trudeau himself—had read some of Patterson's earlier articles on the river in the well-known *Beaver*, the journal of the Hudson's Bay Company and now of Canada's Historic Society.[38]

In any event, when Trudeau was shown the proposed plans for the first phase of the Nahanni National Park Reserve, he apparently remarked, "Is that all?" The national parks people apparently decided not to follow up on this opportunity for a larger park. The result was the small Nahanni National Park Reserve of 1976. It was received well in some quarters: for example, in 1978 the Nahanni was designated by a federal–provincial committee as a Canadian National Heritage River and, later, as a United Nations World Heritage Site in 1988.

The small initial 1976 Nahanni National Park Reserve was, however, not satisfactory to some people in the Canadian national park agency as well as nongovernment conservation organizations including the National and Provincial Parks Association and its successor, the Canadian Parks and Wilderness Society. This society continued to lead the public struggle that had been underway since the early 1970s and, ultimately, the reserve was expanded in 2009. Table 2.1 illustrates the scope and continuity of its public campaigns.

The work of the Canadian Parks and Wilderness Society and other groups is described in more detail in the next chapter, along with other fundamental changes that facilitated expansion. Of major importance is the revolution in scientific and scholarly thought, methods, and practice that made an exceedingly powerful scientific case for a larger Nahanni National Park Reserve. Also of great importance was the shift from top-down to co-operative planning among the national park agency, the Canadian Parks and Wilderness Society, other nongovernment conservation organizations, and, particularly, the Dehcho First Nations.

Chapter 3

The Struggle for Expansion: New Ideas and Approaches in the 1980s and 1990s

While research has played a role in understanding and planning for landscapes of national parks and protected areas for decades, its type, sophistication, scale, and significance have grown considerably since the setting aside of land for the first phase of the Nahanni National Park Reserve in 1976. Improvements in theory and method in the ecological, earth, and social sciences have been increasingly applied to the understanding, planning, and management of Nahanni and other national and provincial parks since that time. Of special interest are changes in the general field of ecology, which was revolutionized, beginning in the 1980s, through the introduction of concepts such as biodiversity, landscape ecology, conservation biology, and population viability.[1]

The idea of biodiversity made it possible to identify and more fully understand the behaviour and importance of indigenous species and communities and their role in planning and managing wildland ecosystems. Landscape ecology led to a recognition of connectivity among natural areas as key to the maintenance and resilience of genetic, species, and community diversity in different parts of a landscape or region. Conservation biology prompted greater interest in the role and behaviour of wolves and other large carnivores in maintaining ecosystems and in the need to protect their large ranges inside and outside of national parks and other protected areas. The new concepts and theory were tied to advances in genetics, notably the understanding of DNA, which could be used to identify and monitor the behaviour of species through time and space.

Complementary advances in the analysis of satellite images (remote sensing) and computer-driven GIS made it possible to map landscapes, habitat features, and species movements in hitherto unknown detail and with greater speed. The new theory and methods were applied in the Nahanni watershed by John Weaver of the Wildlife Conservation Society, whose field studies joined Scotter's and Ford's as fundamental contributions to the history of the Nahanni National Park Reserve.[2] From 2002 to 2005, Weaver and his assistants collected grizzly bear hair at 225 survey stations distributed in and beyond the Nahanni watershed in what was termed the Greater Nahanni ecosystem. DNA from three samples was analyzed to reveal individual identity, gender, and genetic relatedness among these bears. This data enabled the mapping of grizzly bear density and indicated that most of the high-density areas were located outside the initial 1976 Nahanni National Park Reserve. Hair collected from an individual bear at widely separated locations showed that grizzly bears moved in and outside the reserve, with likely home ranges of 500–1000 km^2 or more. As a result of their freedom to roam through a large and intact landscape, as yet little disturbed by human activity, the Nahanni grizzly bear populations possessed the second-highest genetic diversity recorded in North America up to that time. Overall, this important research demonstrated that a watershed-scale expansion of the reserve was necessary to protect a viable population of the wide-ranging grizzly.

Weaver also did innovative research on caribou. Three major caribou herds are now recognized as using the Nahanni watershed for seasonal and entire annual ranges: the Nahanni, Coal-LaBiche, and Redstone. Previous research and telemetric tracking studies of these animals were mapped seasonally by Weaver and revealed that caribou wintered near Virginia Falls in the heart of the initial reserve, then migrated in spring

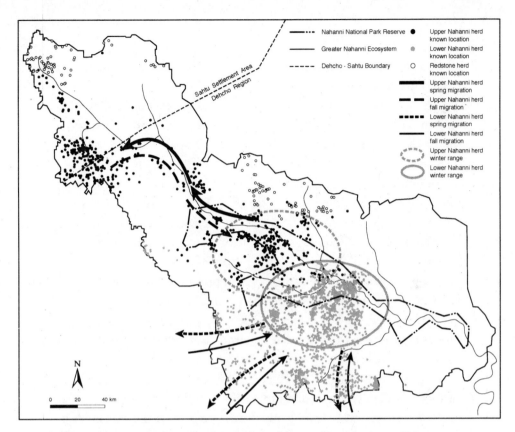

Figure 3.1. Schematic of Woodland Caribou Herd Seasonal Distribution and Movements. Adapted from Weaver (2006 and 2008).

upwards of 240 kilometres to the Nahanni headwaters to calve and raise their young. This key calving area was proposed for inclusion by Parks Canada in one of its alternative plans for the Náátsʹihchʹoh National Park Reserve. But when it was actually established in the northern watershed as a companion to the Nahanni National Park Reserve, it did not include the caribou calving area, thereby weakening the protection value of the new reserve. This issue is discussed again later in Chapter 8.

From 2004 to 2007, additional tracking of caribou wearing satellite radio collars showed that members of the Lower Nahanni or Coal-La-Biche herd spent much of the year along the southwest edge of the Nahanni watershed and adjacent Yukon before migrating upwards of 327 kilometres into the heart of the Nahanni National Park Reserve, south of Virginia Falls. Overall, then, the monitoring and mapping of caribou using the new technology showed that parts of their summer and winter ranges lay outside the initial 1976 reserve, making a strong case for expansion (Figure 3.1).

John Weaver also did wide-ranging field studies of Dall's sheep, an animal that is strikingly prominent in the conservation history of the Nahanni. It is discussed more fully in Chapter 6, along with the discovery of caves high in the walls of First Canyon by the adventurer Jean Poirel and his companions in 1966. These caves were explored more fully later by Poirel, and in detail by Derek Ford. In the Grotte Valérie, one of the larger caves, the skeletal remains of more than one hundred sheep were found; some carbon-14 dated at more than two thousand years old. During his research on Dall's sheep, Weaver found ewes and newborn lambs using caves in previously unmapped karst areas north of First Canyon and the original 1976 reserve boundary. Further mapping of Dall's sheep showed that most of their major ranges lay outside this boundary, supporting reserve expansion, as did the unique limestone and karst features themselves.

Weaver's mapping results from his field studies of the iconic grizzly, caribou, and Dall's sheep unequivocally demonstrated that the original park reserve was too small and narrow to protect these animals in their extensive movements to key habitats beyond the reserve borders. Weaver recommended that the entire South Nahanni River watershed and adjacent karst lands—some 38,000 km^2—be included in an expansion of the reserve. In doing so, he was trying to take advantage of a rare opportunity to match the scale of a protected area with the scale of animal needs and the natural presence of a supportive ecosystem.[3]

Of considerable concern, however, in the 2009 expansion agreement is the provision to exclude certain lands within the new reserve boundaries and allow zinc and other mining to develop, for example in the karst country north of the South Nahanni along the tributary valley of Prairie Creek (Figure 1.1). This property was located and under development before the initial phase of the Nahanni park reserve in 1972. Hard rock mining may also continue at Tungsten, or Cantung, along the western boundary of the extended reserve within the watershed of the Flat and Nahanni rivers. Arrangements have been made to phase out sports hunting areas in the expanded reserve, although some Parks Canada staff say some operators wish to retain their outfitting licences for the possible development of other types of recreation and tourism.

Another new concept that has contributed very strongly to Nahanni National Park Reserve planning and management is ecological integrity.[4] This concept was introduced in the 1980s with the strong support of conservation organizations such as CPAWS, and became the fundamental mandate for Canadian national parks in a 1988 revision of the National Park Act. The definition of "ecological integrity" can be quite complex. Some of the key elements are the maintenance of indigenous species and communities, and the capacity of ecosystems to sustain their basic biological, geological, and other processes, independent of the need for human intervention or management. In other words, the system has the capacity to regulate itself. It is self-sustaining and resilient after fire or other disturbances.

In the United States, the concept of ecological integrity is paralleled by the idea of intact wildlands or ecosystems.[5] These systems are considered to be functioning now as they were in the past. They are seen as diverse and resilient systems capable of long-term survival. The time horizon for these intact ecosystems is rather elusive, with historical studies of land use and landscape change being relatively rare, and the knowledge of the systems often being based on current scientific understandings and interpretations. Intact wildlands or ecosystems are discussed rather thoroughly for the Canada–Mexico Rocky Mountain chain in the ecologist Cristina Eisenberg's *The Carnivore Way*. One benchmark she refers to as an indicator of the early state of these systems is the journals of the famed Lewis and Clark expedition across the northern plains and the Rockies to the Pacific in 1803–1805.

In Canada, the ecological integrity concept rose in the context of scientific, citizen, and planning concerns about the impacts of expanding development on national parks in the 1980s. Banff National Park was especially affected, resulting in extensive ecological and other studies led by Parks Canada and ensuing planning and management changes. In the 1990s, the minister responsible for Parks Canada moved to advance the ecological integrity mandate by appointing an Ecological Integrity Panel, a group of concerned scientists and knowledgeable persons who conducted nationwide consultations while reviewing national park policies and practices in the light of the ecological integrity concept. This panel made numerous recommendations for its implementation throughout the national park system.[6]

Ecological integrity is a fundamental concept in the 2010 Nahanni National Park Reserve Management Plan completed after the 2009 expansion of the reserve.[7] It builds on the advances in theory and method made in the 1980s and 1990s, as well as on new planning and management documents such as the *State of the Park* report completed for Nahanni in 2009.[8] The *State of the Park* report made recommendations on wildlife and other issues and was a foundation for the development of the 2010 management plan.

The zoning system in the plan includes special ecological areas to protect highly sensitive features and habitats such as the Rabbitkettle Hot Springs, its tufa and travertine mounds, and surrounding terrain. Derek Ford considers the Rabbitkettle Hot Springs mounds to be the finest known to him in Canada. He sees the particularly outstanding north mound as threatened by river erosion and feels it should be protected by rip-rap barriers. Parks Canada policy is to let nature take its course. The mounds are sacred to the Dehcho people and home to distinctive plants and other species, including some usually found only in warmer habitats to the south. The hot springs and other highly significant sites were zoned as special ecological areas in early management plans and remain so in the 2010 plan.

Most of the Nahanni National Park Reserve was zoned as wilderness in 2010, as it was in earlier plans. The intention then was to limit disruptive human activities and protect the sights, sounds, and nature of what was then widely thought of as "pristine wilderness." In the 2010 plan, the intention is to protect wilderness, but more specifically the ecological integrity or resilience of the expanded reserve. The concept of ecological integrity provides a scientific basis for monitoring and studying changes in the indigenous plants, animals, geologic features, and processes making up the park ecosystem as opposed to the more nebulous concept of wilderness.

In this sense, wilderness can be seen as essentially static, the central idea being to keep the system in an undisturbed state so visitors can appreciate the classical awe and wonder of remote, historically wild landscapes—the wilderness experience. The concept of ecological integrity is generally supportive of the idea of wilderness but is more dynamic. It recognizes and allows for the formative changes that affect vegetation, animals, soils, and other features as they are altered over the decades and the centuries by floods, snow, ice, storms, earthquakes, fire, and other inherent ecosystem processes.

The basic idea in ecological integrity is that the landscape, or surface expression of the underlying park ecosystem, is in constant short- and long-term flux through time and space. From an ecological integrity standpoint, then, the Nahanni landscape, or wilderness, would not be expected to be generally uniform and undisturbed, but rather a patchwork or mosaic of plant, animal, and habitat types that fluctuate unevenly with fires, storms, floods, or other disturbances over large parts of the region. One manifestation of this in the 2010 management plan is that forest fires are allowed to burn, without attempts at control by humans, except near places like the village of Nahanni Butte, where they may pose threats to safety and social and economic well-being.

To what extent it will actually be possible to adhere strictly to the guiding concept and so exclude fire control is a key question. The idea of ecological integrity can essentially be viewed as neutral in the sense that fires, floods, erosion, and other inherent ecosystem processes should be allowed to work wherever, whenever, and to whatever extent they occur. However, this ideal runs up against some serious challenges mostly related to human values and activities. One clear example is the acceptance of fire control near Nahanni Butte for safety and economic reasons. Another is the proposal to control erosion of the Rabbitkettle mounds because of their geomorphic uniqueness and beauty. The argument could be extended to the unusual plant and biological characteristics of the mounds as well. A third example is the threat that climate warming and rising aridity will increase fire frequency and extent, leading to unwanted changes in wildlife habitat and calls for fire control.

In the early 1800s, moose are said to have been uncommon in the Aishihik region west of the Nahanni in central Yukon. By the 1880s, moose had become more numerous and the formerly more plentiful caribou uncommon. Some attributed this change to the Animal Mother. Others concluded that incoming prospectors and newcomers caused more forest fires, destroying the lichen-rich forests preferred by caribou, replacing them with fresh green growth attractive to moose.[9] Climate change and increased human activity could have similar effects in the Nahanni and lead to pressure to control fires.

Theoretically, the concept of ecological integrity should hold for the effects of long-term use by Indigenous people, as they have been an integral part of the Nahanni ecosystem for thousands of years. Such use has of course been seen, since at least the early twentieth century in North America, as incompatible with the wilderness ideal, which basically limits or excludes the effects of human activity from "pristine nature." If we wanted to try and represent nature as it was before the last glaciation and human invasion from Asia more than ten thousand years ago, then this perception would be understandable. But to do so would be to leave out the early spread of humans from Asia and their very long role in North America's ecosystems.

In this sense, the people of the Nahanni region—the Dehcho and Sahtu—are Athabascan, or Dene, members of a linguistic group thought to have been living in Alaska, Yukon, and bordering areas for thousands of years. On the basis of language, DNA, and archaeological evidence, the archaeologist Peter Bellwood[10] thinks the ancestral Dene may have migrated from Asia to the Americas 9,000–12,000 years ago, crossing the Bering Straits land bridge between the two continents before the bridge was flooded by rising ocean levels fed by massive volumes of meltwater from disintegrating alpine and continental glaciers.[11]

Since the late 1970s and early 1980s, the long role of humans in protected wildlands like the Nahanni has been increasingly recognized in Canada. One influence in this direction has been examples from other countries where relatively lightly populated and little-disturbed wildlands are known as "inhabited wilderness."[12] In Canada, recognition of the role of Indigenous people in creating, using, planning, and managing national parks has also been necessary for reasons of political and social justice. This recognition was spurred by legal decisions made in the early 1970s that tended to support First Nations' land rights. This, in turn, contributed to the federal government's decision to set up the mid-1970s Berger Commission with its recommendation to delay the Mackenzie Valley pipeline for ten years, giving Indigenous people time to prepare for development. All this made it very clear that scientists, planners, conservationists, politicians, and decision makers had to recognize Indigenous land rights and to plan co-operatively for their place in northern parks in particular. Furthermore, it soon became clear that centuries of experience and the Traditional Ecological Knowledge (TEK) of the Indigenous people could make very significant contributions to planning and management.

The village meeting and outreach activities of the Berger Commission reinforced a trend to move beyond traditional, centralized, top-down, or corporate planning, with its emphasis on identifying and achieving the goals and objectives of one organization or group of organizations such as government and industry. Broader consultative or civic approaches came into play, attempts to deal with the needs of more of the groups often excluded from but affected by development proposals and projects.[13] This was accompanied by a growing interest in finding ways of reducing the uncertainties often associated with more specialized and focused corporate planning. Examples of the newer thinking are ongoing, informal, transactive or interactive planning among affected parties, as well as more formal adaptive planning and management. This advocates proceeding in a series of steps, guided by monitoring and assessment of effects and ensuing consultations with concerned groups about these as well as unanticipated issues.[14]

These changes in planning theory and approach took root at about the same time as major changes were occurring in ecological and other sciences, as well as land use studies. The trend to break away from centralized corporate planning emerged strongly in the 1980s, in large part because governments cut budgets and reduced their involvement in fields such as parks, conservation, and social programs. The changes encouraged concerned private and government organizations and individuals to engage in interactive and adaptive planning, initially in order to bring more resources and interests to bear on issues no longer being effectively addressed by governments, although their ongoing use led to more effective planning.

The interactive process was adopted in efforts to expand the Nahanni National Park Reserve. The shift accelerated after the introduction of the 1987 reserve management plan, which was still basically in the top-down corporate planning mode.[15] It focused on federal governance of the reserve by the Canadian national park agency, now Parks Canada, with little involvement by the Indigenous people, who wished to retain some control and use of their homeland.

Interest in expansion of the reserve led Indigenous people and other major players to begin working interactively. The key players were Nahanni National Park Reserve superintendents such as Chuck Blyth, predecessors such as Erik Val, and ecologists, along with other staff in Parks Canada and the Canadian Wildlife Service. Others were CPAWS, with a newly created chapter in the Northwest Territories; inspirational, hard-driving, national leaders like Harvey Locke, innovator of the Yukon to Yellowstone Conservation Initiative (Y to Y); and Alison Woodley, an indefatigable conservation leader at the national office. Prominent also was Nahanni River Adventures, a conservation-oriented ecotourism company led by Neil Hartling. He brought two other Nahanni canoe and rafting companies into not always unanimous involvement by creating the Nahanni River Outfitters Association.

All these groups began to interact and co-operate in three basic ways. One was to exchange information more widely, for example by newsletters and the Internet. The second was to share promotional activities or collaborate in one another's activities. The third was to work together on a program or project. Eventually, the key players took up areas of emphasis and more specific roles. Parks Canada focused on the public policy process, making the scientific case for a watershed- or ecosystem-scale reserve big enough to protect the hydrologic integrity of the Nahanni and the large ranges of iconic mammals such as woodland caribou and grizzly. Parks Canada supported research and the securing of evidence, putting a case forward within government policy discussions about the expansion. Disagreements arose among Parks Canada, Indian and Northern Affairs, other government and private interests in Ottawa, and locally about the scale of the proposed expansion of the reserve, with the reserve superintendent, Chuck Blyth, playing a strong role in the expansion push.[16]

The Canadian Parks and Wilderness Society had supported a big wilderness and watershed approach since establishing the initial reserve in the 1970s. In discussions with the Dehcho First Nations, CPAWS eventually recognized traditional Indigenous use as part of its wilderness approach. CPAWS' main role was promotional and educational among thousands of members and citizens, notably in southern Canada, as well as with political decision makers. Northwest Territories and Yukon chapters were active locally, "on the ground," throughout the expansion effort. CPAWS also invested considerable effort engaging in regulatory reviews of the mining proposals in the watershed and in raising public awareness of the threat mining posed to the integrity of the watershed. Key to CPAWS' efforts was its close relationship and work with the Dehcho First Nations and with Parks Canada staff. CPAWS was most influential on a national basis with people sympathetic to the wilderness idea.

Nahanni River Adventures, and to varying degrees other outfitters, worked to protect the quality of the Nahanni for canoeing, rafting, and backcountry tourism. Their interests related to uses such as adventure and ecotourism and to the views of northerners and other Canadians less attuned to the wilderness idea. Hartling was known locally and interacted informally with other players, including Chuck Blyth, the reserve superintendent until his recent retirement.

Hartling also had good relations with the Dehcho. In earlier days, while he was camped near the shore of the Liard River, he and another traveller saved a man and his family who were en route to the village of Nahanni Butte at the mouth of the Nahanni. Their motor had broken down and they were drifting without paddles or lifejackets toward the Beaver Dam Rapids. Later, when Hartling was trying to secure a rare licence to guide river trips on the Nahanni, the rescued man helped him meet villagers and get the vital support he needed for the licence. Subsequently, he worked with the Dehcho and Grand Chief Herb Norwegian on the expansion of the Nahanni National Park Reserve.[17]

Table 3.1 is a selected list of conservation and expansion activities undertaken by Nahanni River Adventures and recorded in its regular newsletter, *Northern Currents*.[18] The newsletter is sent to numerous past and potential clients, as well as other concerned or influential persons. The list is reminiscent of the range of activities undertaken by CPAWS (see Table 2.1), reflecting the fact that CPAWS and Nahanni River Adventures coordinated closely in their campaign work. In addressing their efforts to groups and individuals with somewhat different interests, CPAWS and Nahanni River Adventures brought the case for expansion to a wider span of Canadians, as well as to people in the United States and other countries.

Nahanni River Adventures and CPAWS advertised and collaborated in holding Nahanni River visits for influential people such as Dehcho Grand Chief Herb Norwegian, the late Jack Layton and Olivia Chow of the New Democratic Party, Prime Minister Stephen Harper and John Baird of the Conservative Party, and Justin Trudeau, son of Pierre and subsequently leader of Canada's Liberal Party, who became prime minister in October 2015. A 2005–2006 CPAWS national tour brought together leaders such as Norwegian and Trudeau, scientists like Derek Ford and John Weaver, and songwriters and performers such as Sarah Harmer to support the campaign for protection of the Nahanni watershed. This large-scale and very influential year-long tour, known as Nahanni Forever, was driven by Harvey Locke of CPAWS. He anchored it and served as the master of ceremonies at all eighteen cities it visited, building a high level of public and political support for the expansion of the reserve. An important collaborator in the 2005 national tour was the Royal Canadian Geographical Society (RCGS). It linked the tour with its annual Fraser Lectureship in Northern Studies, with events offered in more cities than usual, including Kingston, Halifax, Waterloo, Hamilton, Montreal, Whitehorse, Vancouver, Calgary, and other centres across Canada. The events were well attended, involving thousands of members of CPAWS and RCGS supporters and concerned people.

Herb Norwegian was part of this and other events and had the opportunity to exchange ideas and views with key players, including government officials, members of CPAWS, and other conservation groups. Norwegian was one of the early Dehcho leaders in favour of

Table 3.1.

Nahanni River Adventures Public Communications for the Nahanni

Prairie Creek mine; write to prime minister and other ministers regarding dividing up of environmental assessments on the mine, lack of cumulative assessment, and uncertainty about integrity of surrounding area; potential cleanup costs to taxpayers (Spring 2002)

Update of Nahanni Prairie Creek mine; write to prime minister and other ministers about road issues (Summer 2002)

"Greater Nahanni Ecosystem Issue": mining represents most serious threat to ecological integrity of Nahanni; Prairie Creek inactive for twenty years; Canadian Zinc purchase and plan to open mine; need to clean up old tailing ponds; creek already contaminated; letter to Minister of Indian and Northern Affairs and Minister of Canadian Heritage, copied to Neil Hartling and Alison Woodley of CPAWS (Fall 2002)

"Nahanni National Park Issue Update": visionary Dehcho move to set aside 60 per cent of land base as a basis for park expansion, requesting readers write support letters, sample letter provided (Spring 2003)

"Nahanni Update": a call for letters supporting expansion to outgoing Prime Minister Jean Chrétien, copied to the Minister of Indian and Northern Affairs, Minister of Canadian Heritage, and local Member of Parliament (Fall 2003)

"The Grizzly Project and How You Can Contribute": on John Weaver's grizzly survey and its relevance to park expansion (Spring 2004)

"Nahanni National Park Update": on Parks Canada–Dehcho Memorandum of Understanding to expand reserve (Fall 2004)

"A New Prime Minister, A New Challenge": on meeting Paul Martin, Jean Chrétien's successor, and the need for people to write him supporting expansion; "Nahanni National Park Update": on confusion regarding cleanup of closed Century Tungsten mine; Prairie Creek mine application; concern about environmental impact assessment (EIA) and permit approvals (Winter 2004)

"Nahanni Mine: Derek Ford on Prairie Creek Mine Threats to Karst, and the UN World Heritage Award" (Fall 2005)

"Nahanni River Watershed Protection. THE JOB IS NOT FINISHED": in support of the Náàts'ihch'oh Reserve; and a call to write politicians, sample letter provided (Fall 2008)

"Nahanni Park Expanded" (Fall 2009)

reserve expansion, advocating for the protection of South Nahanni wilderness against the destructive effects of mining and other development, helping to ensure the Dehcho could use the land for hunting and other traditional activities in the future. Participation in collaborative and co-operative activities helped gain support from other players for traditional Indigenous activities as part of the 2009 expansion. The expanded park offered an avenue for young Indigenous people to learn about the ways of the past and to become aware of its values and uses now and in the future. The Dehcho are currently co-operating with the local Fort Simpson High School and Nahanni River Adventures in taking young students down the Nahanni annually.

Ways and means of working co-operatively were central to the 2009 Nahanni National Park Reserve expansion. The thinking of governments and NGO conservation organizations also gradually moved from ideal toward inhabited wilderness. By 2001, interaction and adaptation between Parks Canada and the Dehcho First Nations had built the inhabited wilderness idea into a simplified ecosystem model of the Nahanni, with the Dehcho or Dene shown as upper-level carnivores along with animals such as the wolf, eagle, and grizzly (Figure 3.2).[19] Government and NGO conservation organizations steadily became more interested in working with First Nations to protect potential park lands.

Precedents for negotiations were set in earlier so-called land claims settlements with Indigenous people that gave them varying degrees of control over park, mining, and other land use developments on ancestral lands, or Crown lands, depending on your point of view. An early example was the 1984 Inuvialuit Agreement with the people of the northern Mackenzie Valley, which led to the establishment of Inavik National Park. Later comprehensive land claims agreements with the Gwich'in and Sahtu also contained provisions relating to national parks. Another outstanding example was the federal government agreement in the 1990s to establish the separate, largely self-governing territory of Nunavut for the lands occupied primarily by the Inuit of the central and eastern Arctic.

An excellent example of the co-operative approach to national park reserve expansion was the convening in the 1990s of various Dehcho

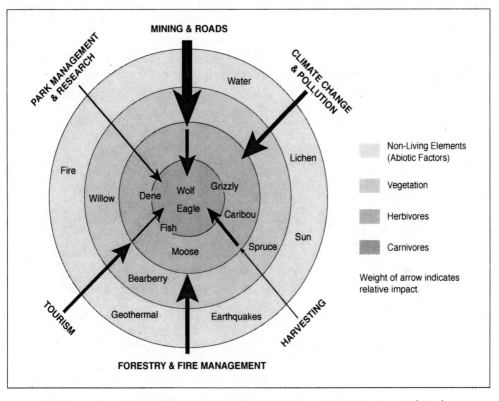

Figure 3.2. Simple Ecological Model of Nah?ą Dehé. Adapted from Parks Canada (2009).

First Nations, with the support and participation of the Northwest Territories chapter of the Canadian Parks and Wilderness Society, to articulate a Dehcho vision for their traditional lands, including hunting, trapping, conservation, spiritual and other values, and to co-operate in regional land use planning, including the national park reserve. Another bridge-building effort was the creation of the Nah?ą Dehé Consensus Team, a joint Parks Canada–Dehcho group formed to work together on reserve management and planning, including the completion of the Ecological Integrity Statement for the Nahanni National Park Reserve in 2001. This statement set out not only the simplified ecosystem model, which included the Indigenous people, but also the ecological integrity goals, objectives, and targets for the reserve. CPAWS sat on the consensus team for many years. Another joint Parks Canada–Dehcho team was formed to implement the 2003 decision to move forward on the reserve expansion.

In 2003, Parks Canada and Dehcho First Nations[20] signed a memorandum of understanding that stated Parks Canada would work co-operatively with affected Dehcho First Nations and other concerned parties toward completing within three years a feasibility study on:

- the addition of lands to the Nahanni National Park Reserve, or Nah?ą Dehé;

- recommending an amendment to the federal National Parks Act for a new boundary;

- guidelines for land use and development in the rest of the Greater Nahanni Ecosystem through a Dehcho land use plan; and

- moving, as part of the Dehcho final agreement, to full national park status under the National Parks Act.

The summary of the targets of the joint Ecological Integrity Statement are listed below. They combine Parks Canada's scientific and First Nations' cultural and natural perspectives, as well as those of major NGO conservation organizations such as CPAWS:

- preserve the ecological integrity of Nah?ą Dehé;

- establish Nah?ą Dehé as a model of co-operative management with First Nations of the Dehcho;

- improve the reserve's representation of the Mackenzie Mountains Natural Region;

- maintain natural ecological processes such as fire and flooding as primary forces shaping the ecosystem;

- maintain biodiversity (i.e., naturally occurring plant and animal communities);

- recognize and respect traditional human use as an integral part of the ecosystem;

- maintain wilderness quality and spiritual sense of place of Nah? ą Dehé;

- encourage visitor use and engagement within limits of ecological integrity; and

- use interpretation, environmental education, and training sessions, as well as daily personal and media communications, as a means for achieving ecological integrity.[21]

The various co-operative efforts of the 1990s and 2000s culminated in a series of documents and Nahanni National Park Reserve management plans that reflected progressive agreement on the key elements required by Parks Canada and First Nations for a park expansion.[22] These requirements were played off against the interests of mining and other development groups inside and outside government, as well as those of the conservation NGOs. Federal Environment Ministers such as John Baird and Jim Prentice played a strong supporting role at this time. The result was the 2009 expansion agreement that included much of the South Nahanni watershed and adjacent lands on the karst plateau to the north (Figure 1.1) but left out mining claims and operations at Tungsten on the upper Flat and on Prairie Creek. Permits were curtailed for outfitters that had provided sport-hunting opportunities. Indigenous people were to continue their traditional harvesting with due attention to conservation safeguards.

First Nations hunting and traditional rights were incorporated into the 2009 expansion. These activities are listed in the 2003 *Interim Park Management Arrangement* prepared by the joint Parks Canada–Dehcho consensus team.[23] The following cultural activities and "sustainable, traditional renewable resource harvesting activities" are included:

- hunting of mammals and birds;

- trapping of fur-bearing animals, fishing for freshwater and anadromous fish;

- gathering of traditional Dehcho First Nations' foods;

- gathering of plants used for medicinal or ceremonial purposes;

- cutting of trees for ceremonial and artistic purposes;

- conducting, teaching, or demonstrating ceremonies of traditional, spiritual, or religious significance;

- seeking cultural and spiritual inspiration;

- travelling into and within Nahanni National Park Reserve by motorized or nonmotorized vehicles for the above stated purposes;

- use of shelter or facilities essential to the pursuit of the above activities but not including Parks Canada operational facilities.[24]

The Dehcho people of Nahanni Butte have since developed traditional harvesting protocols for the reserve or Nah?ą Dehé. These protocols are definitely in line with the agreements made with Parks Canada at the time of expansion. The protocols are lengthy and apply to hunting, trapping, fishing, the harvesting of medicinal plants, and the use of motorized boats and vehicles. The protocols are quite comprehensive. Only the protocols considered most significant and indicative of the approach of the Dehcho people of Nahanni Butte will be given here. A preamble says that laws from the Creator were given to the Dehcho to live by. The most important law was respect for Creation—Mother Earth. The Dehcho were put here by the Creator to care for Mother Earth. In this spirit, the Nahanni Butte Dene Band encourages all traditional users to follow the protocols out of respect for the land and the community of Nahanni Butte.[25] Key protocols include the following.

- Traditional land use will be practised in a manner that allows the next person the opportunity to experience the site in the same way.

- Hunting and fishing will be for Dehcho First Nations members only, with some exceptions for fishing.

- Traditional land users will call the Nahanni Butte Office ahead of time and check in and out in respect for the community and safety.

- A Nahanni Butte member will, if possible, travel with the traditional user for safety reasons and to share knowledge.

- Meat will not be wasted and animal hides will be brought out.

- Hunting will not be allowed for commercial purposes, but secondary products such as moosehide may be sold.

- Unusable parts of fish and river animals will be placed in the river and other animal waste dispersed out of sight on the land. Unusable sheep parts will be buried under rocks.

- All fires should be out before leaving camp.

- Trees may be harvested for personal use and survival but not for commercial gain.

- Only Dehcho First Nations members will be allowed to use motorized boats and snowmobiles for traditional land use purposes.

- If a Dehcho First Nations member wishes to snowmobile for traditional use purposes, another Nahanni Butte member must accompany him.

- Access by aircraft for traditional use purposes is not allowed. Dehcho First Nations members should not be hunting with aircraft.[26]

Part II

WHY AND HOW THE NATURAL QUALITIES OF THE NAHANNI WERE CONSERVED IN THE PAST

Chapter 4

The Nineteenth-Century Fur Trade: The Early Years

A t this point we are left with a lingering and very fundamental question. In their studies of the Nahanni ecosystem, Parks Canada researchers found that, with the exception of a few exotics such as the coyote and cougar from the south, wildlife species and ecological processes were the same as in the past. The ecological integrity of the system was essentially unchanged. However, this conclusion is not based on any detailed historical studies. In the following chapters an historical analysis will be undertaken, not with expectations of finding any observations of possible fine-grained changes in species and ecological processes but rather in upper-level ones, such as wolves and other predators, whose presence is built on the health of prey and other lower-level species in the system.

The analysis focuses on the years after the arrival of the fur trade and is overwhelmingly based on historical documents, since archaeological research is still limited in the Nahanni watershed. The principal interest is the effects of humans, although some changes emanated from natural events such as the Little Ice Age (c. 1500–1900). We are aware of these because of our knowledge of global patterns of climate change, but these changes are not well understood in the Nahanni Valley.

As outlined in the Introduction, the historical analysis is organized in terms of eras: the early fur trade (Chapter 4), the later fur trade (Chapter 5), and the mixed economy including mining (Chapter 6). Each era tends to introduce a distinct set of economic, technical, and ideological ideas and practices that have the potential for different effects on the species and ecological processes at work in the Nahanni system. Each era is also built around the travels and observations of some remarkable travellers, traders, and scientists whose wildlife and other observations can be compared with one another to determine the extent and nature of any changes. The historical analysis is not, however, intended to be an attempt at a comprehensive study of the history of the Nahanni, but rather of any major land use and ecosystem changes. Chapter 7 offers a very brief summary of the findings, concluding that the natural diversity, resilience, and ecological integrity of the watershed remained high during two centuries of development activity. The bulk of Chapter 7 involves a detailed discussion of the reasons why the Nahanni escaped the widespread and often intense changes that affected so much of the surrounding lands and waters.

We know that fur traders from Montreal reached and wintered on Lake Athabasca by the late 1700s.[1] At this time, the Hudson's Bay Company was still conducting its trade from posts along Hudson Bay. The inland penetration of the Montrealers began to sap the Indigenous traffic to the Bay, and the Old Company began to expand westerly to compete for fur.

In the ten years after their arrival on Lake Athabasca, the Montreal traders moved north along the Slave River to Great Slave Lake. It was this lake, in 1793, from which Alexander Mackenzie made the first arduous and momentous fur trader's voyage down the river now bearing his name to the Arctic Ocean. The first known trading post on the Mackenzie was built in 1796 about eighty miles downriver from Great Slave Lake.[2] In 1800, John Thompson, a Montrealer with the North West Company, built Rocky Mountain House (or Fort) on the west side of the Mackenzie near the mouth of the North Nahanni River. A series of short-lived posts were soon built close to and up the Liard

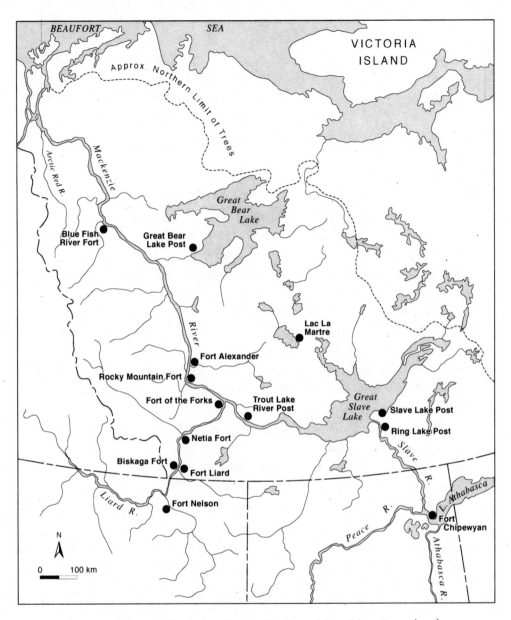

Figure 4.1. Mackenzie Valley to 1850, Fur Trading Posts. Adapted from Stager (1971).

River, in locations where they could conceivably tap the fur and trade of the South Nahanni Valley and its peoples.[3] The main posts were Fort of the Forks at the confluence of the Liard and Mackenzie (1802–1815), Netla Fort, on the Liard close to the mouth of the South Nahanni (1805–1806), and Biskagu Fort, upstream on the left bank of the Liard opposite the Biskagu or Muskeg River (1806–1811). John Stager mapped these in 1971, with dates slightly different than Keith's (Figure 4.1).[4]

We can gain insights into the effects of the trade in the North and the Nahanni region through the journals and observations of early traders and recent historical studies based on these sources. The first Montreal trader known to have reached the borders of Lake Athabasca and the Far North was the infamous Peter Pond, a man renowned for his endurance, persistence, and aggressive nature. Historian Barry Gough has recently described Pond's life story.[5] In 1778, Pond built a post south of Great Slave Lake on the lower Athabasca River, not far from its entrance to the great lake of the same name. In doing this, Pond opened the arduous, twelve-mile-long Methy Portage, bridging the gap between the south-flowing North Saskatchewan and the north-flowing Mackenzie River drainage.[6] Pond established trapping and trading relations with the Indigenous people of the surrounding regions, building on the earlier efforts of the Hudson's Bay Company. He secured excellent returns, bringing an estimated eighty thousand fine beaver skins out to the North Saskatchewan River and Cumberland House for the long transfer to Montreal.[7]

Pond continued to operate on the lower Athabasca for several years, creating a network of outposts and mobile traders who covered much of the Lake Athabasca region. Pond did not operate for long in isolation. He was part of a competitive group of Montreal traders including the Frobisher brothers and Alexander Mackenzie, who vied for wealth by forming shifting alliances in their competition for fur. Independent traders, or pedlars, also competed with these alliances and added to the take of beaver and other wildlife. Game was needed to feed the rising number of traders, so the big operators soon formed Indigenous supply networks for moose and other animals. The Athabasca area was home to wood bison that were hunted to make the dried meat and berries, or pemmican, that had long fed the Saskatchewan River trade. Bison herds as far away as the Peace River Country were hunted by the northern traders, with the meat moved along the Athabasca River as it flowed north from its source in the Rocky Mountains.

In recounting the Peter Pond story, Barry Gough also describes the beginnings of the environmental, social, and economic effects of the fur trade on the North, making observations similar to those of James Daschuk in his monumental *Clearing the Plains*.[8] Rivalry among the Montreal traders and Indigenous groups led to unrest, conflict, and violence in the North Saskatchewan and Great Plains country, and this spread to the North. The excessive use of alcohol and bad behaviour were issues recognized by leaders such as the intrepid Alexander Mackenzie.

The bringing of Old World diseases hitherto unknown to the Indigenous people, who were consequently unusually susceptible to them, was a great calamity. Outbreaks spread quickly ahead of the traders, making it difficult to know how high Indigenous populations were before their arrival. The great spread and range of outbreaks is illustrated by the smallpox epidemic of 1786. This disease is said to have arrived at Cumberland House on the lower North Saskatchewan in December 1781, carried by an Indigenous woman from the Mandan settlements along the Missouri. The disease then spread east and north to the Churchill and Athabasca rivers and Great Slave Lake. Flight offered no escape; it "destroyed with its pestilential breath whole families and tribes."[9] These observations are echoed by the eminent historical geographer, Arthur Ray, in his account of the rapid spread of the smallpox epidemic of 1837–1838 from St. Louis on the Missouri to Fort Edmonton on the North Saskatchewan and beyond in about six months.[10]

The social and economic effects of the outbreaks on Indigenous people are particularly difficult to estimate numerically but seem to have been profound. The effects on the fur trade were considerable, with both the Montreal and Hudson's Bay Company traders taking big losses. According to Gough, in 1782 the Hudson's Bay Company paid a dividend of 5 per cent. But no dividend was paid for 1783, 1784, and 1785, with a small one finally paid in 1786.[11]

All this is not to suggest that Indigenous populations in northern Canada and elsewhere in North America did not suffer from the effects of disease before Europeans arrived. Shepard Krech, in *The Ecological Indian: Myth and History*, wrote of scars on disinterred bones of Indigenous people "holding the memory of pre-Columbian endemic pathologies." Yaws, endemic and venereal syphilitic and other diseases apparently affected many people who lived in densely settled sedentary farming communities along the Atlantic seaboard. And tuberculosis was also found in the New World.[12]

Yet the effect of these indigenous diseases reportedly did not have the impact of the introduced and hitherto unknown afflictions that could fell Indigenous people before they actually met Old World people. Krech gives examples of major outbreaks spreading throughout North America as Euro-Americans carried diseases forward in the seventeenth century and afterwards. According to Krech, in the last decade of the eighteenth and first six decades of the nineteenth century, numerous diseases hit the Dene and other Athabascan-speaking people of the Mackenzie River region.

Given the state of medical knowledge at the time, the often-general nature of the symptoms, and the incomplete reports of fur traders, Krech found it difficult to identify many of the outbreaks. But he thought they included afflictions labelled as pox, measles, dysentery, whooping cough, and influenza. He cited one outbreak that killed many people, including some three dozen Dene. This was considered to be "a great number," presumably because it constituted a relatively large proportion of a lightly populated hunting and fishing people spread thinly through the northern forests.[13] Given the likely occurrence of these epidemics every few years or so, the Indigenous kill of wildlife was reduced, although this was quickly compensated for through the rising toll by the newcomers.

In *Clearing the Plains*, James Daschuk sees the prairies and the North as virtually transformed by the coming of the fur trade, with its market economy, competitive way of life, and vast gathering of fur for a large new external market. The effects of this new system were compounded by the interaction with other ongoing transformations such as the introduction of Old World diseases and climate change, notably the Little Ice Age, which Daschuk thought made life more difficult for wildlife and humans.

Previous to the coming of the trade, wildlife and the ecosystem were lightly burdened by an essentially subsistence and sharing economy, with relatively little demand from external markets. Daschuk concludes that, in a few decades, competition among the incoming traders from Montreal depleted fur-bearers, as well as large animals used for food both by the traders and Indigenous people. He underlines how the people suffered from hunger, poor nutrition and health, poverty, and population and social collapse. Daschuk says that as the search for furs moved into marginal production areas in the North, local Indigenous populations "were not only threatened by both European and aboriginal aggression but displaced from their seasonal subsistence cycles, suffering from terrible malnutrition and succumbing to pathogens that spread along the fur trade routes."[14]

The trade reached the Mackenzie Valley and Liard quickly (Figure 4.1). Indigenous people were displaced, and conflict ensued. Dunne-za (Beaver) peoples of the Peace River Country came into the Liard watershed, reportedly killing twenty-two "Nahanne," who likely were Kaska living along the Liard lowlands. At Mackenzie's post (Fort of the Forks), three or four "Christians" succumbed to starvation in the winter of 1812. Indigenous producers turned on the traders, killing five of them and their families.[15]

More details on the early fur trade years in the Liard–Nahanni area can be found in Montrealer fur trade journals kept by men such as Willard Ferdinand Wentzel.[16] Apparently originally from Montreal, he joined the North West Company in 1799 and served more or less continuously in the Liard River area from 1802 to 1815. Most of his time was spent at the Fort of the Forks, where he worked as a clerk, occasionally taking exploratory journeys up the Liard. He was an experienced trader who dealt successfully with fierce competition, notably from the XY Company, a rival Montreal firm. Wentzel left us three documents that illuminate the Montreal trade and its effects on the land and people of the Liard region: the Fort of the Forks journals for 1805–1806 and 1807–1808, and his 1821 summary of his experience in "Account of the Mackenzie's River With A Chart."[17]

Among other things, the fort journals show that diseases were a problem not only for Indigenous people but also wild animals. They were suffering from "some form of distemper," "with great numbers found all over, some unable to rise themselves upon their legs and others dead."[18] Diseases among the Indigenous people were very serious. On February 9, 1806, for example, some people came to the Fort of the Forks and reported that outbreaks were raging with "astonishing fury among them." Several had died.[19] The year 1807 appears to have been a dry year in the fort area, with great fires said to have almost overrun the whole country.[20] No mention is made of the cause of these fires, but the coming of the fur traders likely led to more of them.

Relying on his approximately two decades of experience in the country, Wentzel's 1821 "Account of the Mackenzie's River" provides a useful summary of the fauna, flora, Indigenous people, and general geography of the Mackenzie and Liard River area at the time the Montreal traders merged into the Hudson's Bay Company.[21] He says the Liard River is the richest in fur species and large animals in the Mackenzie River region: "It produces buffaloe, Moose Deer, the stag, Rein Deer, and Mountain Sheep and Goat." For the trader, its principal attractions were "the numbers of its beaver, black, brown and grizzly Bear, lynxes, Martins, otters, Minks, Wolverines, black, silver, cross; and red foxes and wolves."[22] The area was also "favourable to the culture of foreign vegetables," "potatoes, turnips, cabbages, radishes, beets, lettuce, carrots, barley and even Peas have been known to thrive with little care."[23]

Wentzel saw the potential of the Liard early on and worked to extend the trade upriver, leading to the establishment of posts such as Netla and Biskagu (Figure 4.1). In 1805, the river posts were reported to have done well with 112 packs secured—at about ninety pounds of fur per pack—approximately three-quarters of the returns being beaver.[24] According to Wentzel, the other posts in the Mackenzie's River area did well for a time, but the trade fell off. He attributed this "to the most erroneous system of conduct on the part of some of the managers of Mackenzie's River, contributing to the ruin of the trade, the loss of some company personnel," and "Indigenous contempt for the trader's morals and character."[25] The Indigenous peoples were pushed very hard to secure fur, to the neglect of game and shortage of food: when not productive of fur, they were seen as lazy and were subject to mistreatment and abuse. In some situations they reacted violently. Many withdrew from the trade. In his 1971 "Fur Trading Posts in the Mackenzie Region up to 1850," geographer John Stager put these pressures in a wider context, giving early recognition to the high costs of the fur trade in the far northwest. The exchange of fur and supplies between Montreal and the Mackenzie region involved thousands of miles of arduous travel by canoe. It took at least four years from the launching of supplies at Montreal to the arrival of the furs to pay for them. The necessary capital required much credit and interest before any profits. Stager concluded the Mackenzie trade was marginal, both geographically and economically.[26]

To what extent the Nahanni people were affected by these circumstances is uncertain. The people who came to Fort of the Forks and other nearby posts were mainly the Dunne-za, the Slavey, and Dogrib, who were generally located to the south and east of the Liard. The Nahanni are not mentioned much in the Liard River post journals and do not seem to have been significantly involved in the trade. In spite of attempts to reach them, including an unsuccessful expedition by Wentzel himself in 1807, the Nahanni people remained elusive. The valley and watershed, with their game animals and fur-bearers, quite possibly were little affected by the trade. However, it is difficult to believe that the Nahanni escaped the contagious outbreaks of smallpox, other European diseases, and some of the repercussions these had on hunting, trapping, and wildlife.

The traders' difficulties in dealing effectively with the Indigenous peoples in the Liard Valley and other parts of the Mackenzie basin were generally compounded by a decline in yields because of growing Indigenous reluctance to trade, high take of the most accessible animals, interference with supplies from Montreal in the War of 1812, and the rising costs of operations relative to returns. Competition from the Hudson's Bay Company also began to grow steadily after 1804. In 1815, the North West Company withdrew from the Athabasca and Mackenzie districts. The Liard country was left largely untapped for a time, although it was probably subject to some hunting and trapping by people such as the Dunne-za from the Peace River region.

Like the Liard, the Peace River offered a major route through the Rockies into the interior of British Columbia. It had been followed in the late eighteenth and early nineteenth centuries by Northwesters such as John Finlay. He crossed the Rocky Mountains and undertook preliminary exploration of the river now bearing his name in 1792. The Peace River efforts seem to have run into the same kinds of difficulties that plagued the Mackenzie–Liard country. Harvesting efforts fell off, not to be revived substantially until the rise of the Hudson's Bay Company, following its great amalgamation with the Northwesters in 1821–1822.

George Simpson, the vigorous new governor of the combined Hudson's Bay Company, immediately began to review operations and plan for expansion throughout western North America.[27] Mackenzie's post, later known as Fort Simpson, was built near the ruins of the North West Company's Fort of the Forks in 1822 and efforts again were made to develop the trade along the Liard and in the Nahanni Valley. The Nahanni were "unknown people," not directly involved in the trade, as apparently was also the case earlier during the Montreal era. According to Cooke and Holland in their general historical summary of northern exploration in Canada, the Hudson's Bay people, at the time of the establishment of Mackenzie's post, tried to reach the Nahanni in early 1823.[28] This effort failed and a new trader, John McLeod, tried again in the spring of 1823.

Cooke and Holland state that McLeod and his party canoed up the Liard and entered the South Nahanni River on June 10. He struggled upstream, eventually leaving the river and continuing westward on foot. After a long search, McLeod met some "Nahanni Indians" "beyond the fourth range of mountains," west of the Nahanni Valley in early July. He promised to return the next year with trade goods from Fort of the Forks, or Mackenzie's Post.[29] He came back in 1824, going west of the Nahanni then returning to Deadmen Valley and the canyons. He apparently found the Indigenous peoples on the nearby Meilleur River (Figure 1.1). McLeod persuaded the chief to go to Mackenzie's Post, where he described his country to the traders and promised to return in spring with furs.

According to Cooke and Holland, trade followed for a few years, but then interest in the Nahanni Valley fell off, in part apparently because of Nahanni reluctance to trade and also because the Nahanni Valley did not offer a workable route to the west and the lucrative returns thought to be available in Yukon and the interior of British Columbia.[30] The Hudson's Bay Company moved west, up the accessible, yet turbulent, Laird, bypassing the Nahanni.[31] The journals of John McLeod have not yet been published. An early attempt to secure a readable documentary copy was unsuccessful. So a search was made for an alternative source of information likely to be relevant to the Nahanni region. The choice was to use the journals of Samuel Black, who was chosen by George Simpson to reopen the way along the Peace River Valley into British Columbia's interior. Black undertook his journey in 1824 and his journal was published in 1955.[32] His account of the country and its people offers another window into possible land use and landscape conditions in the mountainous Liard and Nahanni region during the new HBC regime.

Black, a rugged former Northwester, had a reputation that more or less matched his name. Earlier, as Montreal traders, he and his friend Peter Skene Ogden were major intimidators of Hudson's Bay staff involved in the trapping and trading of fur. They harassed and threatened them, as well as Indigenous peoples inclined to trade with the Hudson's Bay rather than the North West Company. When the North West and Hudson's Bay companies amalgamated in 1821, Black and Ogden were left off the list of Northwesters invited to join the new combined company.[33]

However, both Ogden and Black were energetic and vigorous men. Black was a large strong man, adventurous and hard-driving. George Simpson, governor of the new firm, was eager to open new fur ground to obtain yields needed to offset declines caused by past exploitation and allow for recovery measures in older "exhausted" trapping areas. Simpson therefore took Ogden and Black on board, assigning Ogden to open up territory in the Snake River country south of the Columbia River. Black was to explore beyond the Rocky Mountains in the little-known and rugged lands of the Finlay, Stikine, and upper Liard River area. He began his journey from Hudson's Bay, going west along the North Saskatchewan and Athabasca rivers to the upper Peace River. Black spent the winter there, familiarizing himself with the country and recruiting a crew of eight, including a hunter, fisherman, and interpreter to accompany him on his trip to the Finlay.[34] Black was hardy, determined, and ambitious, especially for exploration. George Simpson thought he was just the man to open new ground and obtain the additional furs needed by his company.

Black prepared a very detailed journal that was edited by the historian E.E. Rich and published by the Hudson's Bay Record Society in 1955. It has an instructive introduction by R.M. Patterson, who, about a century later, also travelled into the Finlay River country where Black made his 1824 journey. Black's predecessor, John Finlay, apparently had only briefly visited the river in 1792.[35] But Black went further upriver and beyond the watershed into the Pacific-bound Stikine River drainage. He pressed north as far as the Turnagain River, which flows into the Liard and, eventually, the Mackenzie. The Turnagain and the upper Liard country lie perhaps 250 kilometres west and south of the highlands bordering the South Nahanni and its west bank tributaries such as the Flat and Meilleur rivers.

Black was given rather general instructions on what he was to accomplish during his journey. He was asked to answer three major questions regarding: 1) the prospects of travel to the northwest; 2) the numbers of beaver; and 3) the possibility of maintaining a post at the head of the Finlay.[36] Black, a loquacious man of "good Scottish education," fortunately went beyond this, giving many details on the geology, landforms, forests, animals, and people of this mountainous country. Black's journals show that the Indigenous peoples in the Finlay travelled extensively, mainly by foot, for hunting and subsistence, as did the people met by John Mcleod in his earlier search for Indigenous people in the Nahanni Valley area in 1823.[37] All in all, it seemed reasonable to use Black's Finlay journal as a proxy for the study of land and life in the nearby South Nahanni area during the early years of the HBC fur trade era.

After a long and difficult journey, Black concluded that beaver and other fur-bearers were not numerous enough to attract or support the trade. Nor were the game animals plentiful and reliable enough to maintain a trading post. Beaver were generally only encountered in those reaches of the valley where gentle slopes, thicker sediments, slower stream flow, and poplar and other vegetation provided a workable habitat for the sustenance and engineering of these animals. Their trails could be quite extensive. The beaver built "roads" extending, in at least one case, well up the mountain slopes to harvest trees. To quote Black, "where soft ground with wood eligible for the Beaver had been accumulated Beaver were to be found, otherwise except in such places here and there the whole country is one continued Mountain and Valley of Rock and Stone and can by no means come under the denominations of a Beaver country in the common acceptance of the word."[38] Black also stated that the mountains were "so barren of the means of subsistence that trappers will always be compelled on the approach of winter to go to the plains to support themselves."[39]

Food sources such as caribou, mountain or Dall's sheep, marmot, and other animals were found in the mountains, but unevenly and with difficulty in winter. Black thought the mountains might be trapped from foothills or plains posts where moose were more plentiful and bison could be harvested. Hudson's Bay people might do this job themselves, or perhaps use the Iroquois. They had already moved with the fur trade west from their St. Lawrence homeland and were hunting in the Rocky Mountain region. Black saw the mountainous country as difficult habitat for travel, both by men and animals. The reindeer, or caribou, had "great powers in this way . . . The Indians in such cases follow the Reindeer roads and the deer, in turn, follow the Indian's roads . . . the Mountain Sheep and Goats often take the best windings to reach the summits of the Mountains, but often eccentric and choose intricacies not to be followed by man. The bear hobbles about among the Rocks, Woods and wet places in all directions."[40]

Caribou, as well as Dall's sheep, were hunted along with marmots and other animals by both the Indigenous peoples and Black and his men. Methods of Indigenous hunting included old pounds or enclosures for driving and "ensnaring Reindeer."[41] But game was generally scarce. The First Nations peoples seemed to travel in small groups and live off food sources of little interest to the traders. For example, in late May, when the lower ridges of the mountains were still completely covered in snow, Black encountered some Indians in the lower Finlay Valley who had been living on "a Partridge or a hare now and then—their principal subsistence was Roots and Herbs."[42]

These observations are generally similar to those made of Indigenous people of other parts of the Rocky Mountains.[43] Among them are the Sheepeaters of northwestern Wyoming and the Yellowstone National Park area.[44] These people apparently arrived in this area as late as 1800. They were preceded by other First Peoples with generally similar subsistence patterns and ways of life. According to Janetski, the Sheepeaters seem to have followed a two-phase migratory pattern.[45] They tended to winter in the valleys and lower borderlands, moving in summer to the higher mountains where they lived to a substantial degree on new roots and bulbs such as the camas, as well as blue and other berries. They ate these fresh, or made ground mush for storage and eating later in the year.

Much of Yellowstone mountain country is heavily forested, but substantial areas are in high-level tundra, sparsely treed savannah or parkland, and grassy prairie. These diverse plant communities are attractive to animals such as bighorn sheep, deer, and black and grizzly bears. Bison and elk apparently migrated into the lower and middle valleys and slopes in summer. The Sheepeaters hunted all of these animals but appear to have relied considerably on sheep, which reportedly were numerous in the higher mountains.

Sheep seem to have been captured through group or communal drives between low lines of stones and trees into natural or man-made traps. Remains of many of these drive lines and traps can still be found in decayed condition in Yellowstone National Park or adjoining parts of Utah, Montana, and Colorado.[46] They were used by Indigenous hunters in the Yellowstone and nearby areas for thousands of years before the arrival of Euro-Americans. The lifeways of the Finlay River people seem to have been generally similar to the Sheepeaters, although we have relatively little detail on the kind of pounds, enclosures, or traps they used and how frequently they did so. It appears the Finlay people may have used drives and traps to hunt caribou as much as sheep.

Bears of the Finlay country, including what appear to have been "great brown, gray or white grizzlies," were generally elusive, seemingly avoiding human contact. Black does not mention any attacks by or upon bears like those recorded by explorers such as the Americans Lewis and Clark in their early 1800s journeys in the Missouri country. Black and members of his party were prepared to kill them on at least one occasion. Their companion, an old Indian, would not consent to it, "such is the Idea of the Indians concerning Bears."[47] For the Indigenous peoples to kill the great grizzly would have been difficult because they had few firearms at the time, although they did have iron-tipped weapons. The metal reportedly was obtained relatively recently by trade with Indigenous people who lived between them and the trading posts that the Russians had built at Sitka and other sites along the Pacific coast of Alaska and British Columbia in the late 1700s and early 1800s.

Black reports only the one example of a contrary attitude toward the killing of bears, so it is difficult to give much weight to this evidence. However, prohibition of, or limits upon, killing of bears or other animals were not uncommon among the Indigenous people of North America. In his *North American Indian Ecology*, J. Donald Hughes gives much detail on Indigenous attitudes and behaviour toward animals generally.[48] According to Hughes, animals were seen as closely related to humans. Both were part of a complex and interrelated world. Animals' consent was considered necessary for killing. This was preceded by careful rituals. Ceremonies were held to placate the hunted animal and secure success. There appears to have been a rather pronounced tendency to give special respect and care to powerful animals such as the eagle, the wolf, and the bear.

The great bear, or grizzly, was particularly strong and dangerous to hunt, having attributes such as great energy and size that the Indigenous peoples respected and wished to acquire. The black bear seems to have been more commonly and easily hunted. An entire tribe of people could participate in important seasonal hunts such as the spring emergence of bears from hibernation or the start of the fall hunt when these animals were generally well-fed and in prime condition.[49]

Aside from spiritual and ceremonial considerations in hunting the bear, we also have to consider some practical ones. The old Indigenous man who would not consent to Black and his men killing a bear may have felt the situation was unusually risky for an attack on such a powerful animal, or perhaps that he and the Hudson Bay people simply had not had time to go through the rituals necessary before such a hunt. To the extent that such attitudes and limitations were longstanding, they help to explain the large population of bears and other animals in at least parts of the continent at the time of the arrival of Europeans and Americans. Their frequently aggressive attitudes and firearms soon took a heavy toll on them.[50]

In his *Make Prayers to the Raven*, an ethnographic study of the Koyukon, an Athabascan people living in the Koyukuk River Valley, a tributary of the Yukon, Richard K. Nelson casts more light on the beliefs, understandings, and behaviour of northern Indigenous people toward bears and other wildlife.[51] Nelson warns that his findings are not necessarily applicable to other Indigenous groups. During his lengthy residence with the Koyukon, listening to their oral histories and participating in hunting, fishing, and other activities in the 1970s and 1980s, Nelson gained a remarkable grasp of their wildlife beliefs and practices. He offers detailed information on their ideas and behaviour toward animals ranging from small fur-bearers such as the weasel and muskrat, through to herbivores such as the moose and caribou, to large mammals such as the otter, lynx, and black and brown bear or grizzly.

The bears were among the most revered of animals. The black bear had somewhat lower status than the grizzly but was hunted as a prime source of meat and fur in spring and fall. The grizzly was generally avoided because of its size, strength, energy, and inclination to attack humans when disturbed. Such thinking could well have been behind the elder Indian's reluctance to attack a bear when urged to do so by Samuel Black.

On July 15, 1824, while in the upper reaches of the Finlay River, Black met with Indians of a clan or tribe different from his Indigenous guides. These strangers knew of "Nahanni people" who had come into the upper Liard watershed, bringing "Muskets, Powder and Ball, axes, etc." to trade for skins, including those of the siffleur or marmot. Some of the Nahanni people wore clothes like Black's, notably Russian sheeting trousers said to be lighter than canvas or sailcloth.[52] It may be that these Nahanni people included "Creoles," offspring of Russian men and Indigenous women living at posts on the Pacific coast. The Russian expert, Natalie Stoddard, stated the "Creoles" wore Russian clothing and may have become involved in interior trade.[53]

Two days later, on July 17, Black was told by some other Indians that the Nahanni people he had heard about earlier likely were not those met by John McLeod in the Nahanni Valley the year before— in 1823—showing that news could spread quickly and widely among both the Indigenous people and fur traders. According to these other

Indigenous informants, the Nahanni mentioned to Black were from the north and had obtained their trade goods from "the people of the sea," or Russians, via intermediary people living closer to the Pacific.[54] Here it is difficult to sort out who the term "Nahanni" refers to, since the name seems to have been applied to people of somewhat different groups, clans, or tribes. They may have been part of a larger confederacy that hunted and traded over a large area beyond the Liard and the upper Finlay country. A possible analogy is the Plains Blackfoot confederacy, which consisted of tribes such as the Peigan, Bloods, and Blackfoot, hunters in the western plains of what is now Canada and the United States. Nahanni identity is addressed again in Chapter 8.

Intriguingly enough, the poor condition of Indigenous peoples encountered by Black could have been due, at least in part, to the introduction and early spread of European diseases by the Russians. In his seminal *Ecological Imperialism: The Biological Expansion of Europe, 900–1900*, Alfred Crosby tells how they brought numerous diseases with them into Siberia during their great advance in the sixteenth, seventeenth, and eighteenth centuries, including smallpox, measles, scarlet fever, typhus, venereal diseases, and breath-borne infections likely to be highly contagious in the close quarters of long-winter dwellings.[55] This transfer of afflictions initially stopped at the Pacific coast but eventually was carried across the sea into North America.

In her ethnological studies of the Russian fur trade, Natalie Stoddard found that one of its unintentional effects was the introduction of diseases such as syphilis and tuberculosis. Outbreaks of these had serious effects on Indigenous peoples. Soon after reaching Norton Sound on the Alaskan west coast in the 1780s, the Russians reported that Indigenous populations had dropped due to the introduction of smallpox.[56] This and other diseases could, however, have been introduced by other Europeans, especially Spaniards exploring the North American west coast beyond their stronghold in southern California, then part of Mexico.

Aside from the early 1770s voyages of the great English explorer James Cook, sailors and traders from a number of other European countries and the east coast of the United States, including Boston, had voyaged and traded along the northwest coast of America by 1800.

Like the Russians, these people were interested in obtaining furs for sale in the lucrative Chinese market. The Americans began to compete in the sea otter trade in 1788. By 1793, at least eight American ships were trading along the coast with less frequent arrivals of French, Portuguese, and other vessels. So, while the Russians seem the most likely source for the introduction of Old World diseases to British Columbia's coastal areas following their arrival in the late 1700s, other newcomers likely contributed as well.[57]

Samuel Black does not make specific reference to disease outbreaks among the Indigenous peoples he encountered. His lack of comment may have been due to his familiarity with the effects during his decades of experience with Indigenous people in the fur trade on the Great Plains. Nevertheless, many of the Indigenous groups that Black encountered were short of food, starving, thin, and gaunt. Some came from areas once having plenty of reindeer, or caribou, which had been driven away or killed by Indigenous people using snares. The decline could have been due to heavy hunting by local people, displaced nomads from neighbouring areas, or intermediary Indigenous peoples seeing opportunities to hunt and trade Russian goods with interior tribes, or a combination of these effects.

Certainly, Black's journal leaves an impression of movement of different Indigenous groups into the upper Finlay and Liard in the early 1800s, disturbing wildlife and earlier ways of life. On the other hand, Black's observations also suggest that the Indigenous peoples in the mountains had long lived close to the edge in an environment less favourable than that of the plains. The Indigenous peoples frequently ate small mammals like the marmot, or roots and other plants. They also relied considerably on trout and other fish caught mainly in wood-fibre nets in lakes scattered across the Finlay region. However, this supply seemed to be precarious and was quickly depleted, at least temporarily, by fishing pressure. A main source of subsistence for Black's party appears to have been dried buffalo meat, or pemmican, brought with them from east of the Rockies. Black resisted pressure from the Indigenous peoples to share this nutritious fare with them.

One other question of considerable interest is whether Black's journal can shed light on the frequency and extent of wild fires in pre-fur trade times. Ecologists want this information so it can be compared with more recent fire observations and conclusions. Studies of recent forest fire history suggest that fires in the Nahanni were relatively limited in extent in the 1960s, 1990s, and 2000s, and more extensive in the 1970s and 1980s.[58] The 1980s was a decade when high temperatures and aridity were relatively common. Most of the 1970s and 1980s fires were in the southern and southwestern area, where human activity is more frequent. Theoretically, fires could be due to careless or deliberate burning by humans, but, on the other hand, also to lightning, drought, or climate change.

Black's observations are of limited help in making early-nineteenth-century comparisons with such patterns, although careless and accidental effects of the traders are a major message left by his journals. On August 29, for example, Black returned to a cache made during an earlier trip upriver. He found it "destroyed by fire and every article we left in it reduced to ashes by the moss and pointed wood having taken fire after our departure—although every precaution had been taken to get the fires properly extinguished, some sparks had been lurking in the moss in some of the encampments—the Powder had exploded and the lead melted into lumps."[59]

Black describes what appear to have been large fires caused by the passage of his party through the mountains. On July 9, he was "sorry to observe that some of our fires coming up has completely desolated those fine valleys of Wood." Much of the land "is completely burnt and left a dreary waste discovering the bare rocks through the Black stems of burnt trees."[60] Black rarely refers to older burned stands, leaving the impression that Indigenous, or lightning-caused, fires were not very numerous or extensive in the Finlay, Stikine, and upper Liard country in the years before the arrival of Europeans. However, it is not possible to estimate fire frequency from his journal.

Recent research on fire histories in the Nahanni National Park Reserve itself, using the Canadian Forest Service Large Fire Database for 1959–1999, as well as fire scar studies and other evidence, can be compared with this conclusion, which is of course based on the observations of only one early Euro-American explorer, Samuel Black. For example, the Large Fire Database indicates that about 11,494 hectares burned in the Nahanni National Park Reserve in 1959–1999. A total of eleven fires over two hundred hectares reportedly occurred, with four in 1983 and three being subject to control efforts.[61] All of the fires were considered to be caused by lightning.

The fire scar studies yielded an estimated mean fire frequency return interval of about twenty-one years for the period of 1813–1974 (161 years). On the basis of a different analytical method, this interval was estimated at twenty-eight years. In these fire scar studies, no estimate was made of lightning as opposed to human-caused fires. Overall, the available evidence suggests that since early Euro-American times, periodic fires occurred on average four or five times a century.

After analyzing Samuel Black's journal I went north, in August 2013, for the raft trip down the Nahanni. En route, I stopped in Yellowknife and visited the Cellar Bookstore, where I found a copy of Patterson's *Those Earlier Hills*.[62] This book is a historic collection of many of Raymond Patterson's early travel essays republished from previous copies of the Hudson's Bay Company periodical, *The Beaver*. One essay on "The Nahany Lands" is an edited version of Patterson's 1961 account of J.M. McLeod's 1823 and 1824 forays into the Nahanni River basin. In preparing this essay, Patterson had access to an unpublished version of McLeod's journal.

During the Yellowknife stop, I also had discussions with some knowledgeable local people about their understanding of the history of the Nahanni Valley and the efforts to create a Nahanni National Park Reserve. One of them later suggested that useful information on the early fur trade and its effects on the Nahanni might be found in the nineteenth-century Fort Simpson and Fort Liard journals in the Hudson's Bay Company Archives (HBCA) in Winnipeg. I contacted the archives and found that the journals for these posts were quite voluminous. I decided to concentrate on Fort Simpson because this was the older post of the two and had served as a depot for the Liard–Mackenzie River region.

Most importantly, HBCA staff informed me that the Fort Simpson journals included copies of John McLeod's unpublished reports of his 1823 and 1824 expeditions to the Nahanni. I was able to go to the archives for about one week in early December 2014. I found, on arrival, that an attempt to review all of the Hudson's Bay Company Fort Simpson journals was impossible. They consisted of daily entries made from

1822 to the 1890s. So I selected the 1822–1823 journal, as it contained McLeod's expedition report, and then reviewed journals at approximately ten-year intervals for 1832–1833, 1843–1844, and 1863–1864 in the expectation they would reveal any basic changes in the fur trade and its effects, particularly on the Nahanni.

The archives also held past copies of the Hudson's Bay Company's periodical, *The Beaver*. The summer 1961 issue included Raymond Patterson's "The Nahany Lands," later republished in *Those Earlier Hills*. This essay had a sketch map of McLeod's 1823 and 1824 journeys that was omitted in the version of McLeod's trips published in *Those Earlier Hills*. This sketch map is useful as it helps sort out McLeod's confusing descriptions of the unknown and unnamed country through which he was travelling (Figure 4.2). Patterson prepared the map based on his experiences in the Nahanni, guided by McLeod's references to major landmarks such as the series of mountain ranges he crossed during his journey. Other issues of *The Beaver* contained useful articles on men such as Robert Campbell, the tough Hudson's Bay Company traveller and explorer who undertook early forays into the upper Liard River Valley, west of the Mackenzie Mountains and the headwaters of the Nahanni watershed, where he encountered numerous Nahanni people.[63]

The following summary and interpretation of the early fur trade and its effects on the Nahanni Valley and its people rests on all the foregoing sources: the 1823 Fort Simpson journal and report on McLeod's first foray into the Nahanni; the Fort of the Forks or Fort Simpson journals for 1832–1833, 1843–1844, and 1863–1864; and Patterson's "The Nahany Lands," as republished in *Those Earlier Hills*, as well as the original version in the 1961 issue of *The Beaver* and other articles in this now defunct Hudson's Bay Company periodical.

A review of the 1822–1823 Fort Simpson journal provides far more detail than the brief account I discussed earlier from Cooke and Holland. McLeod's explorations were sparked by Indigenous visitors' descriptions of the Nahanni as an "unknown people," said to inhabit a mountainous region rich in furs. A short-lived winter exploration did not locate them. But this party reported that the country through which they travelled had many beaver, as well as moose and other game needed to support traders. This initial party likely travelled west along the Liard lowlands into the lower Nahanni River and the branching channels of the Splits, good habitat for beaver, muskrat, and other fur-bearers, as well as moose.

John McLeod's journey was undertaken a few months later, in early June 1823, and lasted for about one month. McLeod started from Fort Simpson with about four or five men. They went up the Liard to the Nahanni River's mouth. Along the way, the group grew to about fifteen or twenty people, including Indigenous and Metis voyageurs, hunters, and an interpreter. Some of these people appear to have hunted in the Nahanni previously, perhaps during the North West Company years, and knew of Nahanni people. McLeod started up the river in his big canoe loaded with men and supplies. En route, he sent hunters out and they returned with moose and other game. After a few days, the party stopped in the Splits below the First Canyon, cached their canoe and some supplies, and then set off cross-country to the northwest. They were plagued here by frequent and debilitating attacks by mosquitoes. In the ensuing weeks, they crossed deep valleys, mountains, and level uplands as they proceeded west in the direction of the Liard Valley. Unlike Black's Finlay River party, McLeod's group subsisted on moose, caribou, bears, mountain goats (Dall's sheep), and small animals. Game was plentiful much of the time, notably caribou and Dall's sheep in the grassy limestone uplands of the Tlogotsho Mountains. Sometimes animals were scarce, for example in steep, rough, mountain terrain.

McLeod and his men lit signal fires to attract the Indigenous peoples, although no mention is made of any getting out of control. Eventually, they found a band of about twenty Nahanni. The two groups were cautious with one another initially, but this soon broke down. McLeod gave the Indigenous leader a hat, coat, and other accessories of a chief. His people got beads, trinkets, and standard trade fare to entice them to trade for more goods in the future.

The Nahanni traded "a few Martens, some Beavers, Cats and a Bear skin or two." This might indicate that the Nahanni had already been touched by the fur trade, perhaps earlier with the Northwesters. The Nahanni leader, White Eyes, told McLeod that his people were not involved in the Russian trade network. The Nahanni did not have guns

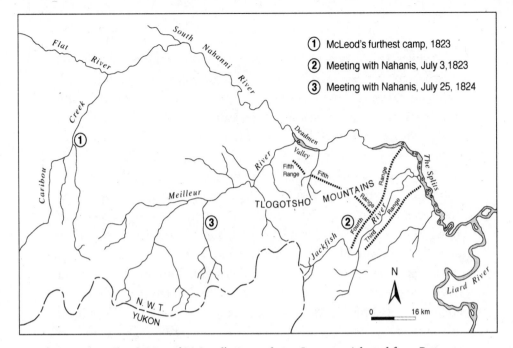

Figure 4.2. Sketch Map of McLeod's 1823 and 1824 Journeys. Adapted from Patterson (1961).

or metal tools, signs of exchange with the "white man." The furs traded with McLeod may have been caught by the Nahanni for their own use or traditional exchange with neighbours. White Eyes gave McLeod some prime marten furs that he believed might pay for the cost of all the presents given to the Nahanni.[64]

When White Eyes was asked about people and lands lying ahead, he said that his band had separated three years earlier from the main body of the Nahanni who lived along the upper or west branch of the Liard. He also said that "beyond the mountains over which he travelled" he was acquainted with two different tribes "of Indians whose languages likewise were different than his own." While he was "ignorant of any larger Chain of Mountains on the west," White Eyes reported that neighbouring lands were "level and frequented by immense herds of Rein Deer (caribou) such as we ourselves killed." He spoke in a rather vague way "about many Large Lakes, beside many smaller ones where Beaver were abundant" and black and grizzly bear numerous.[65]

The Nahanni and HBC men spent about two days together, socializing, celebrating, eating, and dancing. On his departure, McLeod asked

White Eyes to meet him again the next year in the same area. Patterson's sketch map suggests this was south of the Meilleur near the Jackfish River, not far west of the mainstream and the Splits (Figure 4.2). In the meantime, the Nahanni leader was encouraged to hunt and bring furs to Fort Simpson. McLeod then went back to the Splits, recovered his cached canoe, and ran the Nahanni and Liard rivers to the fort.

Once there, McLeod summarized his impressions of the Nahanni and their country. He considered them to be manly and good hunters, "smart, active and quick, conscious of their free and independent state." They were inclined to be peaceful, but not fearful or mean. They were clean, hospitable, and sociable. White Eyes, their leader, was tall, strong, and confident, with a beard that made him look like "an old Roman Sage." McLeod apologized because his limited scientific knowledge prevented him from providing details "on the natural products of the country." He referred generally to a few trees such as fir and poplar, as well as shrubs such as "Boxwood." Smaller growth included "alder, White and Red Willow and dwarf birch." Fruits included "Cranberry, Blueberry, Juniper Berry and a small Red Berry," reminding us of Raymond Patterson's forages for fruit during his 1927 and 1928–1929 sojourns in the Nahanni Valley.[66]

McLeod described "mountains of Saline Rock, of a Dark, Greenish Texture." On the summits no trees grew. Some places were covered with "a kind of grass" on which numerous Dall's sheep fed, presumably the uplands of the Tlogotsho Mountains. Between almost every large range were "small Brooks formed by the droppings from Adjacent Heights but no trace of the Beaver were discernable on either, excepting the Nahanni River itself, along which we frequently saw vestiges of a fresh Date." The beaver were probably found in the Splits and lowlands along the lower River. McLeod concluded his report by saying that the Nahanni, a land of "projecting rock" and "rugged and swampy Valleys," is "a forbidding aspect for Civilized Man, difficult and laborious to travel through."[67] These findings were unlikely to generate much interest among the leaders of the Hudson's Bay Company in establishing a post in the Nahanni Country.

Chapter 5

The Nineteenth-Century Fur Trade: The Later Years

McLeod returned to the Nahanni in the spring of 1824 for his promised rendezvous with White Eyes and his band. On June 8, he left Fort Simpson with a starting crew of five. Other people joined the party as it went along for a total of perhaps twenty. McLeod encountered considerable ice along the Liard banks. Upstream tracking of the canoe was difficult and dangerous. At the mouth of the Nahanni River, McLeod sent men out to hunt for "Mountain Goat" on nearby Nahanni Butte. We do not know whether they were successful.

He proceeded upriver, once again caching the canoe and some supplies before striking out across country, meeting White Eyes and his band near the Meilleur Valley area. The Nahanni had not made any hunts worth mentioning. They blamed privation and severity of the winter.[1] McLeod tried to talk White Eyes into crossing the mountains to Beaver Creek, a tributary of the Liard, where Murdoch McPherson, the chief trader at Fort Simpson, was exploring the country. White Eyes refused because he did not want to let any of his people put themselves within reach of the Fort Liard Indians. McLeod did, however, persuade White Eyes to come with a son and nephew to Fort Simpson.

White Eyes' entire band accompanied them as far as the summit of the Fifth Range (Figure 3.2), where the Nahanni took advantage of the traders' guns to make a large kill before they returned to the fort. As Patterson put it: "that magnificent hunting ground of the Tlogotsho did not fail them." McLeod spotted a caribou herd with his glass. His men and some Nahanni went to "surround them." In less than two hours, they killed nine caribou, a harbinger of the toll that the introduction of firearms would take on wildlife populations. McLeod's men took some meat, and "after the most tender farewells among the Nahanni" they were on their way.[2]

En route to the Splits and his canoe, McLeod saw many Dall's sheep. Conditions made it difficult to reach them, even with firearms. Indigenous people with bows, arrows, spears, and projectiles would likely have found it even more difficult to kill many of these sheep, although snares and traps sometimes were successfully used to catch these animals, as was seen earlier in the use of game drives by the Sheepeater people of the Yellowstone region. No evidence seems to be available of the use of game drives among the Nahanni. At the time of their first contact with McLeod and the fur trade, a kind of rough rhythm seems to have existed between Indigenous hunting technology and large game populations, a rhythm that the firearms and equipment of the "white man" eventually disrupted to the detriment of the game as well as Indigenous people.

Raymond Patterson used McLeod's journals to count the game taken during each of McLeod's month-long 1823 and 1824 journeys. The numbers are considerable. In one month, in 1824, thirty-four large animals were killed: sixteen caribou, fifteen sheep, and three moose. The total in 1823 was thirty-five killed: "23 caribou, nine sheep, three moose and a bear besides a few odds and ends."[3] These totals, and the animal descriptions in McLeod's journals, support his claim that game in the land through which he travelled was plentiful, although, as we have seen, sometimes uncommon due to steep terrain and habitat variations.

After McLeod's 1823 and 1824 journeys, the HBC does not appear to have sent any more expeditions to the Nahanni country. The rough terrain was likely one reason. Another was the apparent lack of enough beaver in the mountains and uplands to support a fur trade post. The lower Nahanni River was also difficult to navigate because of fluctuating water levels, complex and constantly changing channel patterns, and forest debris in the water. Easier travel was available along the Liard to more productive fur ground in Yukon and British Columbia.

The Nahanni people do not seem to have responded well to McLeod's attempts to pull them into the HBC trade network. A small number of Nahanni appeared at Fort Simpson in the first few years after McLeod's journeys. Their infrequent arrivals are described in the post journals. These indicate little participation in the trade. One entry, in late November 1832, recorded the arrival of two Indians sent to the fort by travellers who had spent the summer and previous winter with the "Nahannay." Nothing is said about any trade in fur. An April 1833 entry declares that "two emaciated Nahanny Indians made their appearance . . . four nights from their camps," apparently without any fur to trade. They had suffered severe privation throughout the winter. Like other starving people who came to the post from time to time, they were "in need of provisions."[4]

The demands placed upon the fort by hungry Indigenous peoples were frequent and heavy enough to cause traders to worry about whether their meat supplies were sufficient to meet the needs of the post itself. The direct demands of the fort and its fishing, hunting, and trapping operations undoubtedly reduced game previously available to Indigenous people, contributing to their need to come to the post for food. How far this effect of the post might have extended is a question. But one would expect it generally to fall off rather steadily with distance. Hard winters, changes in habitat and animal numbers could produce food shortages as well. Rabbits were a major source of food, especially in winter, and their numbers fluctuated cyclically over the years. Predators such as lynx rose and fell with them. Caribou numbers also have fluctuated over the decades.

The Hudson's Bay Company Fort Simpson journals for 1832–1833, 1843–1844, and 1863–1864 show that the nature of the trade and its effects changed considerably during the later nineteenth century. However, little evidence can be found to indicate any significant effects on the Nahanni and its people. The situation was different for the low-lands around Fort Simpson and their extension west along the Liard. These lands were the site of Fort Liard and other trading posts. Hunting and trapping were concentrated within a hinterland that undoubtedly expanded and contracted with fur, game availability, and other circum-stances. The posts attracted Indigenous people who came off the land and settled around them. Lower Indigenous populations and less use of remote areas such as the upper Nahanni likely also gradually reduced pressure on outlying parts of the watershed.

The Fort Simpson journals describe ongoing trade activities and broadly illustrate the foregoing effects. In the early 1830s, about twenty people lived at the fort, with the number falling in summer when fur was poor and activities reduced. Other people—hunters and fishers—lived more or less continuously at outlying camps near enough to the post to permit the regular bringing of food as well as some fur. Still others, living perhaps three or four days away, were an outlying part of the fort's network, participating to some extent in hunting, fishing, and trapping for the trade as part of their traditional nomadic round of activities.

Workers cut and worked wood in the vicinity of the post to main-tain the facilities and build canoes and boats for river transport. The demand for fuel wood was very high in the long cold winters. Large volumes of wood were burned to make charcoal needed to construct and repair guns and other tools for the post, as well as trade with the Indigenous peoples. Some charcoal likely was used for heating. The demand made it necessary to construct more than one charcoal furnace, with some operating "at a distance."[5] It is difficult to put numbers on these activities and their impacts, but over the years more intense and wide-ranging effects fell upon the forests and wildlife. With time, also, supplementary ways were found of maintaining the post. Among these was agriculture.

Since the late seventeenth century, the HBC governors in London had encouraged the growing of crops to cut the costs of shipping salt pork and other food to overseas posts.[6] Seeds of grains such as wheat, rye, barley, and oats, as well as garden plants, were sent to Hudson Bay in the belief they would help feed the posts in North America.

The grains generally did not do well in the northern climate. Efforts to grow garden crops were more successful, especially root crops such as potatoes and turnips. The 1832 and 1843 journals at Fort Simpson reveal that much of the spring was devoted to clearing ground, tilling, planting, raising, harvesting, and storing crops. Potatoes were raised with some success at Fort Simpson. But losses came with frosts, floods, and other hazards, including rot in storage bins. Post women laboured to sort the good from the bad. Irregular returns made it necessary to put continued pressure on caribou, moose, rabbits, birds, and other game.

Agriculture increased activity at Fort Simpson, with questionable returns. It involved clearing and maintaining cropland and defending crops against hazards such as insects, birds, and other wildlife. Agriculture led to the introduction of exotic plants. Fire likely was used to clear and maintain fields and conceivably could lead to big wildfires, especially during warm chinook winds. Cattle and livestock were also raised at Fort Simpson. While undoubtedly beneficial in terms of milk products, they brought more clearing and habitat changes. The effects of the trade at Fort Simpson occurred at other posts such as Fort Liard. These posts were part of the river transport system maintained for decades by the HBC. Furs and supplies moved among them regularly, as did changes affecting the bordering lowlands, with relatively little apparent impact on the more inaccessible Nahanni.

By the 1860s, major changes had taken place in the economy, technology, and transport. The HBC trade at Fort Simpson and other posts was threatened by the invasion of steamships coming down the Mackenzie River from the Arctic and, ultimately, the Pacific coast. These boats were part of a general northern movement to harvest whales, seals, and other marine mammals, profiting from their oils, pelts, and other products. In the Mackenzie Valley, the focus was on getting terrestrial furs from Indigenous people in exchange for liquor. The 1863 Fort Simpson journal reflects the frustration of the clerk about the exploitation of Indigenous people by alcohol. The people came from considerable distances to trade furs directly with the steamship traders for grog. The numbers bringing furs to the HBC post fell accordingly. Another consequence was widespread drunkenness, unrest, conflict, and violence in the community that had grown up around the post. It is difficult to determine what effects all this had on our focus of interest: the Nahanni watershed and its people. The 1863–1864 post journal generally does not refer to their arrival at the fort. However, Indigenous peoples arriving to deal with the steamship traders are not usually referred to by name. The clerk focused on the seductive and destructive effects of rum on the Indigenous peoples generally, and on company losses in trade. The illicit trade and its consequences probably spread upriver to Fort Liard and beyond. Some effects may have reached the Nahanni watershed from this direction.

Evidence left by the HBC explorer and trader Robert Campbell suggests this could have been occurring from an early date.[7] Campbell made an exploratory trip into the upper Liard country in 1836. While going down the Dease River about five miles from its junction with the upper Liard, Campbell met a Nahanni who told him about a nearby rendezvous run by "an Indian despot who made his living by acting as an intermediary in trade between interior Indians and the Russians on the Pacific Coast."[8]

Despite warnings of danger, Campbell and two Indigenous companions went to the rendezvous. From the top of a hill they caught their first glimpse of the great camp. It was the largest concourse of Indigenous peoples Campbell had ever seen, gathered from all parts of the western slopes of the Rockies and Pacific coast. Each year they apparently met to trade with "Shakes," the powerful chief whom the Nahanni seemed to regard with awe. This forest potentate acted as an agent for the Russians situated on the Pacific coast. He held sway over an immense number of Indians of different tribes.[9]

Along with an Indigenous man who understood some English, Campbell went into the tumultuous camp and met Shakes, a tall, powerfully built man. Campbell impressed him and other Indigenous people with his firearms, including a demonstration with a double-barrelled percussion gun previously unknown to them. Some of the Indigenous people knew Dr. McLaughlin and James Douglas, leaders of Hudson's Bay Company activities in the Columbia River country far to the south. Campbell sent notes to them via Indigenous people and later heard these letters reached the two men. All of this attests to an extensive early network of contacts and trade in what is now Yukon, British

Columbia, and Washington state. Elements of this network undoubtedly were in place before the coming of the fur trade, which intensified and expanded the exchange system.

At the most fundamental level the rendezvous, and the Russian trade network of which it was part, were expressions of major economic and social changes underway in northwestern North America in the middle decades of the nineteenth century. The network reflected Indigenous attempts to marry their historic practices with the arrival of Russian traders from the west and Europeans and Americans from the east. Prior to the arrival of the newcomers, the Indigenous trade likely was relatively light, involving extensive exchange of dried fish products, fish oils, chert and tool-making rocks, otter, beaver, and other commodities between west coast and interior peoples. After the arrival of the newcomers, the Indigenous peoples adapted and extended the system to their advantage. The system became a broad interacting network wherein tribes closest to the newcomers set themselves up as intermediaries for maximum profit while bringing more distant tribes into the trade. Shakes is an example of an Indigenous entrepreneur who organized and benefitted from these opportunities.

The Russians and their associated trade network were, nevertheless, a major threat to Indigenous sources of fur and the westward expansion of the HBC trade empire.[10] The Russian Fur Company was not just a business competitor like the old North West Company. It was the powerful spearhead of national expansion from the Russian homeland and Muscovy west of the Urals, across Siberia to the Pacific.[11] The expansion was led largely by Cossacks, who, while crossing great rivers like the Yenesei, Ob, Lena, and Amur in the seventeenth and eighteenth centuries, heavily exploited fur-bearers such as the sable, otter, weasel or ermine, marten, fox, and other animals long highly valued in Europe and the Ottoman Empire. As they advanced, the Cossacks and a growing number of Russians, Germans, and other entrepreneurs established a network of posts, block houses, and winter quarters[12]. Like the English, Canadian, and American trappers and traders in the early nineteenth century in the North American west, the Russians exploited the land and people, obtaining fur by trade, extortion, or tribute.[13] Imposing a fur tax on Indigenous people augmented the impact. Hundreds of thousands of furs were shipped west to Muscovy. Eventually, the Russian monarchy organized the various competing entrepreneurs into one large powerful enterprise, the Russian American Fur Company.

In his classic study on *Feeding the Russian Fur Trade*, James R. Gibson provides some relevant details on the character and implications of Russian Trans-Siberian expansion.[14] This was undertaken quite quickly with only about fifty years between the defeat of the Mongols, the removal of their blockade east of the Ural Mountains, and the arrival of the first Cossacks on the Pacific coast in 1639. By the 1730s, Russian expeditions under Vitus Bering had arrived in North American coastal waters. They reached the Commander and Aleutian islands, as well as Kodiak Island in the Gulf of Alaska, by 1763. A permanent post was built there in 1784. By 1799, the Russian American Fur Company had established "a number of others at the mouths of rivers or at the heads of bays along the continental and insular coasts."[15] By 1817, this company had five hundred Russian trappers and twenty-six sailors at sixteen posts. Fort Ross, approximately fifty miles north of the Spanish post of San Francisco, was built in 1812.

According to Gibson, the Russian advance across Siberia to North America was motivated by the search for land, gold, adventure, the scientific and imperial ambitions of the great czar, Peter the Great, and, ultimately, fur. In contrast to the beaver in North America, the main target was the sable, an arboreal martin, whose rich fur was sold in the thousands in Europe, the Middle East, and, by the mid-1700s, in China, through trade at Kyakhta, a post in the Amur River basin south of Lake Baikal. The Russian drive was fuelled by fur, which once depleted led to rapid movement onto fresh fur ground.

Once established in the North Pacific and the Bering Strait, the Russians shifted their hunting to the numerous sea otter, or "sea beaver," near the islands and along the Asian and North American coasts. Indigenous people were quickly incorporated into the trade. Intense hunting and trapping continued. The toll was high. Further expansion followed. According to Gibson, from 1743 to 1800, one hundred ventures were outfitted by the Russians to the Commander and Aleutian islands and the Alaskan coast in search of furs, primarily sea otter but also seals. In 1787 alone, twenty-five Russian vessels manned by one thousand men and owned by five merchants pursued this fur trade. These "Siberian Argonauts" reaped a rich harvest of "Golden Fleece." The recorded catch of sea otters from 1743 through to 1798 amounted to 186,754 pelts or about ten pelts per day.[16]

Much of this fur was sold in China at a substantial profit. The main commodity was sea otter. But terrestrial fox and other skins were also traded for tea, cloth, porcelain, and other Chinese goods. During the 1780s, through private trade alone, "up to 10,000 Russian carts, handled by some 3,000 men annually, hauled Chinese goods north from Kyakhta in Manchuria to Irkutsk" in Siberia.[17] Given the long history, national drive, and experience behind the Russian west coast trade, it is not surprising that Samuel Black found evidence of early and expanding Russian trade in the interior of British Columbia in 1824. Nor is it surprising that Robert Campbell came across the great rendezvous in the upper Liard country in 1836, decades after the expansive Russians had begun to trade for fur in North America.

By the early 1820s, Russian trade led to tension with the HBC over plans to expand its west coast operations.[18] John McLaughlin, chief factor in the Columbia District, and Governor George Simpson envisioned building a system of trading posts north along the west coast and wanted to build one in the Stikine Valley in northwestern British Columbia. Simpson apparently reached an agreement for such a post with local Russian authorities while on the west coast in 1825. But they later opposed it. Discussions and negotiations continued for years. Simpson finally went to Moscow in 1838, reaching an agreement with Baron Wrangel and the Russian Fur Company for the extension of trapping areas into the Alaska Panhandle, the selling of food to Russian posts, rental payments, and the placing of a Hudson's Bay establishment on the Stikine.

An old Russian post on the Stikine was transferred to the Hudson's Bay Company in 1840 and operated fitfully until 1849.[19] It is doubtful trade from this post ever extended very far into the interior of British Columbia. The deal lessened tension between the two companies for a time, although it was only the Russian sale of Alaska to the United States in 1867 that ended the conflict. The various negotiations and agreements between 1825 and 1838 seem to have done little to hinder the expansion of the Russian fur trade network into the upper Liard and the great rendezvous encountered by Robert Campbell in 1836.[20] Moreover, agreements between the two great companies likely had little effect on independent Indigenous responses to the opportunities offered by the fur trade. The Indigenous system had a dynamic of its own.

At the rendezvous, Robert Campbell met the remarkable chieftainess of the Nahanni who was later highlighted in Michael Mason's *The Arctic Forests*, the book that motivated Raymond Patterson to make his first visit to the Nahanni in 1927.[21] "She had a pleasing face lit up with fine intelligent eyes, which, when she was excited, flashed like fire."[22] She had the force of personality and character to earn the respect of her people, many of whom were with her at the rendezvous. These Nahanni appear to have been the parent group from which White Eyes told John McLeod his band had separated during their meeting near the Meilleur Valley area in 1824.

Such separations probably were not unusual, perhaps sometimes triggered by a divisive event, recalling that White Eyes told John McLeod he wanted to stay away from the Indigenous people, likely Kaska, in the Liard Valley. In fact, these separations often occurred among nomadic hunting peoples in other areas. Indigenous people in the Great Plains or in the Shield country of northern Ontario broke into small bands to survive on game that was dispersed, elusive, and hard to reach in winter. The people gathered in large camps for social purposes in the spring, summer, or fall, when wildlife was more abundant and easier to kill. The band McLeod met in 1823 may well have been part of a Nahanni dispersal that came together annually at places such as Dease River, or nearby Dease Lake, where game and fish were numerous enough to support a large camp at least seasonally. The Nahanni band met by McLeod had been out of touch with others for about three years. Yet bands may not have been able or inclined to meet every year. The traditional coming together of many bands, as well as neighbouring people, would offer entrepreneurs like Shakes an excellent opportunity to promote and profit from the fur trade.

To what extent the people at the great camp hunted and trapped in the Mackenzie Mountains and the upper Nahanni watershed, as part of the Russian trade network, is an important question. We have no documentary evidence upon which to base an answer and lack relevant archaeological work. The ethnological research of Catharine McClellan, an anthropologist and long-time student of Yukon Indigenous people, helps fill the gap.[23] In 1973, McClellan collected Indigenous oral histories from throughout Yukon. These showed that the Indigenous peoples generally survived by moving through a round of seasonal habitats each year. An example is the Kaska, who at least sometimes appear to have been labelled as the Nahanni. They lived at the upper Liard, Francis Lake, and nearby headwaters of the Pelly River during the nineteenth century, the prime fur trade era. The Kaska are described in McClellan's oral histories as hunting beaver in the spring before coming together at good fishing lakes, possibly including Dease, to catch trout. They fished in summer as well, with only the Pelly River offering salmon as it was a tributary to the Yukon and benefitted from the annual migratory run from the Pacific.

In summer and fall, many families went high in the mountains to trap marmots in snares and deadfalls, drying them to store for the winter. The Kaska caught wandering caribou in corrals likely resembling those mentioned in Samuel Black's 1824 expedition to the Finlay River country not far from the upper Liard. According to the Kaska, some buffalo—or wood bison—once were found in the Yukon drainage.[24] By the nineteenth century they were uncommon, perhaps because of Indigenous hunting. I found no reference to bison in the Fort Simpson journals I reviewed. Using McClellan's research, we can estimate that the Nahanni or Kaska were hunting in the mountainous western headwaters of the Nahanni River in the nineteenth century as part of the extended Russian trade. We do not know whether they reached the mainstream, nor the kind and amount of their take of wildlife.

By the 1870s, areas around the Nahanni Valley had begun to open up to new economic activity, including prospecting and mining. As we saw earlier in Chapter 2, this culminated in the great Yukon Gold Rush of 1896–1899 and subsequent mining activity. Trapping for fur continued, but it was part of a mixed economy. Both the newcomers and Indigenous peoples exploited an array of activities to earn an income and livelihood.

Chapter 6

Mining and a Mixed Economy

Then he opening of Yukon and Alaska to mining began thousands of miles to the south in California. The discovery of gold in the foothills of the Sierra Nevada Mountains in 1849 attracted thousands of people from all over the world. Some found gold but still wanted more. Others were not successful, yet caught gold fever and went in search of prospects elsewhere. A major move was to the north, along the mountain ranges of western North America. Strikes were made in the 1860s and 1870s in the Cariboo country and Cassiar Mountains of British Columbia. Movement further north was stalled by the power and control of Russia and the Russian American Fur Company in Alaska, and by the British Crown and Hudson's Bay Company in northern Canada. Both of these great companies were committed to keeping the country wild to maintain their fur empires.

The main mode of travel was along rivers. Settlements were small, concentrated around fur trade posts in the valleys. Great tracts of outlying lands remained wild, the habitat of nomadic hunting peoples. Many of them had become involved to some degree in trapping fur and hunting meat for the companies. Roads were essentially nonexistent. Overland travel followed ancient Indigenous paths and game trails. Travel difficulties were compounded by thousands of square miles of rough mountainous terrain, exceedingly difficult to penetrate.

The grip of Russia, Great Britain, and the two companies loosened in the late 1860s and 1870s. Alaska was purchased by the United States in 1867. The Russian American Fur Company was succeeded by the American Commercial Company based in San Francisco. In the same year, the founding of Canada led to the 1870 transfer of Rupert's Land to the new nation. The Hudson's Bay Company remained in the hands of its British board of governors. It continued to operate in Yukon and other parts of the North, albeit on lands now controlled by a new government. Both the United States and Canada were committed to expansion and national growth.

Limits on the spread of the mining frontier were greatly eased. The Canadian government, in particular, was committed by its new constitution to protect Indigenous people, a commitment that, in practice, carried little force and did not impede the mining advances. Even with the lowering of the political and economic barriers posed by Russia, Great Britain, and the two great fur companies, the mining movement north was initially quite slow.[1] The great distances to be travelled, and vast mountain systems such as the Pacific Coastal Ranges along the southwest and west coasts of Alaska and British Columbia, were major impediments to incoming prospectors.

The slow buildup to the great Yukon Gold Rush was a time of ongoing fur trade expansion into southwestern Yukon, northern British Columbia, and Alaska. During the 1830s and 1840s, the HBC continued to search for new fur ground. In the 1830s, its traders were still working their way down the Mackenzie River. After establishing Peel River Post, or what is now Fort McPherson, on the lower river, expansion moved west over the Mackenzie Mountains and down the Porcupine River. Alexander Murray built Fort Yukon at the junction of the Porcupine and Yukon rivers in 1847. In the south, Robert Campbell moved from the upper Liard Valley and Francis Lake down the Pelly to its junction with the Yukon, where he built Fort Selkirk in 1848. The fixation of Campbell and other traders was fur and the trade. Campbell found some gold near Fort Selkirk, yet did nothing about it. Missionaries at Fort Yukon also heard of rich nearby gold deposits but went on with their religious work. Traders at the fort were too involved with fur to look for this gold. Their attitudes were not supportive of the development of prospecting and mining.[2]

The stage was set for the arrival of the first few prospectors from the south. A leader was Andrew Hayes, an American. He panned the Yukon River for gold in 1873 without much success. Others followed with similar results. Hayes and two colleagues set up a trading company originally affiliated with the American Commercial Company. They built Fort Reliance on the Yukon River, not far from Forty Mile Creek and the Klondike. Nuggets were found on Forty Mile in the early 1890s. Major discoveries were made at Circle City farther up the Yukon, close to the Arctic Circle. About $400,000 worth of gold was brought into Circle City in 1894 and $1,000,000 in 1896. Prospectors George McCormick and Skuckum Jim made the big strike on Klondike Creek in 1896. The Great Rush was on, and essentially over by 1899.

Many men were still eager to find more gold. They took the search to surrounding lands, including the Liard and Nahanni watersheds. Some of them may already have passed through the Nahanni and Flat valleys, en route to Yukon in 1897 or 1898. Others may have heard of the Nahanni country while in the Klondike. Still others, including Indigenous people and Metis, may have gotten a local brand of the fever upon hearing about the great riches found in the Klondike.

As we saw in Chapter 1, Pierre Berton studied the rush to Yukon and the Klondike (Figure 1.2).[3] He analyzed traffic from Edmonton and the east in some detail, as did J.G. MacGregor in a study published in 1970. Berton estimated that a total of 766 men, women, and four thousand horses had tried to reach the Yukon Valley through Edmonton and the Liard and Mackenzie valleys. He concluded that 166 men ultimately got to the goldfields via either river, with no women or horses completing the trip. MacGregor estimated 775 people attempted the journey, with 160 reaching Yukon with no women or horses.[4]

Neither Berton nor MacGregor identify the South Nahanni as an important route to the goldfields. Berton does say that there were Klondikers "deep in the South Nahanni Valley with its caves and canyons," but he makes no estimate of the number going this way.[5] MacGregor does not mention any use of the South Nahanni by Klondikers. He does refer to one party overwintering further down the Mackenzie in the lower valley of the North Nahanni. They returned to the mainstream in the spring, going down the Mackenzie to the Peel and Porcupine river route across the mountains to the Yukon Valley.

In reminiscing about his more than forty years as a trapper, sometime prospector, boatman, construction manager, and airplane pilot, Dick Turner, a Yukoner, wrote at some length about the great gold rush to the Klondike.[6] He thought that after reaching the Liard or Mackenzie rivers, gold seekers took "any stream" over the Mackenzie and northerly Richardson Mountains to Yukon. He thought some of them must have worked their way up the South Nahanni.[7] His chief informants were men who had participated in the great gold rush. Some had reached the Klondike and spoke of stories going "round the Yukon about gold found on the South Nahanni and Flat Rivers by men who had come that way."[8]

Turner believed that most of those using the South Nahanni probably went upriver only as far as the major west bank tributary, the Flat, where they turned upstream, went west over the mountains to the upper Liard country, and on to Yukon. Few seem to have travelled up the South Nahanni's main stem, past Virginia Falls and on, for hundreds of kilometres, through the Mackenzie Mountains to the goldfields. It is important to recognize that much of Turner's evidence is conjectural and anecdotal, relying on testimony from what appears to have been only a small number of participants in the gold rush. When the evidence provided by Berton, MacGregor, Turner, and also by Raymond Patterson, is considered as a whole, it does not seem likely that many more than one hundred people used the South Nahanni route, and most of them did not reach the Klondike.

Old paths and abandoned cabins are sometimes seen as possible relics of the Klondikers' passage to Yukon. The journey could be a long one, with some travellers overwintering along the way, taking a year or more to complete the journey. In his return visit to the lower South Nahanni in the 1950s, Raymond Patterson spoke of some "old, old cabins" hidden away in the upper Flat Valley, "the work of Klondikers perhaps. They are built of upright logs and have fireplaces of clay and stone set in the centre of their floors. They stand amongst tall, black spruce from which hang long venerable beards of gray-green moss. A sense of eld and of decay and of tragedy prevails that haunted spot."[9] Jack Stanier, a former Klondiker and resident in the Liard Valley in the 1920s and 1930s, told Dick Turner about going into the mountains from Fort Liard in 1934 and finding a cabin in the bush with three frozen bodies of long-dead men still in their bunks. He thought they might have been Klondikers, a questionable conclusion given the passing of the years.[10] But it was stories and rumours that drew men to scour the land for gold.

In about 1900, an Indigenous man brought a gold-bearing nugget into Fort Liard. In 1904, gold was discovered near the Flat Creek junction with the Nahanni. The search continued for years. Prospectors such as Willie and Frank McLeod and Martin Jorgenson were found dead in 1908 and 1915, respectively.[11] The promise of gold and other minerals was at least partly responsible for the exploration and mapping by government geologists such as J. Keele in the upper Nahanni–Mackenzie mountains in 1910. The mysterious deaths of the McLeods and Jorgenson led to investigations in the Nahanni by the Royal Canadian Mounted Police (RCMP) and eventually to the establishment of a patrol station at Fort Simpson. In 1910, a government Indian agent was appointed. A treaty was signed with the Indigenous peoples of the Mackenzie District in 1921–1922. The treaty was unsatisfactory, prepared in haste for a poorly defined Indigenous population. It was misunderstood by both sides and implemented without inclusion of some verbal agreements made in meetings with the Indigenous people.[12]

The gold search ebbed and flowed for years in the Nahanni Valley, with brief and uncertain discoveries made in 1927, 1929, and 1933. Legendary figures in the bush tradition built their reputations at this time. Hardy individuals such as Klondikers Poole Field and Jack Stanier, as well as later arrivals such as Gus Kraus and Raymond Patterson's mentor, Albert Faille, worked the valley from the 1920s to the 1960s, mainly below Virginia Falls. Indigenous trappers and hunters may have searched for gold in a large part of the upper valley in the first decade of the twentieth century. Subsequently, prospectors appear to have concentrated their activities more and more in the lower valley.

Arrangements for the discovery and exploitation of gold and other minerals underwent revolutionary changes in the 1930s. Advanced technology began to take a strong role. Aircraft were introduced. Air photos quickly followed. The efforts of individual prospectors were overtaken by companies and corporations more capable of financing, organizing, and developing mineral discoveries. In 1928, a company known as Northern Aerial Minerals Exploration Ltd. flew people in to investigate earlier claims along the Flat. The year 1933 saw the formation of the Liard and Fort Simpson syndicates. The Liard and Nahanni Gold Syndicate followed in 1939, with links to eastern Canadian funding and mining expertise. The discovery of galena near Prairie Creek led to another local eastern Canadian initiative: the Clarke-Eaason Corporation.

Americans became heavily involved, with diverse interests in hard rock minerals and oil. One company, the Canadian Tungsten Mining Corporation, uncovered sufficient prospects for this uncommon mineral to build a townsite, airport, and an all-weather road from the Liard into the upper Flat Valley and the borders of the South Nahanni watershed in the 1960s. Numerous companies were active in the South Nahanni region, and the proposal for a dam at Virginia Falls was put forward to provide power needed for mining.

Dick Turner tells of many of the basic changes that took place in the region with the rise of large-scale mining as a scientific and technical enterprise in the 1930s, 1940s, and 1950s. Turner was seventeen in 1930, near the start of the Great Depression, when he left Calgary to go north with his older brother Stan to earn enough to return to "civilization fat and prosperous." An adventurous year among the wonders of the North was a powerful magnet, strengthened by visions of a cornucopia of big game. Turner wrote of reading an article on the Nahanni in the *National Geographic Magazine* that extolled the Flat Valley as "teeming with game . . . Herds of caribou and moose could be seen at almost any time from the aircraft crossing the streams and lakes." What began, however, as a one-year adventure turned into a northern life lasting more than half a century.[13]

Turner followed the same general route north as Raymond Patterson had three years earlier. He and his brother travelled by train to Waterways and canoed the numerous streams and lakes leading to the Mackenzie River and its junction with the Liard at Fort Simpson. After resting a day or so, they continued upstream to Fort Liard and began long hunting, trapping, and prospecting careers. Contrary to expectations, they did not encounter any big game during their lengthy journey until they killed a moose just before reaching Fort Liard. The lack of game must have largely been due to a long history of trapping and hunting since the fur trade began in the Lake Athabasca–Great Slave Lake country in the late 1700s.

In the 1930s, the Turners exploited moose, caribou, beaver, marten, fox, minx, and other animals along the Liard, a list reminiscent of Wenzel's 1820s observations. Wolverine and wolf were unwanted "pests," preying on traplines. The grizzly was dangerous and best avoided. The main travel method was dog teams. Their pressure on game for food was greatly reduced by the introduction of snowmobiles in the 1940s. The Turners joined what appear to have been less than one hundred other settlers dependent on hunting, trapping, and a little agriculture.

By the early 1940s, hunting and trapping were not enough to support the Turners. The reasons for this are not entirely clear. They probably included a decrease in wildlife, the pressures of marriage and children, a desire for a higher standard of living, and new economic opportunities offered by corporate mining and related activities that came to the Northwest Territories and Yukon in the 1930s. Dick Turner eventually went into the river transport business, building a boat and working primarily for the incoming mining and oil companies. He got involved in construction, notably the building of the Canol pipeline. It stretched from the oil fields at Norman Wells on the Mackenzie River, west through the wild country along the Keele River, to Yukon and Whitehorse. Petroleum was needed there to fuel planes being ferried to Russia to fight the Germans in the Second World War.

When Turner arrived at Fort Liard in 1930, it was still a small, old-time trading post. Eight white men lived there: two Mounties; three representatives of the Hudson's Bay Company and its competitor, the Northern Trading Company; a Catholic priest and a lay brother; and a white trapper. The fort's buildings were strung for two miles along the river banks to ease access to river travel and water. About 250 nomadic Indigenous peoples were within one hundred miles of the post. They lived as they had for 150 years since the beginning of the fur trade, by hunting moose and other game. When their activities depleted these resources, or seasonal or other changes made habitats less desirable, they moved to more favourable ground. Beaver, marten, and other fur provided the means to replace traditional bush huts with tents and other equipment, as well as new pleasures such as the portable gramophones whose music filled the air at their camps.

During his years on the Liard, Turner saw less game and trapping. The economy changed from one dependent on furs to one reliant on jobs and wages.[14] The changes extended to education and preparation of Indigenous children for employment in the new society. Families were separated from their children and traditional ways. Psychological and social problems arose from church and government efforts to integrate Indigenous people into what was viewed as the modern Canadian economy and society.

Turner was aware of stories of gold along the Nahanni. He knew of the McLeod brothers, whose apparently headless bodies were found in 1908 below the Second Canyon in what is now called Deadmen Valley. Their deaths remain a mystery. Possible causes include slayings by legendary mountain Indigenous peoples, other trappers, or prospectors, or starvation, with their heads removed by grizzly bears. No trace was found of the gold they were rumoured to have panned while working the Nahanni and its tributaries.

Former Klondikers such as Jack Stanier and Poole Field continued prospecting into the 1920s and 1930s. They engaged in trapping, odd jobs, and business. Where and how often these men travelled in the Nahanni is not clear. Much of their prospecting seems to have been caused by rumours of gold on the Flat, with small rushes ensuing in hopes of finding more. They staked claims that could be sold later to others with a yearning for riches. Jack Stanier and a companion apparently flew into the upper Flat in 1933, a quick and easy means of travel unavailable only a few years earlier. Stanier believed that some old sluice boxes on the upper river were the work of the McLeod brothers before their untimely deaths in the early 1900s. Memory and hope die hard in the gold business. Stanier apparently found some gold that set off a small rush.

In 1934, Dick Turner and three other men went up the Flat to find gold. Here they met Raymond Patterson's old friend, the redoubtable

Albert Faille, who joined their search. Big game was seen often. They lived on caribou, moose, and other animals.[15] On one occasion, Turner climbed into the uplands, saw a band of Dall's sheep, and shot a big ram. Its great horns had to be left behind because of the steep descent to camp. It was spring and the meat turned out to be too tough to eat. Turner and Faille wanted to press on upriver. The others refused. Turner staked some claims and later sold one to a traveller passing through the Liard Valley.

When Turner encountered him in 1934, Faille was in his forties. He was a mountain man in the spirit of the legendary American trappers who roamed the Rocky Mountains of Wyoming, Colorado, and New Mexico during the 1830s and 1840s. They depended on elk, deer, and other game for food. They overwintered while trapping for fur, coming out to trade in spring at rendezvous in the Green River Valley or posts along the Platte or Arkansas rivers.

Like them, Faille overwintered in the Nahanni watershed, coming out in spring to trade at posts along the Liard. Sometimes he was not seen or heard of for a year or more. Much of his activity centred on the Flat and lower Nahanni valleys. He is known to have travelled into the upper Nahanni beyond Virginia Falls. But we do not know when and how long he did so. Some of his activity above the Falls was in the vicinity of Rabbitkettle Creek, "one of the best game areas in the Nahanni Mountains as well as a good trapping area."[16]

In the Flat Valley, Faille built a string of four or five cabins about fifteen miles apart to provide shelter while he was running his traplines. He was constantly eager to find gold, but trapping was his economic mainstay. Faille's experiences appear to have been unusual, yet they show how far a dedicated trapper could roam in search of fur and gold. His domain covered hundreds of miles along the Flat and lower Nahanni, as well, at times, as the valley above the falls. He harvested many animals. But we do not have the numbers to assess his kill of beaver, marten, lynx, or other fur-bearers, nor the moose, caribou, sheep, and other game on which he lived. If Turner's descriptions of game along the Flat in 1934 are any guide, the effects of trappers and prospectors such as Faille on wildlife were not heavy enough to significantly lower their numbers and diversity. Ecological integrity was still high.

Other trappers and gold seekers did work the Nahanni in Faille's time. We are uncertain as to how many did so or how frequently. The upper valley was more lightly used and apparently little disturbed. The lower valley was becoming a thoroughfare for hunters, trappers, prospectors, and pleasure seekers. Motorized scows were used sometimes for trips to the falls. Sport hunting was coming into vogue. One of Turner's sons was apparently in the guiding business by the 1960s. Dall's sheep on the Tlogotsho uplands were a principal quarry as horn and trophy animals. Little mention is made of Indigenous people. Turner does suggest the Nahanni were in decline in the 1930s, apparently partly because of intermarriage with other Indigenous peoples or whites. On the other hand, Turner and other observers seemed to focus on the white man rather than Indigenous people.

Four journeys illuminate the state of the Nahanni in the 1940s, 1950s, 1960s, and 1970s. The first, in 1948, by E.G. Oldham, superintendent of forests and wildlife in the Northwest Territories, was discussed in Chapter 3. Oldham extolled the richness of wildlife in the valley.[17] While flying over the watershed, he saw many moose and caribou. He also heard reports of sheep and other animals, notably bears. He was enthusiastic about the wild state and potential of the valley, and recommended it as a national park candidate.

The problem is we do not know the areas Oldham flew over, nor exactly which parts of the river and its watershed he thought worthy of national park status. Nor do we know what he meant by a national park. If the model was Wood Buffalo National Park north of Lake Athabasca, then his vision would be quite different from the image most people have of a national park today. This image would portray a highly regulated area in which lumbering, mining, power development, hunting, trapping, and other activities were strictly controlled. Yet, in Oldham's time and for years thereafter, Wood Buffalo was essentially a bison reserve in which lumbering, hunting, and other practices were ongoing.

In his book, *Nahanni*, Dick Turner refers to a visit to Fort Laird by a "Mr. Odham," a wildlife official whom he and other trappers met to discuss their objections to government regulations on the take of beaver and other fur-bearers as well as big game. Turner does not give a date for this meeting. It likely occurred during E.G. Oldham's 1948 tour of the Nahanni. At the meeting, Turner stated it was necessary for trappers to ignore or evade some regulations if they were to make a living, often with the knowledge and tacit concurrence of the RCMP and game guardians. Oldham apparently agreed that some regulations were too restrictive. Changes were soon made, including the establishment of official traplines and fewer restrictions on moose.[18] All of this reflects the bind in which wildlife officials like Oldham found themselves. For better or worse, the trapping life in the North was not always amenable to strict regulation. Yet the kill of fur-bearers and game could seem too high to be sustainable, especially given the traditional needs of Indigenous people.

The second journey bearing on wildlife and other changes in the Nahanni was the return of Raymond Patterson in 1951. His observations are more detailed and significant than those of Oldham. In his article, "South Nahanni Revisited," Patterson records his joy on coming back to the lower Nahanni and the Flat where he met Albert Faille again after so many years away.[19] But the dominant tone is sadness and loss because of the landscape changes since his last sojourn in 1928–1929. Patterson was especially concerned about signs of extensive forest fires. A big one on the Flat near one of his longtime cabins caused Albert Faille to decide not to return to that area in the future. Things were not the same.

Mineral exploration, tourism, careless visitors, and even old-timers like Albert Faille, all seem to have interacted to accelerate landscape change. Faille had been in the wolf business the winter before Patterson's return. He had been weakened by scurvy and killed a pack of seven assertive wolves near his Flat River cabin not long before Patterson's arrival. Faille's kill of wolves might not have had much overall impact in earlier days, but it can be seen as having more significance as growing numbers of people added to the take of wildlife.

Patterson wrote evocatively of the changes after a long hike from First Canyon onto the Tlogotsho uplands: "That stretch of the plateau was covered with sheep droppings in 1928: in 1951 there was not a sign of any kind except an occasional old track. The wild game from observation and from all reports had been cut, in 25 years, to one third of its former plenty—probably even less. Various cycles of scarcity had probably coincided with an increased wolf population, better rifles in general use and greater pressure from humankind. And the paw of the ape had been laid heavily on that lovely river." Much of the Splits country had been devastated by fires in recent years and all of the Second Canyon—"eight miles of the most magnificent river scenery—wrecked, a desert of scarred and fire-blasted rubble and scree."[20] In August 2013, the Nahanni traveller could still trace pine stands slowly succeeding burned forest, as well as younger growth following more recent fires in the 1980s.

Patterson's observations are quite different from those of Oldham, who visited the Nahanni only three years earlier. Oldham wrote, in general terms, of a valley rich in wild animals with no sign of fire or human activity. One possible explanation for the difference is that Oldham's observations were made from a plane and possibly apply, in the main, to the more isolated area above Virginia Falls. Patterson's observations were made on the ground and apply to the lower valley and the Flat River country. The impression of a growing difference in human effects in the lower, as opposed to the upper, valley is heightened by the observations of Jean Poirel in 1964 and John and Joanne Moore in 1978.

Poirel was a Quebec physical education instructor with a deep interest in wildlands discovery and travel. In the early 1960s, he kayaked the Mackenzie River, where he heard about the natural wonders of the Nahanni and decided to explore it from source to mouth. In June 1964, he drove with three companions from Montreal to Watson Lake, Yukon. Here he and one of the other men took a flight over the Mackenzie Mountains into the headwaters of the river. They then did the unthinkable and parachuted into a small basin they thought was the source of the Nahanni. Landing on steep mountain slopes, they hiked for miles across ice, snow, and rock to join their two companions, who had been flown in, along with the expedition's supplies and equipment, to safer ground near the Nahanni mainstream.

In the following weeks, Poirel and his party completed a remarkable journey along the length of the river to its junction with the Liard and the village of Nahanni Butte. In approximately the first third of the journey they struggled through forest, swamp, muskeg, and very cold water along otherwise impassable riverbanks. In the second third of the journey they travelled by float and dinghy over relatively gentle waters to Virginia Falls. The final third, through the canyons and swift waters to the Splits and Nahanni Butte, was also made by water.

Above Virginia Falls they found no sign of past or present human activity, including Indigenous people. The land was largely covered in spruce forest and swamp. The first pine, poplar, and aspen were recorded in the vicinity of Virginia Falls, along with remnants of a few old burns, possibly a marker of past human activities. Wild animals seemed plentiful. They observed or saw signs of moose and ducks, as well as otter, beaver, muskrat, wolf, and black and grizzly bears. The animals were often quite large. Black bear were troublesome because of their attraction to camp supplies and equipment. The grizzly was a threat considered more likely to attack them, as on one occasion when they came across a large female and her cubs. Fish seemed easy to catch.

Signs of humans began at Virginia Falls. A portage was located on one side. At the base they found the camp of Albert Faille. He was then in his seventies and had been trapping and prospecting along the Nahanni for about forty-five years. Faille was waiting for the arrival of Dick Turner, an old friend, now a pilot, who was bringing supplies. Continuing downriver, Poirel and his men met two members of the Royal Canadian Mounted Police, one a Metis auxiliary. They also encountered members of Mines and Surveys Canada, harbingers of the rising interest in large-scale mining along the Nahanni. This was about the time of the construction of the Tungsten mine in the upper Flat Valley and the plans to build a power dam at Virginia Falls, although Poirel does not mention this project. A few Indigenous people apparently were involved in the Mines and Surveys crew. Otherwise, Poirel does not report having met or seen signs of Indigenous people in any part of his journey.

He did see a few Dall's sheep in the canyons.[21] Caribou seem to have been numerous below Virginia Falls, although they apparently were not seen above them. This may simply be due to happenstance. Caribou are intrinsically nomadic. To attribute human cause to the distribution observed by Poirel is problematic since neither the animals nor humans were reported above the falls, whereas both were observed below them. Toward the lower end of First Canyon, Poirel's team visited Gus and Mary Krause, old-timers who had a cabin at Nahanni hot springs. Here the adventurers enjoyed homegrown potatoes and vegetables, as well as a dip in the hot springs.

Poirel said little about caves in the canyon walls during his 1964 trip. He returned several times between 1970 and 1974 to explore them and adjoining karst terrain.[22] He and some companions located and explored numerous caves, ultimately discovering the Valerie system, a series of subterranean branches and chambers hundreds of yards long. The Valerie caves contain many spectacular features, notably large ice columns, stalactites, stalagmites, and terraces, as well as the surprising remains of about 120 Dall's sheep. Some were carbon-14 dated at approximately 2,500 years old.[23] The origin of these animals and the cause of their deaths are rather mysterious. The general view is that they wandered into the caves, moved down the slippery ice slopes, and could not get back to the surface again. In this and other cases, Poirel's explorations led to follow-up research by others, notably the geomorphologist Derek Ford, who established the global stature of Nahanni's caves and karst and supported their protection in the Nahanni National Park Reserve. In 1970, Poirel was invited to meet Prime Minister Pierre Trudeau, who was in the valley in the lead-up to the creation of the initial Nahanni National Park Reserve in 1976.

Poirel's Nahanni trip was undertaken at about the same time that George Scotter and his colleagues were beginning the biological and ecological studies that eventually became so important in creating the initial 1974 national park reserve and expanding it to watershed scale in 2009. Some biological work extended along the length of the river. But the biologists left few descriptions of land use and its effects in the upper valley. Their research concentrated on the lower Nahanni, possibly because development pressures and threats were greatest there or because protecting Virginia Falls, the canyons, swift waters, and the scenery became the focus of government interest in establishing the first phase of the Nahanni National Park Reserve.

The lower valley definitely bore signs of past and present uses. While working near the junction of the Nahanni and the Flat in the late 1960s and early 1970s, Scotter saw geologists and mining people passing through or over Deadmen Valley en route to potential mining sites in the greater Nahanni region. Scotter also saw remains of cabins built by

Indigenous trappers and other travellers. Campsites and other signs of sports hunting and fishing parties were also found, marking the growth of a wide-ranging industry that had already begun to undermine the Nahanni ecosystem by, for example, trophy hunting Dall's sheep and other animals, potentially reducing the quality and quantity of wildlife populations.

Field evidence supporting the extension of the reserve to the upper valley was apparent by the late 1970s, even though its natural riches were extolled in these years and beyond. In 1977–1978, Joanne Moore and her husband John spent their honeymoon year in the upper valley about thirty miles above Rabbitkettle Creek.[24] They flew in with ample supplies, built their own cabin, and otherwise looked after themselves. They hiked, snowshoed, climbed, and explored the surrounding country, enduring the cold winter and spring mosquitos. The couple saw much diverse wildlife, including moose, caribou, marten, wolverines, black and grizzly bears, and eagles. They observed seasonal variations in animal behaviour, for example caribou escaping the winter cold of the sun-deprived valley by climbing into warmer air on mountain slopes. They witnessed the gathering of large numbers of wolves in winter to co-operate in running down large animals such as moose.

The Moores' most spectacular wildlife observations were made along the river in the spring of 1978, on the way out to Virginia Falls and, eventually, Nahanni Butte: wolverine, moose, black bear, otter, porcupine, beaver, eagle, widgeon and other waterfowl, geese, sandpiper, and songbirds often in migration to summer breeding grounds. Most of these observations were made above Virginia Falls in areas then outside the initial national park reserve. Once within it, especially below Virginia Falls, the Moores were preoccupied with the scenery and successfully canoeing the challenging rapids and swift waters of the canyons. They did not report as much wildlife. They apparently only saw and tracked one Dall's sheep.

In her account of this year in the wild, Joanne Moore, like others before her, focused on the natural wonders and beauty of the landscape and the challenges of survival in a remote land. However, she did record planes flying in and out of the upper valley country in support of mineral exploration. Supplies were flown in and stored for summer crews. Camps had been operating for years. Pressure was building to find gold, copper, zinc, or other metals in quantities and qualities sufficient to pay for road construction and other development like that at the Tungsten mine and townsite, built on the upper Flat River in the 1960s. Not much is said directly about the threat these activities posed to the wild landscapes that were so highly valued by the Moores.

The story of their Nahanni sojourn, *Nahanni Trailhead*, has been printed several times and has reached thousands of readers.[25] With its focus on natural diversity and richness, the book undoubtedly increased general appreciation of the upper valley and the greater Nahanni. The Moores do not seem to have been as interested in potential threats, notably from mining. No mention is made of hunting or other signs of Indigenous people. The arrival of canoeists is described in the spring, with little apparent question about the impacts that more newcomers could have on the valley.

How far mining exploration and other developments would have gone, and what effects they would have had on the still wild upper valley, is now a moot question. The 2009 expansion of the reserve substantially curtailed mineral and other threats to the upper valley and much of the watershed. However, potential impacts remain because of projects such as the Tungsten mine on the upper Flat and the Prairie Creek mine, to be discussed more fully later.

Problems could arise through injudicious recreational and tourism development. However, Parks Canada has established controls on tourism, limiting outfitter numbers in the valley, setting quotas on trips, and regulating waste disposal and other effects of raft and canoe travel.[26] During my August 2013 raft trip downriver from Virginia Falls, we saw only one other tour party, followed strict camp and waste disposal procedures, and encountered little waste or sign of human disturbance.

Chapter 7

Conserving the Ecological Integrity of the Nahanni for More than Two Hundred Years

The successive observations of nineteenth- and twentieth-century traders, prospectors, adventurers, and researchers ranging from John McLeod to Joanne Moore and George Scotter are generally similar in their descriptions of the Nahanni ecosystem, albeit with minor variations from place to place due to fires and other processes affected by the fur trade, prospecting, and a mixed economy. These small-scale variations were integrated into a still vibrant self-generating system that remained high in ecological integrity over the two hundred years of post-fur trade history in the Nahanni region. The reasons seem to fall into three groups. The first arises from what can be called the dynamics of the fur trade, mining, and other activities. The dynamics are part of the unfolding of the activity and not necessarily deliberate or planned. They are part of the workings of an enterprise. The second group arises from deliberate or planned attempts to control the effects of a new activity by its originators or responsible authorities. In the case of the fur trade or mining, these are mainly companies or governments. The third group consists of deliberate or planned attempts at control by hosts, in this case the Indigenous people.

Examples of the first group include encounters of the fur trade and mining with difficult terrain, harsh climate, the uneven distribution of resources, competition or conflict with rivals, and change in markets or economic and political conditions. Terrain was a major barrier to the fur trade and mining in the Nahanni, especially in the early stages of their development. The Nahanni is surrounded by mountains and hard to penetrate. The obvious entry route, the Nahanni River, is difficult to traverse given the Splits, deep canyons, swift waters, and Virginia Falls. The upper valley is a cul-de-sac, with no ready way of passing over the mountains into Yukon. These obstacles, and long cold winters, make travel difficult. In the cold season, game is scattered and hard to find and kill.

Food could be in short supply. This proved to be the case when McLeod returned to the Flat in 1824 to meet with White Eyes and trade for the fur he expected the Nahanni would have secured during the winter. He found they had trapped very little, citing "privation" as the reason. As a result of such difficulties, the HBC bypassed the Nahanni River for the more accessible and lucrative Liard route into the interior of northern British Columbia and southern Yukon.

As far as competition and conflict are concerned, these sometimes worked to the detriment of beaver, other fur-bearers, and game. An example is the scorched earth policy pursued by the Northwesters and HBC before the 1821 amalgamation. On the other hand, competition between the Russian and the HBC trade networks may have buffered fur trade activity and possibly offered some protection for wildlife on the western slope of the Mackenzie Mountains and headwaters of the Nahanni. Changes in the demand for beaver in the 1840s and 1850s reduced pressure on the animal. This general market change does not appear to have been of fundamental importance in protecting beaver in the Nahanni. The discovery of gold in Yukon in the late 1800s eased the pressure on fur somewhat as attention shifted to the potential offered by minerals. In the Nahanni, during the 1920s, 1930s, and 1940s, prospecting seems to have unfolded through periodic rushes into areas such as the Flat.

As in the case of the fur trade, the diversity and ecological integrity of the Nahanni were protected against heavy mining impacts by the difficulty in gaining access to the country and finding worthwhile deposits. This changed with the arrival of airplanes, air photo mapping, other advanced technology, and the shift from solitary prospectors to corporate enterprise in the 1930s. Exploration methods improved, leading to the initial development of the Tungsten and Prairie Creek deposits in the 1960s. Joanne and John Moore saw numerous signs of wide-ranging mineral exploration in the upper valley during their winter stay in 1977–1978. The establishment and expansion of the Nahanni National Park Reserve in 1976 and 2009, respectively, resulted in a general prohibition of prospecting and mining in most of the watershed. However, the Tungsten and Prairie Creek mines not only remain as threats to the sites themselves, but also cause damage via the construction and operation of access roads, truck traffic, water disposal, toxic pollutants, and other effects.

The second group of reasons for the protection of the ecological integrity of the Nahanni watershed was deliberate attempts to control the damaging activities by companies and governments. Some examples are the early Hudson's Bay Company conservation policies, government establishment of the Arctic and Mackenzie Mountain game reserves, and the game regulations. Of these changes, the game regulations have been more consistently successful. Their effectiveness was reduced by uncertainty about the funding, nature, and degree of control that should be used and by concerns about their effects on livelihood.

As we saw earlier, the new combined Hudson's Bay Company introduced a conservation policy after amalgamation with the Northwesters in 1821. George Simpson and his council created a quota system. Targets were set for the number of beaver to be taken annually from districts in the company's vast territories. The intention was to allow for recruitment or recovery of heavily exploited lands, and to sustainably manage new ones. The possibility of doing this arose from the company's apparent ability to control the yield because its major rival had been eliminated; the yield could be regulated without interference through trapping by competitors.

Some success may have been achieved for a time. But there were difficulties with the plan from the beginning. How was the yield to be estimated for inadequately understood wildlands? And how was the yield target to be set and implemented? Trappers were predominately Indigenous people and not likely to adhere to a beaver quota that limited their profit, especially if the furs could be taken to different posts. HBC traders may not have been keen to limit the trade to an estimate they did not think was accurate.

That such obstacles handicapped the implementation of the policy can be seen in the day-to-day operations of a post such as Fort Simpson in the 1830s, 1840s, and 1860s. Indigenous peoples coming in the spring with a winter catch of beaver, marten, and other furs did not have any rejected by the trader on grounds of a quota. And how could a trader allocate any quota, especially when his customers still pursued an essentially traditional nomadic lifestyle some distance from his post? The various clients who came to the post may have been competing with one another for fur ground and yield. How was the trader to control such competition and its effects? At least partly for such reasons, no mention is made of any quota system at Fort Simpson nor any impacts on the Nahanni watershed.

An example of an unevenly successful effort to conserve wildlife in the North generally was the extensive Arctic Game Preserve system. This was originally established by the federal government in the early twentieth century to conserve caribou, muskox, and other game animals for the subsistence of the Inuit and other Indigenous people. The muskox and other animals had been heavily hit by the wide-ranging and intense hunting by whalers, trappers, prospectors, and other outsiders who came in increasing numbers to the high Arctic and the North in the nineteenth and early twentieth centuries. Their take of animals was great enough to threaten the survival of the Inuit and other Indigenous peoples, a concern to the government since if the animal populations fell to too low a level it would have to absorb the costs of feeding the people. The federal government was also interested in using the creation of the Arctic Game Preserve to support its efforts to demonstrate Canadian sovereignty against the contending claims of Denmark and other Nordic countries (see Figure 7.1).[1]

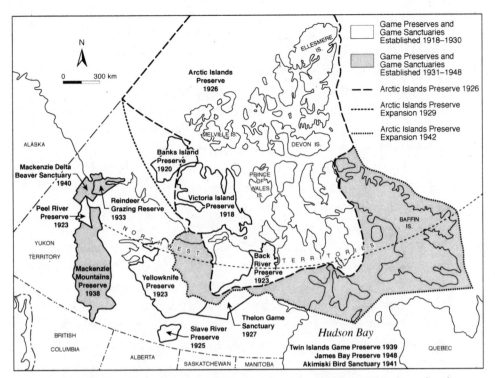

Figure 7.1. Bird and Game Preserves and Sanctuaries, 1918–1948. Adapted from Scace (1975) and Hunt (1976). Original map prepared by R. C. Scace.

The Arctic Game Preserve system was extended to include the South Nahanni River area in 1938. The Mackenzie Mountains Game Preserve was created, running approximately east from the Mackenzie Mountains to the Mackenzie River and north from the Liard to Arctic Red River. Its establishment arose from concerns about the depletion of fur and game due to increased trapping and big game hunting. Newly introduced airplanes provided easier access to areas such as the upper valley of the Nahanni than did arduous travel by foot, canoe, and dogsled.

Some of the earliest calls for a preserve came from hunters and backcountry adventurers, notably members of the 1935 and 1937 Nahanni River expeditions led by Harry Snyder, a well-to-do Montreal businessman.[2] Snyder and his team were not Northwest Territories residents and therefore not eligible for a permit to hunt caribou and other large animals. However, permission was given to Snyder to hunt for scientific purposes. The principal interest was mountain sheep, notably "the black-tailed sheep," and Snyder did send specimens to the National Museum in Ottawa.

A large-scale influx of more mobile trappers and big game hunters was apparently in the process of killing enough animals to threaten the viability of existing populations. Unlike animals in many parts of the Northwest Territories and Yukon, these animals had survived depletion largely because of inaccessibility and isolation. In the 1930s and 1940s, Albert Faille and about eight other trappers were said to be working in the watershed on a regular basis. They had built cabins in the lower Nahanni and Flat valleys. The preserve proponents said the upper valley was much less exploited, even by Indigenous people. It was described as a natural refuge for wild animals and an area of replenishment for wildlife depleted from surrounding lands. It was also seen as appropriate for Indigenous hunting. At the time, the Indigenous people were concentrated along the Mackenzie River, and any kill of animals reaching the upper valley was likely to take only a small part of populations there.[3]

A major reason given by advocates of the preserve was the need to protect the mountain sheep, which apparently had already been reduced considerably. A variant known as the black-tailed sheep was of very great interest. They were viewed as distinct from the white or Dall's sheep. The two were, however, exceedingly difficult to distinguish in the field, the black-tailed having a few black hairs on its tail and flanks. It was argued that the threats to this rare animal were strong justification for a preserve.

In examining the proposal for the preserve, the deputy commissioner of the Northwest Territories, R. A. Gibson, undertook a wide-ranging consultation to secure views and advice. The RCMP conducted a survey of the lower valley, finding caribou to be numerous on the Flat. Little mention was made of sheep. Scientists were also consulted, including R.M. Anderson at the National Museum of Canada. He was generally knowledgeable about mountain sheep and had the opportunity to examine seven specimens of black-tailed sheep submitted by Snyder after his 1935 and 1937 expeditions.

Anderson found no reason to consider the specimens as representing a distinct species. He noted that several different kinds of mountain sheep had been identified in Alaska, Yukon, and British Columbia based upon variations in dark shading among the various specimens. He concluded that these variations were insignificant and that the animals were actually Dall's sheep. Nevertheless, he and others supported the establishment of a Mackenzie Mountain preserve because the threats to wildlife seemed very serious. Small numbers of remaining Dall's sheep at the south end of their range in the Nahanni could easily be eliminated.[4]

The Mackenzie Mountains Game Preserve enjoyed only limited success. Its area was huge, consisting of thousands of square miles of rough terrain that was very difficult to protect with the resources and staff available to responsible agencies such as the RCMP. Hunters and trappers could fly in and out of the preserve without knowledge of the authorities. Cabins could be built and trapping and hunting conducted without apparent discovery. An example is given by Snyder, who undertook another scientific hunt near the Gravel or Keele River north of the Nahanni in summer 1939, about a year after the creation of the preserve.[5] He was transported by a local pilot and guided by a crew who were operating on a rather large scale. They had built a big cabin near a mountain lake and were charging clients $100/day, a very high rate in a time of economic depression. They informed Snyder "over the campfires" that they had killed numerous sheep and other animals, as well as trapping for hundreds of marten, one of the species R.M. Anderson thought well worth protecting. They used an airplane to fly supplies in and furs out.

Of the four or five men involved, only one was apparently eligible for a territorial hunting licence. He seems to have been, at one time, a resident of the Yellowknife area. He was using the permit of a person with a similar name who apparently was an old-age pensioner living in Inuvik. The efforts of the RCMP, Snyder, Gibson, and others on this matter are reminiscent of the search for the proverbial needle in the haystack.[6] The preserve did not seem to have much support among local residents and appears not to have been taken very seriously by them. In his book, *Nahanni*, long-term resident Dick Turner does not discuss the preserve. Yet he was at times very upset about the effect of the territorial regulations on trapping and hunting, seeing them as a threat to his livelihood. It is not surprising that the Mackenzie Mountains Game Preserve was abolished in 1953 after newcomers secured a strong role on the territorial council. This preserve deserves more research, but it remains a major step on the road to the Nahanni National Park Reserve.

Somewhat more success was achieved by the government game regulations. In his book, *Hunters at the Margin: Native People and Wildlife Conservation in the Northwest Territories*, John Sandlos gives a detailed historical account of the rules of the federal and territorial governments.[7] Sandlos sees the regulations as aimed principally at northern Indigenous people and, in large part, as an attempt by the federal and territorial governments to exert greater control over them: an ironic situation given the federal government had used the need to protect game and ensure the livelihood of Indigenous people as one rationale for setting up the Arctic Game Preserve and justifying its claim to sovereignty of the Arctic Islands against Danish as well as other Nordic claimants.[8]

According to Sandlos, the Indigenous people were perceived as being very destructive of game and as committed to an ancient way of life standing in the path of modernization and commercial development. This was the reasoning behind, for example, the introduction of reindeer ranching in the Northwest Territories, an enterprise similar to the Sami reindeer grazing economy of northern Norway and Sweden. Canadian biologists, wildlife managers, and other officials largely supported these developments. They wished to use and conserve game and other wildlife in accordance with scientific principles rather than what they saw as the ineffective customary knowledge of Indigenous people.[9]

Of central interest to the scientists and professional wildlife managers, as well as the federal and territorial governments, were bison, caribou, and muskox. They found these iconic and meaty herbivores to be heavily hit by fur traders, sport hunters, adventurers, miners, and Indigenous people. Neither the Mackenzie game preserve nor the new regulations were entirely successful in stemming losses, although the muskox did increase in the Arctic and the bison were protected in 1922 by the establishment of Wood Buffalo National Park. In these and other efforts, government action was greatly limited by low budgets and insufficient staff. This was especially true in the 1930s, when government funding was cut back because of the economic collapse during the Great Depression.

Sandlos shows the regulations were reasonably successful in controlling the decline of big game animals, especially in the Wood Buffalo National Park area and the higher Arctic.[10] Fluctuations in the caribou populations continued because of the insufficiently recognized cyclic effects of disease, floods, storms, deep snow, hard winters, and the rising toll enacted by newcomers in the 1940s, 1950s, and 1960s. Dall's sheep and other wildlife of the Nahanni were not the focus of government game regulations to the same degree as the bison, muskox, and caribou. The decline of Dall's sheep was significant in the lower Nahanni as recounted by Raymond Patterson.[11]

Several reasons may lie behind the lack of apparent human impact on the wildlife population of the upper Nahanni Valley. One is the distance, the canyons, and the rugged terrain that hindered access from lands along the Liard and Mackenzie valleys. The Kaska people of the upper Liard and Francis Lake in southwestern Yukon are known to have hunted for caribou, marmot, and other animals in the fall and early winter in the mountains on the border of the Nahanni watershed.[12] But they are not said to have actually hunted in the upper Nahanni Valley, perhaps because of distance or rugged terrain. We also know that for centuries Mountain Dene moved up the Keele River to hunt and fish in the mountains on the northern border of the Nahanni.[13] Oral evidence suggests that nineteenth-century Dene moved from the Mackenzie Valley up the North Nahanni River to hunt and fish in fall and winter before following the South Nahanni back to the Liard and Mackenzie in the spring. Such annual trips downriver would have involved taking some moose, migratory birds, and other animals. But the toll likely need not have been very high relative to the size of wildlife populations.

This takes us to the third group of reasons for conserving the diverse wildlife and ecological integrity of the Nahanni watershed: the beliefs, policies, and practices of the host people. This is undoubtedly a major reason for the continuing healthy state of the system over the centuries. The taking of wildlife was tempered by conservation activities carried out traditionally by Indigenous people of the region, including identifying group leaders whose tasks involved preventing overhunting and protecting the harvest for the future. The Indigenous people seem to have extended these controls on their impacts on wildlife to the newcomers. Pierre Berton suggests the Dene people of the Mackenzie and Liard valleys used tales of the deaths of prospectors, such as the McLeods, and of potential attacks by giant denizens as deterrents to newcomers intending to prospect, hunt, or visit the Nahanni.[14]

Researchers such as Hugh Brody have written about the conservation ethic of Indigenous people such as the Beaver or Dunne-za, Athabascan people who lived for generations in the Peace River Country.[15] Brody stayed for eighteen months with these people in the early 1970s as part of a research team studying and mapping Indigenous use of traditional lands then under pressure for minerals, ranching, and other uses by new-comers. Brody hunted and travelled with the Dunne-za and found their knowledge of and respect for wild animals was high. The people generally lived with and used the animals in ways likely to sustain these resources for the future. Like other hunter-gatherers, the Dunne-za saw the hunt as more than mere hunting; it was being part of a vitally important rela-tionship where people depend on animals and these allow themselves to be killed. Animals agree to become food because of the respect the hunters and their families show the land and the animals in particular.[16]

The experience of Richard K. Nelson, the anthropologist who lived with the Koyukon, another Athabascan group of central Alaska, was cited earlier in regard to Indigenous attitudes and behaviour toward bears. Nelson's studies were very comprehensive and underline the many ways in which people like the Koyukon protected wildlife. Of particular interest is his framework, or checklist, of the main mea-sures used in conserving plants and animals. While Nelson cautions against too readily transferring findings for one group to another, his framework likely has general value, at least among Athabascan north-ern peoples.

The Koyukon husbanded resources through spiritual beliefs and field or ecological experience.[17] Their conservation ethic was expressed through measures such as range and territory, responses to competi-tion, avoiding waste, and practising sustained yield. Only a summary of these measures can be presented here.[18] In thinking about them, it is important to realize that the Koyukon ecosystem, or habitat, was quite complex and dynamic. Adjustment to change was normal.

Range and Territory

Outbreaks of fires, floods, diseases, and other forces changed the kind and supply of wildlife continually over the short and long term. Sometimes the system worked to produce a relatively rich food and resource base accessible only a short distance from the village or camp. In such situations, the hunting range could be comparatively small. In conditions of greater scarcity, the range had to expand. Furthermore, with the Koyukon the range generally was not exclusive or private. People went where they needed to go to get food. The idea of territory apparently came into play after American arrival, largely in relation to animals not essential to the human diet. Trapping fur-bearers for commercial purposes is a prime example. Ownership in this case can be seen as giving both motive and means to reduce competition and maintain wildlife populations for the long term.

Competition

Animals such as the lynx, or especially wolves, could compete with humans for key resources such as caribou and moose. Unlike Euro-Americans, the Koyukon did not attempt to eliminate these predators. Wolves were a special challenge. They can exert a heavy toll on moose and other herbivores. Yet, at the time of his research in the 1970s and 1980s Nelson found that the Koyukon were reluctant to reduce or remove this predator. It had been, and apparently still was, perceived as possessing great spiritual and physical powers, capable of killing anyone who slew it wastefully. More contemporary Koyukon apparently saw the wolf in more practical ecological terms. If it became numerous and moose decreased or moved elsewhere, then people tended to check wolf effects by intensifying hunting and trapping, which also could bring greater monetary rewards.

Waste

One of the major tenets of Koyukon wildlife management was to avoid wasting anything from nature. Meat was not to be left unused and wounded animals were to be pursued until they could be killed. Although avoidance of waste was evidently first based on spiritual sanctions, Koyukon people also believed avoidance had practical significance in maintaining wildlife populations. People were encouraged "to harvest only what they could use and to use everything they harvested."[19] These safeguards may have diminished since Nelson's day. However, it is important to realize they definitely were still very much in play in the 1980s and probably later.

Sustained Yield

The Koyukon limited resource harvesting in the expectation that, in the long term, this would lead to higher yields. They avoided young animals and plants, believing their value would increase with age. Large meshed nets were used to catch whitefish on the upper Koyukok River, with the intent of allowing smaller fish to escape and grow toward full size before use. Trappers watched population levels carefully and took measures to ensure continuity; for example, snare and trap sets were arranged to select for larger animals, and catch was limited. Trappers were proud of trapping an area for many years without significant decline.

Some of Richard Nelson's and Hugh Brody's findings on the Koyukon and Dunne-za may not hold completely for other Athabascan or Indigenous peoples. Yet many conservation measures they describe likely found a home among the people of the Nahanni Valley and help explain why the diverse wildlife populations and ecological integrity of the upper valley, in particular, remained high into the corporate mining years of the 1950s and 1960s. And the regulations introduced by the Indigenous people of the village of Nahanni Butte to protect wildlife after the expansion of the reserve in 2009 show that conservation thought and practice remain high today.

Plate 1. The Cirque, Terrace Tower, and glacial moraine in the Ragged Range. Photographer:. Dorothy Stearns. *Courtesy of Parks Canada.*

Plate 2. Cirque of the Unclimbables Mt. Harrison. Photographer: Fritz Mueller. *Courtesy of Parks Canada.*

Plate 3. Lotus Tower and the Cirque of the Unclimbables in the Ragged Range. *Courtesy of Harvey Locke.*

Plate 4. Aerial view of Tufa Mounds at the junction of Rabbitkettle Creek and the Nahanni. Photographer: Fritz Mueller. *Courtesy of Parks Canada.*

Plate 5. Mount MacBrien towers about 1800 metres above Glacier Lake in the Ragged Range, an area renowned for rock climbing. *Courtesy of George Scotter.*

Plate 6. Pools, steps, and terraces on the Rabbitkettle Mound. *Courtesy of Derek Ford.*

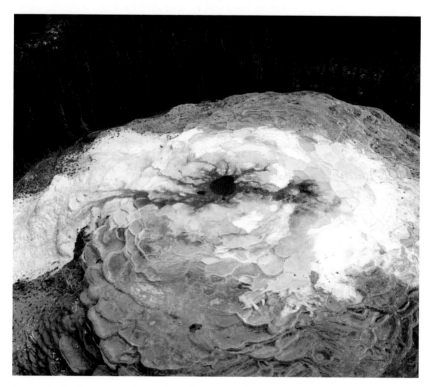

Plate 7. In the thousands of years since the retreat of ice-age mountain glaciers, hot springs have built the majestic Rabbitkettle Mounds, a global rarity. *Courtesy of George Scotter.*

Plate 8. Mist and trembling ground at Virginia Falls. *Courtesy of Bill Caulfeild-Browne.*

Plate 9. The Nahanni flows smoothly from the Ragged Range and Rabbitkettle Mounds through a sediment-filled glacial basin before plunging over Virginia Falls. *Courtesy of George Scotter.*

Plate 10. Rafters about to launch into Fourth Canyon just below Virginia Falls. *Courtesy of Alison Woodley.*

Plate 11. Looking down on the orange red rocks of Fourth Canyon below Virginia Falls. *Courtesy of Alison Woodley.*

Plate 12. Rafters running through Fourth Canyon. *Courtesy of Bill Caulfeild-Browne.*

Plate 13. Steep walls bordering the meandering Nahanni in Third Canyon. *Courtesy of Alison Woodley.*

Plate 14. A well-known landmark, Pulpit Rock, at the end of Third Canyon. Photographer: Wolfgang Weber. *Courtesy of Neil Hartling.*

Plate 15. Prairie Creek in Deadmen Valley between Second and First canyons. *Courtesy of Wendy Francis.*

Plate 16. Rafters taking a meal at a campsite on the way down the River. *Courtesy of Bill Caulfeild-Browne.*

Plate 17. Prairie Creek has deposited a long fan in Deadmen Valley upstream of First Canyon, the site of the McLeod brothers' mysterious death in 1908. *Courtesy of Bill Caulfeild-Browne.*

Plate 18. Canoeists entering the First Canyon of the Nahanni. *Courtesy of Wendy Francis.*

Plate 19. In 1940 Gus and Mary Kraus settled near the hot springs at the end of First Canyon but later moved because 50 Reserve visitors annually was too much. *Courtesy of George Scotter.*

Plate 20. Braided channels, or the Splits, begin at the end of First Canyon and run across the Liard lowlands toward Nahanni Butte. *Courtesy of Wendy Francis.*

Plate 21. A fine Dall's sheep ram; such trophy animals attracted sport hunters even before the 1930s. *Courtesy of Norman Simmons.*

Plate 22. A band of Dall's sheep ewes with young in upland terrain near First Canyon. *Courtesy of Norman Simmons.*

Plate 23. Lengthy migrations of caribou beyond the boundaries of the first 1976 National Park Reserve led to expansion in 2009. *Courtesy of Norman Simmons.*

Plate 24. Dall's sheep ram and ewes on high ground. *Courtesy of Norman Simmons.*

Plate 25. Ancient Dall's sheep remains in the big cave called Grotte Valerie. *Courtesy of Derek Ford.*

Plate 26. Dry polje in Karst terrain north of the Nahanni River. *Courtesy of Derek Ford.*

Plate 27. Grass and tundra of Tlogotsho Plateau south of First Canyon supported large numbers of Dall's sheep, with hunting causing marked decline by the 1950s. *Courtesy of George Scotter.*

Plate 28. Magnificent dry valley in Karst terrain north of the Nahanni River. *Courtesy of Harvey Locke.*

Plate 29. Spectacular Karst terrain in the Ram Plateau, north of the Nahanni River. *Courtesy of Alison Woodley.*

Plate 30. Canadian Zinc's mine on the Prairie Creek floodplain, a major tributary flowing into the Nahanni River. *Courtesy of Harvey Locke.*

Part III

THE STRUGGLE
CONTINUES

Chapter 8

Challenges and Opportunities

We are now at a hinge point in the story of the Nahanni. We have a good understanding of the unique natural wonders of the river thanks to the explorations and travels of people like Raymond Patterson, Dick Turner, Jean Poirel, Joanne Moore, and the detailed research of scientists such as George Scotter, Derek Ford, and John Weaver. We also understand how conservation efforts grew over the years, culminating in the establishment of the Nahanni National Park Reserve in 1976 and its expansion to watershed scale in 2009. We recognize the fundamental importance of research, Indigenous traditional knowledge, and the co-operative approach among the Dehcho, other Indigenous people, Parks Canada, and nongovernmental organizations such as the Canadian Parks and Wilderness Society and Nahanni River Adventures. We are aware of the major reasons why the Nahanni retained its high natural qualities and ecological integrity since the coming of Euro-Americans around 1800. And we recognize the importance of continuing the co-operative approach to the use and conservation of the Nahanni in the future. Yet some major challenges remain, offering opportunities in the years ahead. These challenges can be broken into two groups: those that mainly affect the natural diversity, quality, and ecological integrity of the Nahanni watershed, and those that relate mainly to the Indigenous people involved in the Nahanni National Park Reserve.

The first major challenge to the ecological integrity of the watershed and reserve is mining. It poses threats at Tungsten on the upper Flat River, as well as Prairie Creek, the major north bank tributary of the Nahanni (Figure 1.1). The Tungsten mine has been operating sporadically for decades, opening and closing with the rise and fall of mineral prices. The mine is now closed, an uneconomic enterprise whose fate is in the hands of the territorial government. Considerable, potentially toxic waste has accumulated at the site, the threat of pollution is high, and the issue of rehabilitation and cleanup is still unresolved.

A discussion of the Prairie Creek mine development illustrates the risks and inadequacy of environmental safeguards. Prairie Creek is highly significant for a number of reasons. It drains the limestone formations that house the unique karst topography and cave systems in the lower Nahanni Valley. Prairie Creek also provides excellent habitat for Dall's sheep, which graze on nutritious grasses and tundra flourishing on the underlying limestone. The Prairie Creek area also has a high population of grizzly bears and other wildlife. The site of the mine is alongside Prairie Creek, which drains into the Nahanni canyons. The intention is to exploit zinc, lead, and other minerals found in low concentrations in the bedrock.[1] Much waste rock, tailings, water, and debris will require disposal, with safety an issue, largely because of the release of pollutants, notably mercury, during the recovery of the ores. All of this offers threats to the environmental health of Prairie Creek and the lower Nahanni, the experience and economic benefits of wild river tourists, the health of Indigenous people, notably in Nahanni Butte, and the hunting and fishing economy which they value.

The early developer of the site, Cadillac Explorations, undertook environmental assessments that were approved in 1982. At that time, the site was located about twelve miles outside the boundary of the 1976 reserve. Subsequently, another company, Canadian Zinc Inc., obtained the rights to the site and revised the plan for the mine and associated facilities. In seeking approvals for these changes, Canadian Zinc made submissions to the Northwest Territories' Mackenzie Valley Environmental Impact Review Board, requesting renewed acceptance of the original 1982 environmental impact assessment. The company also applied for land use and water permits for additional changes, triggering several separate environmental assessments to support these proposals. Relevant documents were submitted to the Mackenzie Valley Environmental Impact Review Board and posted on the public registry for public study and comment.

Some replies were received supporting the project, apparently largely in the belief the mine would provide jobs and economic development.[2] The extent of such benefits from mining has, however, often been questioned. For example, in her Ph.D. research Dr. Lindsay Bell tracked employment for students recently graduated from an eighteen-month Hay River underground mining training program and found that only one of ninety students secured work in the industry. She recognized that the results had been influenced by the recession of 2007–2009.[3] However, such declines in the mining industry occur periodically, resulting in job loss and lack of long-term security. Such was the case in 2015.

Many submissions and letters questioned the Prairie Creek project, mainly on environmental and social grounds. These submissions were made in and before 2008, before the Nahanni National Park Reserve was expanded in 2009. The new reserve now includes the lands and waters surrounding the Prairie Creek site, leaving it as a mining enclave within the expanded reserve, an outlier in the Nahanni limestone plateau country with its unique karst topography, caves, underground water, Dall's sheep, and other wildlife habitat.

The reasons for objecting to the mine applications are numerous and complex and can only be summarized here. A very explicit statement of the deficiencies in the company's environmental assessment was put forward by the Northwest Territories' Environment and Natural Resources Department (ENR).[4] The ENR made recommendations on wildlife; sewage treatment and garbage incineration; hazardous wastes including the processing of PCBs and cyanide, oil, asbestos, waste rock, and tailings; as well as mine/mill closure, forest management, silver concentrates, quarrying, waste water disposal, waste management, water sources, and fuel storage. Other comments related to the need for the company to adhere to existing legal codes, such as the National

Fire Code, and obtain additional permits, for example for proposed quarry construction.

A very basic ENR criticism was the need to move beyond particular measures the company planned to take, for example, on wildlife or water management, to overall plans that would show interactive links between the individual technical, land use, monitoring, staff training, and other measures needed for protection. The ENR called for a wildlife management plan that would include means to protect species of special conservation concern such as the grizzly bear, wolverine, rusty blackbird, and short-eared owl. The ENR recommended that Waste Plan and others should be prepared before approval by the review board.

Other worries for the ENR were the danger of floods and their potentially destructive effects on waste water ponds and other facilities, as well as earth movements and landslides, the mine being in a flood and earthquake zone. Quakes in the 6.6–6.9 range on the Richter scale have been recorded in recent years, with major landslides as an aftermath. The ENR also drew attention to the lack of some necessary information in the company's application and asked that these gaps be filled. The organization of the assessment was clearly a concern, the application having been divided among different parts of the project such as roads and the mine. It was, consequently, difficult to identify and deal with interactions and cumulative effects.

CPAWS expressed concern about the mine's impacts as early as 2000. The society argued from an early date for a full-scale environmental impact assessment review in accordance with the federal Mackenzie Valley Resource Management Act. This would require the creation of an independent panel of knowledgeable people who would review scientific evidence and public submissions, hold hearings, and render a decision. This arm's-length, evidence-based approach clearly differed from the process used for the mine, which substantially relied on reports and arguments prepared by Canadian Zinc, the project proponent, and assessment by a standing Northwest Territories review board.

Despite all these fundamental concerns, on December 8, 2011, the review board approved the applications and gave Canadian Zinc the go-ahead to work with responsible government agencies on regulations for developing the mine. Two board members dissented from the majority's decision. They stated that the evidence presented by Canadian Zinc was "inadequate from a legal perspective to provide a sound basis for a conclusion that there will be no significant water quality impacts resulting from this development . . . the majority gave insignificant weight to the evidence, including traditional knowledge . . . especially with regard to the importance of water quality to the Nahanni National Park Reserve downstream communities and the traditional and cultural uses of these areas, including fisheries."[5]

In its decision to approve the mine proposals, the review board stated that the project would not have important environmental effects nor be a significant cause of public concern, these being the two criteria used to determine whether a full-scale federal environmental impact review was necessary. A number of objections were submitted immediately after the board announced its decision. The Dehcho First Nations wrote the federal Minister of Aboriginal Affairs and Northern Development Canada, who had final approval for the mine, to the effect that the Dehcho communities supported the economic potential of the project and the impact benefits agreements signed by the Liidlii Kue First Nation and the Nahanni Butte Band, but wanted assurances of higher standards of water effluent treatment. The Dehcho thought impacts on water quality could be minimized, preferably by using a reference condition approach whereby monitoring would ensure that water quality closely followed water conditions prior to mine development.[6]

CPAWS stated that in spite of the review board's assertions to the contrary, there was considerable evidence of wide-ranging public concern and a very strong case for a comprehensive environmental impact review. As a leading example, Derek Ford, who earlier made the case for the unique qualities of the Nahanni karst, wrote to the UNESCO World Heritage Committee, detailing his scientific and conservation concerns about the proposed mine and its potential impacts on waters, landforms, and wildlife of the reserve. He asked that the committee, which had awarded World Heritage status to the Nahanni in 1978, contact the federal government of Canada at the highest levels, expressing its grave concern about permitting the mine without an appropriate environmental assessment. His letter was featured in the fall 2005 *Northern Currents,* the widely distributed newsletter of Nahanni River Adventures.[7]

On August 15, 2008, CPAWS called attention to its long-time criticisms of the project. CPAWS said its concerns should be taken as expressions of its twenty thousand members across Canada and its 180 members in the Northwest Territories. Its membership was apprehensive about the environmental effects of the mine on a national park reserve, where the mandate is a very high level of conservation and protection of ecological integrity. The society also cited international concern, specifically the United Nations World Heritage Committee's response to Derek Ford's request. The committee cautioned that "various mining, mineral, oil and gas exploration activities around the property could have adverse cumulative effects on the integrity of the property." These could not be systematically assessed by the divided (four-part) land use and water application process being used by the company. The committee also recommended that Canada should protect the entire Nahanni watershed. CPAWS also pointed out that a Northwest Territories public opinion poll in September 2007 estimated that 51 per cent of residents were opposed to allowing the mine to proceed. In May 2008, a Canada-wide opinion poll suggested 64 per cent of Canadians supported protecting the entire South Nahanni watershed in a national park. Twenty-two per cent thought parts of the watershed should be left out for mining development.[8]

Both the Northwest Territories' CPAWS chapter and the national office protested the review board's decision to allow the mine to proceed to development. The local chapter cited the following specific concerns:

- the board has avoided its own responsibility, which is to provide a clear mitigation framework for the safe development, operation, and closure of the proposed Prairie Creek mine;

- the reasons for the decision do not provide the regulating agencies with enforceable measures to fulfill commitments that will prevent environmental impacts during the lifespan of the development;

- the responsible federal authorities' recommendations have not been adequately reflected in the report, including for water quality;

- the Mackenzie Valley Environmental Impact Review Board (MVEIRB) has based its decision on the "assumption" that Canadian Zinc will fulfill a twenty-five-page list of commitments made during the environmental assessment;

- MVEIRB does not make any firm mitigation recommendations and only provides three "suggestions" as to how the project should be managed from an environmental perspective.

The local chapter asked that the assessment be returned to the review board for further study and that "until mandatory mitigative measures are in place, the project should not proceed to regulatory permitting and licensing."[9] The CPAWS national office summarized its earlier concerns and recommendations about the project and repeated its request for a full-scale environmental impact review.[10]

Knowledgeable people in Yellowknife believe the Prairie Creek mine proposal deserves much more study and widespread and intense public discussion. It threatens the environmental and social well-being of the Nahanni watershed. Its threats to the integrity of what is possibly Canada's outstanding northern national park reserve deserve greater public understanding and involvement. That the twenty-five-page list of company commitments will be adequately implemented, monitored, and regulated is hard to accept in light of past experience, budget cuts, and the lack of qualified government staff.

The second major challenge related to the integrity of the Nahanni watershed and reserve is the location of its boundaries, as the previous discussion of the Prairie Creek mine shows. Another significant example is the boundaries of the new Náátsʼihchʼoh National Park Reserve on Sahtu[11] and Metis lands in the northern part of the Nahanni watershed (Figure 8.1). The boundaries of this long-awaited reserve reflect the smallest of the three possible boundaries (Option 3) that had been offered for public comment (Table 8.1; Figure 8.1).

This option was characterized in Parks Canada's public consultation documents as offering "minimal protection to important conservation values" compared to the two larger options offered on scientific and traditional use grounds. These were intended to complement the existing South Nahanni National Park Reserve and sustain a virtually complete South Nahanni watershed ecosystem (Options 1 and 2). Critical habitat areas identified by John Weaver and used by woodland caribou to calve and breed were left out of the final reserve boundary, as was key grizzly and Dall's sheep habitat (see Table 8.1). The smaller reserve also leaves out lands sacred to and long used by Indigenous people. Although some data on Table 8.1 seem overly precise, this boundary decision is not in line with the evidence-based and co-operative process built up since the 1980s. The project requires more research, monitoring, and civic vigilance.

The second group of challenges relates to the Indigenous people of the reserve and involves, first, inadequate knowledge of their identity, geographical behaviour, and land use history, and, second, their future as part of the Nahanni National Park Reserve. Our knowledge of the names of the different peoples and their divisions into clans, tribes, and other groups often arises from contact with early fur traders. They generally did not know or speak the language of the early people they encountered, naming them through uncertain transliterations of Indigenous languages. Various groupings were organized and systemized later by scientists and scholars, notably anthropologists who generally decided whether Indigenous people actually merited a tribal or other title on the basis of evidence such as a distinctive language, territory, and common history. The validity of these decisions was, at times at least, questionable. Names and locations tended to change with time. Some movement can be explained by the push of newcomer advances. On the other hand, as we saw with Richard Nelson's research on the Koyukon, Indigenous people did not always hold European or Canadian views on the boundaries of a homeland.

As for knowledge of the Indigenous people using the Nahanni watershed and surrounding region at the time of the fur trade's arrival, so far only some brief stories are known. For example, stories are told about early Indigenous people who are said to have lived in the highlands

Table 8.1.

Notes on Schematic Options for Nááts'ihch'oh National Park Reserve

OPTION 1: *To best protect conservation values within the proposed reserve while still providing open area around existing third-party mineral claims and leases:*

Covers 94 per cent of the upper watershed; provides habitat for about 94 per cent of the grizzly bear population (about 108 grizzlies);

Protects about 81 per cent of the woodland caribou herd's summer habitat;

Excludes three main mineral claims and lease areas;

Omits 6 per cent of the watershed from the reserve, which contains 20 per cent of the highest mineral potential area.

OPTION 2: *Protects 84 per cent of the upper watershed:*

Includes an estimated 85 per cent of the grizzly population (about ninety-six grizzlies) and 72 per cent of the upper Nahanni woodland caribou herd's summer habitat;

Excludes 16 per cent of the upper watershed, accounting for about 43 per cent of the highest mineral potential.

OPTION 3: *Covers 70 per cent of the upper watershed:*

Includes habitat for an estimated 70 per cent of the grizzly bear population (about seventy grizzlies);

Includes only 44 per cent of the upper Nahanni woodland caribou herd's summer habitat in the reserve.

Adapted from Parks Canada (2010b).

Figure 8.1.
Schematic of
Options for Sahtu
or Nááts'ihch'oh
National Park
Reserve. Adapted
from Parks
Canada (2010b).

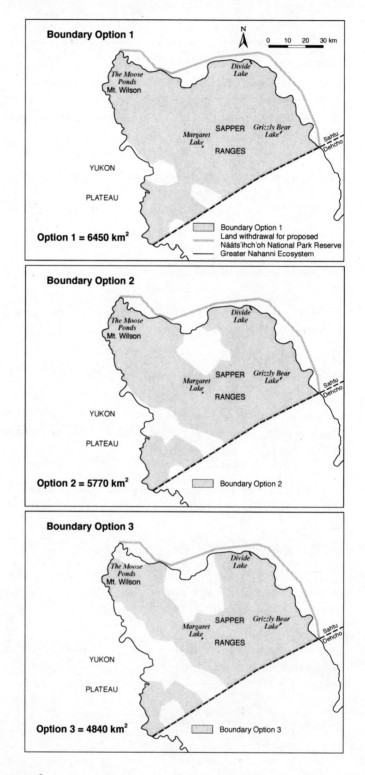

bordering the Nahanni, descending periodically into the Mackenzie Valley to raid people there for valuables, including women.[12] Ford thought these highland people may have lived in sheltered upland karst valleys such as Prairie Creek, where wildlife is relatively plentiful. Ford and Woodley stated that these highland people ultimately disappeared. This brings to mind the story of the Apachean (Apache and Navajo) Athabascan-speaking people of the American Southwest. The scholar Stephen Trimble links the Apache and Navajo to Athabascans living in the North, in Canada, Alaska, and on the Pacific coast. Anthropologists have tried to track their migrations without clear success. They may have moved south through the mountains or across the Great Plains centuries ago.[13]

According to Scotter, mountain people are discussed in Keele's report on his geologic reconnaissance across the Mackenzie Mountains in the early 1900s. They were said to number about one hundred or so Indians who hunted and trapped around the headwaters of the South Nahanni and Keele rivers near the present border between Yukon and the Northwest Territories. Keele described them as a superior class of men who had maintained their old independent way of life before the advances of the white man. Keele apparently thought they might have been the inspiration for legends of evil spirits or gigantic Indians hunting in the country along the Mackenzie Mountains.[14]

In his *Nahanni: River of Gold . . . River of Dreams*, Neil Hartling refers to mountain people, the Naha, who others have called Nahanni. They are said to have dressed in Dall's sheepskins and to have been violent. In contrast, the Dene concentrated along the lowlands of the Liard River. They went into the mountains, usually in winter, returning in moosehide boats in spring. In doing so, they came into conflict with the Naha. This fighting declined late in the nineteenth century, either because the Naha migrated to another locality, were killed off by the Mountain Dene, or perhaps some combination of the two. Hartling says some Naha eventually settled along the Liard lowlands, where they live peacefully with the neighbouring Dene.[15]

Parks Canada tells a slightly different story.[16] According to this account, in the late 1800s Mountain Dene from the surrounding area would travel down the South Nahanni River each spring. They built and used moosehide boats. These were made of six to ten untanned moosehides sewn together over a spruce-pole frame. Entire families, their dogs, and furs came down the river in these boats to trade and visit relatives. They dismantled the craft at the end of the trip and exchanged the moosehides. Upon completion of their trade and visits with relatives, the Dene returned to the mountain country, carrying their gear or loading it onto pack dogs.

These stories of early mountain people are vague. Keele's report suggests they were active into the early twentieth century. They may have been people we know as Kaska, Slave, or even Cree. The European and Canadian advance pushed these people into the South Nahanni, Liard, and Mackenzie River area. Possibly, they were a combination that came together because of a common interest in the old hunting and trapping way of life. Whether these men were very active in the South Nahanni Valley and possibly involved in conflicts over trapping in the early 1920s is another question.

Of particular interest are the people whom fur traders and later arrivals called the Nahanni. They are often viewed as the earliest users of the valley. They were "the unknown people" sought by John McLeod as targets for the fur trade in the 1820s. The name of the Nahanni River likely derived from these mysterious people. Over the years, their numbers are thought to have been gradually reduced by conquest, amalgamation with other Indigenous peoples, or newcomers. Recent land use and Nahanni National Park Reserve agreements were made with the Dehcho and their northern neighbours, the Sahtu.

The anthropologist Beryl Gillespie's article in the *Handbook of North American Indians*, published by the Smithsonian Foundation in Washington, DC, helps shine some light on the history of the Nahanni. According to Gillespie, their name is not an "anthropologically acceptable" label for any tribe, or cultural or linguistic group. It has not been identified as applying to a people consistently associated with a specific language and location. Over the years, the name has been used to refer to an array of people in northern British Columbia, Yukon, and the Northwest Territories. These include the Kaska, Slavey, Tutchone, and other groups. Variants of the Nahanni appellation have been applied to Mountain Indians, Northern Tutchone, Kaska, and other people associated with the Pelly and upper Liard areas, as well as the upper Stikine.

Of more specific interest for this book, Gillespie states that the term "Nahanni" is derived from a word used by several Athabascan groups to refer to certain Athabascan speakers other than themselves. The name was also applied by Europeans and Canadians to people who actually did not think of themselves as Nahanni. The term had a vague mystical flavour. It suggested the unknown or strange. It was used by various Athabascan peoples "for relatively remote or distanced Indian groups" that were considered "evil, untrustworthy or hostile, possibly giants."[17]

All this is reminiscent of the previous brief references made by Hartling and other observers to Indigenous peoples involved in the history of the Nahanni and the Nahanni National Park Reserve. Gillespie's account seems to provide for a deeper understanding of this history. For example, the "unknown people" found by John McLeod in 1822–1823 were very likely the people known as Kaska. Indeed the chief, White Eyes, told McLeod that his band had separated from a parent group in the upper Liard—the land of the Kaska—three years earlier. When Robert Campbell met the Nahanni and the chieftainess in the upper Liard in 1836, he likely was encountering Kaska. Catharine McClellan's oral histories of nineteenth-century Kaska describe their use of the Mackenzie Mountains for summer and fall hunting, supporting the idea that the Kaska came to be labelled as the Nahanni.[18]

All of the foregoing discussion points to the need for more historical, ethnological, and archaeological research and traditional knowledge on the Indigenous people of the Nahanni region. If the research does confirm, for example, that the Nahanni were predominantly Kaska, then a different picture emerges of the land use and environmental history of the upper Nahanni Valley. As users of the mountains and the Nahanni headwaters in summer, the Kaska likely were the people who came into conflict with the Dene during their annual downriver run from a winter in the upper watershed. The conflict may have resulted in the upper Nahanni Valley becoming a land between, a place of risk, less frequently hunted, possibly a buffer zone, where wildlife was often thought to be more plentiful and inadvertently conserved than on land more regularly hunted by people such as the Kaska or the Mountain Dene.

In their study, "Revising the 'Wild' West: Big Game Meets the Ultimate Keystone Species," Paul Martin and Christine Szuter give numerous examples of what they call buffer zones and their effects in the nineteenth-century west. For example, in lands beyond the Great Lakes, disputed by warring Sioux and Chippewa: "The hunters were also the hunted and game thrived. When hunters no longer had anything to fear in the disputed lands, they hunted freely and game rapidly declined." Martin and Szuter also saw "the wealth of wildlife observed by Lewis and Clarke in 1804–05, to the east of the Rockies in the upper Missouri country, as a result of conflict for territory between the Blackfeet and Assinboine making the area risky and dangerous for either tribe to hunt consistently."[19]

In a recent article on "Peace, War, and Climate Change on the Northern Plains: Bison Hunting in the Neutral Hills during the Mild Winters of 1830–34," historian George Colpitts has enriched our thinking about the interaction of Indigenous people and the nature of buffer zones.[20] Mild winters in 1830–1834 apparently led to modified bison grazing patterns on the northern plains of what is now Alberta and Saskatchewan. Larger areas became available for grazing so that bison were more dispersed and difficult to hunt. However, the animals still congregated in more favourable areas like the Neutral Hills. Neighbouring Indigenous people such as the Blackfoot and Cree were drawn together in exploiting these more accessible animals. These circumstances led to co-operation in seasonal hunting camps, as well as the exchange of labour, traditions, and marriages. Given the new insights of George Colpitts, it seems that while the buffer—or neutral—zone sometimes separated people and protected wildlife, under other conditions it brought people together and increased pressure on animals. Seen from this perspective, the buffer zone appears to be a more complex ecological mechanism than was previously thought.

More detailed archaeological work would undoubtedly help lift the veil over Indigenous activities and effects in the Nahanni and other parts of the Mackenzie Mountains in pre- and early contact times. To see this, we can consider the snow-patch studies recently completed by Tom Andrews and his colleagues at the Prince of Wales Northern Heritage Centre in Yellowknife.[21] Snow patches are ecologically significant since they attract caribou and other wildlife seeking to escape the heat and mosquitoes in the warm season. Snow-patch studies in Yukon and other parts of the world show the patches also attract humans in search of food. The Prince of Wales studies are interdisciplinary and represent what could be done in the upper Nahanni. They reveal human history and landscape and ecosystem changes over the centuries.

The Prince of Wales snow-patch work was carried out in co-operation with Indigenous people. The archaeologists used previous land use history studies undertaken for First Nations' land claim purposes, as well as Elders' stories of old-time hunting patterns that involved the use of snow patches. The patches are located in the Selwyn and Mackenzie mountains in the Keele River watershed, perhaps fifty to one hundred kilometres from the upper Nahanni country. The patches are within the current Sahtu Settlement Area and the traditional land use range of the Mountain Dene, who today are concentrated along the Mackenzie Valley.

Ice cores and snow have persisted in some sites for centuries. Eight selected patches were all associated with caribou dung, which sometimes formed a surrounding ring because of melting snow and climate warming. The eight patches were also associated with rarely found wooden artifacts, including throwing dart, bow and arrow, and snare technology. These involved the use of wood, a material that does not readily resist breakdown and is rarely found at archaeological sites.

Drilling in the patches revealed successive dung layers separated by snow and ice. In the case of some dung layers, wooden artifacts were found on open ground where patches had melted seasonally or because of climate change. Carbon-14 dates on some wood revealed a long pre-contact history of snow-patch use by caribou and human hunters.[22] Throwing dart technology dated around 2500–2300 BP (before the present). Succeeding arrow shaft technology dated between 850–230 BP. A snare was found that was dated to approximately 970 BP.

The snow-patch studies conclusively show that Indigenous people were hunting caribou and other animals in the Selwyn–Mackenzie Mountain area, the current lands of the Sahtu and Mountain Dene, for thousands of years. Andrews and his colleagues linked the snow-patch use patterns to old trails of indeterminate age and to oral histories of early-twentieth-century land use patterns of the Mountain Dene. According to the oral histories, the Indigenous peoples spent winters in the lower mountain ranges along rivers like the Keele. Nets were set through the ice for fish. Snares were used to hunt smaller game. Sheep, caribou, and moose were taken with snares, fences, and rifles. In spring, after wintering in the valleys and mountains, the people would travel eastward down the Keele to posts on the Mackenzie River or westward along the Keele into Yukon to trade. Time often would be spent near the posts, fishing. In summer, they returned to the mountains where they usually took up snow-patch hunting, along with fishing and other activities. Andrews and his colleagues believe that a similar pattern could have applied in pre-contact times, with allowance for differences in technology and the absence of trapping and hunting for the fur trade.

A key question is whether the archaeological evidence for these fur trade and pre-contact land use activities extends into the nearby upper Nahanni. In a conversation about the possibilities in September 2013 with Prince of Wales archaeologist Tom Andrews, a pre-Euro-American connection was not ruled out. He noted that reconnaissance surveys by graduate students and other researchers were revealing archaeological sites in places previously considered as unlikely. Detailed archaeological studies of the upper Nahanni Valley area should therefore be a high priority for Parks Canada. They are perhaps the only reasonably reliable way of answering questions about very early Indigenous use of the upper valley, its effects on the ecosystem, and the cultural history of pre-Euro-American times.

The snow-patch approach could be quite fruitful in the mountainous terrain of the upper Nahanni region, notably the Ragged Range country where glaciers are still found today. Any archaeological research that is carried out should be multidisciplinary, including pollen analysis, carbon-14 dating, and other tools that could cast a brighter light on the details and significance of any recovered human artifacts, as well as any environmental changes associated with them. Glacier retreat and climatic change studies have been undertaken recently in the Ragged Range, although these may not be continued in future. Linking such studies into multidisciplinary archaeological work could paint a broad picture of human land use and environmental change in the Nahanni and surrounding areas.

Further multidisciplinary archaeological research in the Nahanni watershed could yield answers to some key questions about human use and its effects on fauna and flora.[23] When did humans first enter the mountains of the region? What was the climate and environment like at that time? Could entry have occurred as long ago as "the early man" or Paleo-Indian era more than eight thousand years ago? Or was the cold climate still too extensive and harsh in the waning years of glaciation, delaying human use until later, milder times? What was the subsistence and behaviour pattern of early peoples? Is it possible to estimate their effects on, or role in, the ecosystem?

At least tentative answers have been given to some of these questions by archaeologists and scientists working in other areas such as the central Rocky Mountains in the 1970s, 1980s, and 1990s.[24] Early man or Paleo-Indian sites were found amid the forested mountains, high tundra, parkland plateaus, and bordering grasslands of Colorado, Wyoming, Utah, and Montana. Their frequency and associated populations seem to have been low. The number apparently increased as the climate warmed. These people appear to have migrated into the mountains in the summer when the snow and cold were less restrictive of their movements. Whether they were ice or snow-patch hunters in the style of the Keele River people is not clear.

A major purpose of early movements into the mountains seems to have been to secure obsidian and other rock suitable for producing effective stone projectile points. Such rocks were quite valuable and were traded extensively in the Great Plains country. The effects of these early people on wildlife have been controversial. Some see Paleo-Indian overhunting contributing to the elimination of the large bison of late ice age times. Others see the animals dying out because of climate and environmental change, or a combination of the two hypotheses.

In about 8000–7000 BCE, the climate in the central Rockies became warmer and drier. People living in bordering foothills and plains moved into the moist, more heavily vegetated mountains to escape the increasing aridity of the grasslands, as did bison and other game populations. About 4000–3000 BCE, this warm dry Altithermal period came to a close and the climate grew cooler and wetter. The number of people seems to have risen, with two broad types of cultural patterns developing in the plains and mountains respectively. The plains people widely adopted communal bison drives as a source of food, leather, and other resources.[25] Those in the plains borderlands near the Rockies moved into the valleys and uplands in summer. The people of the valleys and uplands appear to have hunted in smaller groups, using sheep or caribou traps at higher altitudes.

While this picture of early human entry and use of the central Rockies is subject to question in relation to the Nahanni, it does indicate the kind of fundamental knowledge that further archaeological research could unearth in that general region. Available legendary, historical, and archaeological evidence already suggests that Mackenzie River Dene and other people using the Nahanni Valley and surrounding areas may also have fallen into two groups. First, the Mackenzie Valley Dene are recorded as migrating into the Keele River valley in late summer to hunt, for example, around snow and ice patches, returning later to the Mackenzie lowlands to overwinter. Oral evidence suggests also that the Dene may have hunted and wintered in the upper Keele or North Nahanni valley, returning down the South Nahanni in spring to trade fur and moosehides at Nahanni Butte.

Some of these trips may have been carried out by a second group of more regular residents of the Nahanni country who moved about in the valleys and mountains for the entire year. Derek Ford has suggested that the deep sheltered cave and sheep-rich Prairie Creek Valley could have been a good site for these mountain people. Further archaeological and field research in this country would help to answer some of these questions.

The final major challenge to be discussed here is the future use of the Nahanni National Park Reserve, especially by and for Indigenous people. One of the most significant values of the Nahanni and other national parks is as a source of knowledge for scientists, scholars, planners, decision makers, and citizens, including First Nations who have long inhabited their homeland. The usual practice has been to view national parks and similar protected areas in terms of their values for conservation and recreation, including tourism and as a generator of income for local communities. Education, learning, and research are also often seen as a value of national parks, but not to the same degree as the others. Education is aimed at the tourist and delivered through interpretation programs. These are usually quite general, focused on the neophyte visitor, and often the first program to be cut in a budget crunch.

Seeing national parks as ongoing centres of learning, and the deep research needed to understand and adapt to the changing world around us, is uncommon. Yet, today, deep research is more and more important in order to comprehend climate and environmental change and its implications for wild and human life. National parks are one of the few places where ecosystems have been conserved, and research can tell us the long story of natural and cultural change and the interactions between them. Ideally, national parks are invaluable repositories of natural, archaeological, and historic information, tracing environmental and cultural changes significant to all people, including local communities, Canadian citizens, and people living some distance away. Research and monitoring of natural and cultural changes is an increasingly vital role of national parks, giving information essential for the well-being at the local, regional, provincial, national, and international scales.

Nowhere is this better exemplified than in the Nahanni National Park Reserve. It encompasses a relatively little disturbed and nearly complete watershed and ecosystem, with a unique geology and diversity of indigenous wildlife. It houses an insufficiently understood archaeological and historic record reflective of centuries of human evolution in the North while remaining a homeland for the Dehcho and, in the case of Nááts´ihch´oh, the Sahtu and Metis. Its role as a research and monitoring platform for environmental and land use change is insufficiently recognized yet fundamental to its contribution to conservation, recreation, tourism, and Indigenous ways of life.

It is here that the Nahanni and Nááts´ihch´oh national park reserves can be seen as opening a doorway into a different type of learning experience intended largely for the people of nearby First Nations' communities—although this could be shared with tourists and outsiders in as yet undetermined ways. This idea arose from a conversation with Dehcho Grand Chief Herb Norwegian in the Fort Simpson's Nahanni Inn coffee shop in late August 2013. We discussed the idea of the Nahanni National Park Reserve becoming a research centre, with the study and monitoring of glacial behaviour in the Ragged Range as an example. We also discussed the possibility of the reserve as a place where Dehcho, both young and old, could come into contact with the land in historical ways that young people, in particular, were now often unaware of because of their life in towns. The Nahanni is being used to a limited extent in this way now. Nahanni River Adventures co-operates with local schools and other organizations in offering a student river trip downstream from Virginia Falls annually. Although Herb Norwegian and I did not get a chance to follow up on these ideas after the coffee shop meeting, I have been thinking about the possibilities ever since.

One line of thought is that a return to the land can be seen not so much as a retreat from the sometimes promising but often destructive pushes and pulls of urban life and an increasingly intensive commercial consumer society, but rather as a potential stabilizer and eye-opener to a middle way. In this sense, Indigenous people could participate in experiences on the land that bring back values and ways of life that tie them to their historic past and their heritage, as well as potentially opening up opportunities for the future.

Indigenous leaders began in the 1980s and 1990s to recognize the values and opportunities that national parks and comparable reserves offer to the Dehcho and other Indigenous people. Lengthy dialogues with Parks Canada, conservation NGOs, and other organizations, as well as among the Indigenous peoples themselves, have led to values and uses such as hunting, camping, travel, and spiritual practices being embedded in the Nahanni National Park Reserve agreement, along with opportunities to gain employment with Parks Canada. To what extent these opportunities can be further developed by the Dehcho in association with concerned organizations such as Parks Canada is yet to be determined. This work involves finding means to exploit the heritage opportunities in commercial and occupational ways that are practically beneficial to the Dehcho, offering skills, jobs, and paths of value to them. This vision appears to parallel working with the people and other concerned parties to rediscover heritage through experience on the land.

And the Nahanni offers an opportunity for a learning centre that transcends what people like me have been thinking. My focus was on research in the southern Canadian tradition, science or scholarly based school, university, and advanced studies to help with local, national, and global problems such as climate and environmental change, providing more knowledge of culture, land use, and landscape through archaeological, historical, and other research. Opportunistically, studies by young Indigenous people can be tied to this through field experiences, summer jobs, internships, research positions, and other avenues to economic and social skills. Archaeologists at the Prince of Wales Northern Heritage Centre in Yellowknife have already embarked on this journey, for example by involving young and older Indigenous people in research such as the snow-patch work.

The Nahanni National Park Reserve can offer young people opportunities, first through wildland experiences linked to learning and training in traditional hunting, fishing, and basic survival and, second, through associated tourism, business, marketing, planning, management experience, and training that offer possible paths to the outside commercial world. It follows that officials in national parks and related agencies will have to develop the social skills, knowledge, and funding needed to work with Indigenous people in this way.

Bob Rae, chief negotiator for a group of northern Ontario Indigenous people, has recently issued a call for greater understanding of the life challenges faced by First Nations and the need to think much more co-operatively in learning, business, leadership, and social terms about their future. He made these important points within the context of what he saw as the overly simplistic and too great expectations associated with the so-called Ring of Fire mining project on employment and economic prospects for Indigenous people in the far north of Ontario. As Rae sees it, Indigenous people cannot benefit in the near or long term to any great extent from such projects without gaining the social, economic, and life skills he thinks are needed to exploit mining and other opportunities beneficially in the longer term.[26] This is a useful idea that should take account of Indigenous values and cultures in an interactive, adaptive, and mutual-learning fashion.

Account should be taken of the desire of some Indigenous people to continue to pursue hunting cultures and their own view of the world.[27] Thomas Berger sees this as a way of life that may be the most appropriate for large parts of the boreal forest and Arctic.[28] In *A Long and Terrible Shadow*, Berger writes at some length in justification of the hunting, fishing, and subsistence lifestyle, making the point that it is perhaps the only way Indigenous people in the North can live in a manner that conserves the values of their culture. It may also be the only sustainable long-term use of large parts of the boreal forest and Arctic. Yet many people still have difficulty with the idea of a continuing hunting culture today. They make judgments based on the longstanding notion that progress in the modern sense means Indigenous people will, or should, move up what is envisioned as the socio-economic ladder of economic development such as mining. But, as Vicki Cummings points out in *The Anthropology of Hunter-Gatherers*, the concept of "unilinear development, from hunter-gatherer to farmer (or miner or the like) was very much part of a nineteenth century way of thinking about the world and human development."[29]

According to Cummings, such a view is problematic because it prioritizes the economy over every other aspect of life. It also assumes mining or some other perceived more advanced activity is somehow a better or superior way of life. It continues to promote the notion that hunting and gathering is a distinct activity, separate from mining, as well as business, administration, research, and other purportedly higher activities.

Negotiations with Indigenous people about mining or other development could end in the failure to secure their consent because of concerns about the sustainability of the traditional economy, heritage, and way of life. A recent example is the Lax Kw´alaams' opposition to the construction of a large LNG (liquefied natural gas) terminal close to the mouth of the Stikine River, not far from Prince Rupert, BC. Impacts on fish habitat, especially sanctuary areas for juvenile salmon that have long been a mainstay of the traditional economy, are a major concern. Three meetings organized by this Indigenous group to secure the people's vote on the proposal found that the Lax Kw´alaams are united in their rejection of the project in spite of an offer exceeding more than a billion dollars for their consent by the proponents.[30] The proponents plan to modify the project and continue to seek consent. This rejection is a very strong signal that in some cases money and other economic "benefits" may not persuade all Indigenous groups to back proposed resource developments, especially when they involve basic threats to the environment and their longstanding and valued way of life.

On the other hand, the opportunities for some Dehcho to combine environmental conservation, hunting, and gathering with other activities and a wider lifestyle hold potential. This is especially so in this electronic age, given the successful examples at Gwaii Haanas National Park Reserve on the Haida Gwaii (formerly known as the Queen Charlotte Islands), or with Arctic Inuit and Mackenzie Valley Inuvialuit since they reached agreements with the Canadian government. Here national parks and other conservation reserves can be seen as offering diverse opportunities while retaining the essence of the hunter-gatherer culture or way of life—keeping one foot firmly on the land while scanning for compatible new options, including management and entrepreneurship.

Development of the Nahanni National Park Reserve can clearly be linked to such ideas. Further progress depends heavily on continuing the research and co-operative approach that led to the 2009 Nahanni National Park Reserve expansion. It was the combined research and co-operative approach among Parks Canada, Dehcho First Nations, CPAWS, Nahanni River Adventures, and other groups, along with the support of citizens, that made the expansion possible.

After 2012, the former federal government was heavily criticized for its funding cuts and their effects on research, evidence-based planning, and decision making of the kind so important to the 2009 expansion. In his book, *The War on Science*, Chris Turner found that the cuts were particularly heavy on the basic research, data gathering, monitoring, assessment, and conservation tools previously used to provide sound environmental stewardship.[31] Large cuts were made to Parks Canada, reducing overall staffing and prospects for employment of First Nations people. Arrangements apparently are still pending with the Dehcho on completion of an impact and benefit agreement consequent upon Dehcho contributions to the Nahanni National Park Reserve expansion. Monitoring programs intended to track pollution from the development of the Prairie Creek mine also appear to be in limbo, and the operational definition of co-operative or joint management of the reserve remains to be addressed.

The Dehcho may well be concerned about any lack of commitment to complete the funding, staff, and work arrangements associated with reserve expansion. A recent assessment of ecological integrity in national parks by the Office of the Auditor General of Canada identified a number of significant problems in Parks Canada's overall program.[32] These included failure to complete park management information on time, updating monitoring information, and filling gaps in baseline data on park ecosystems. Such problems were linked to reductions in budget and resources for management and could be one obstacle to meeting commitments with people such as the Dehcho in regard to the establishment of the Nahanni National Park Reserve. Not meeting important commitments with co-operative Indigenous partners has potential future implications, not only for the Nahanni but other northern national park reserves—there is, once again, a strong need for research and civic vigilance and planning.[33] Hope lies with the election of the new federal government of Justin Trudeau in October 2015. This government has promised to improve funding and support for Parks Canada. What effect this will have on funds for benefits agreements with the Dehcho, or for more research and conservation, remains to be seen.

In an essay in the *Literary Review of Canada*, Terry Fenge and Tony Penikett recognize that governments often do not follow through or implement obligations set forth in treaties and agreements.[34] They point out that the government of Canada is not keeping all of the promises it made to Aboriginal people in twenty-four "modern" treaties, mostly in the North, negotiated over the last forty years. They demonstrate the long-time reluctance of the federal government to commit whole-heartedly to the treaty process and its obligations, given a long-standing interest in assimilating Indigenous people into the wider Canadian society and economy, an idea long resisted by many Indigenous people. Lack of commitment to fulfilling treaties has led Indigenous people to protest against the failure to act effectively by both their own leadership and the government, as for example with the cross-country Idle No More demonstrations in the winter of 2013–2014.

Responsible departments and agencies often do not coordinate and co-operate well in addressing and implementing such commitments. Many factors impede the implementation process, including avoidance or delay by government officials of frequently complex commitments involving various departments and fields of interest. Natural Resources,

Environment, Finance, and other agencies, as well as Aboriginal and Northern Development (formerly Indian and Northern Affairs) and provincial and other governments, can all be involved in treaties that involve land ownership, management of lands and natural resources, harvesting, management of wildlife, assessment of resource development, capital transfers and economic opportunities, royalty sharing, establishment of national parks and conservation areas, cultural expression and enhancement, and more.[35]

So the Dehcho do not stand alone in seeking fulfillment of any agreements made as part of the 2009 expansion of the Nahanni National Park Reserve. Fenge and Penikett see one potentially very important road to improvement in the establishment of the independent modern treaty audit and review body recommended by the Land Claims Agreements Coalition created in 2003 to represent all First Nations and modern treaty organizations. Fenge and Penikett thought the establishment of such an independent audit and review body would require the approval and authorization of the prime minister. They saw this as unlikely, given the relative indifference to Indigenous affairs shown by the previous incumbent, with treaties being ignored in the government of Canada's northern strategy of 2009. With the election of the new federal government in October 2015, a more positive stance toward addressing the needs of Indigenous people is apparent, but so far not much concrete action has been taken with respect to agreement with Indigenous treaties and their land use concerns.

Chapter 9

Analogies with Experience Elsewhere

F indings similar to those in this book can be found in the work of others, notably in relation to wilderness, Indigenous people, research, and co-operative planning. An early example lies in the work of Aldo Leopold, the legendary conservationist and author of the famous 1949 *A Sand County Almanac*, which became a near bible for North American environmentalists in the 1960s.[1] Leopold was one of the first graduates of the newly established Yale School of Forestry, where he became an adherent of the utilitarian philosophy of "the greatest good for the greatest number for the longest possible time"—the gospel of Gifford Pinchot, federal chief forester under the great conservationist, President Teddy Roosevelt.[2] Roosevelt created the first forest reserves and the United States Forest Service in the late 1800s and early 1900s. Under Pinchot's banner, they were managed according to the utilitarian doctrine and the associated principle of promoting highest and best human uses, which in this case were considered to be lumbering and cattle grazing.[3]

Leopold took his first job in New Mexico in 1906, where he quickly applied this approach and associated policies of eliminating grizzly, wolf, cougar, and other big predators on cattle and sheep. He also supported controlling fires to protect forests for lumbering. However, Leopold was a keen hunter of elk, deer, ducks, and other game. He eventually became concerned about the road and other programs underway to open up forests for lumbering, grazing, camping, and mass tourism. Leopold saw these programs as the death knell for rugged backcountry hunting in remote forests. He began to devote himself to game and, later, wildlife management, working for the recognition of hunting as a significant use of forest reserves along with lumbering and grazing.

Before departing the Forest Service for a professorship at the University of Wisconsin, Leopold published a groundbreaking article in the November 1921 *Journal of Forestry*, entitled "The Wilderness and Its Place in Recreational Forest Policy." Here he defined wilderness as "continuous stretches of country preserved in its natural state, open to lawful hunting and fishing, big enough to absorb a two weeks' pack trip and kept devoid of roads, artificial trails, cottages or other works of man." Leopold thought such wilderness areas should take up only a small part of the total national forest. In making his case for recreational or hunting wilderness, Leopold argued principally from a social or political rather than the ecological perspective he would become famous for later. He organized co-operative game clubs throughout New Mexico and started a newsletter to increase member awareness of developments and their implications. He wrote for general readers as well as foresters and other professionals, frequently calling for research on contentious issues. His proposal for backcountry hunting areas led to the establishment of the first Forest Service recreational wilderness in the Gila National Forest in New Mexico in 1924. Within ten more years, seventy blocks of U.S. Forest lands were set aside as wilderness or "primitive areas." These were important to Leopold because they offered an alternative to national parks, where recreational hunting was prohibited.[4]

Leopold's thinking continued to evolve after he left the Forest Service. He began to value conservation of big predators, notably the charismatic grizzly, and grew more concerned about the impacts of heavy lumbering and grazing on habitat, vegetation cover, soils, gullying, and erosion. A momentous change came when he and a friend went on a hunting expedition to the Rio Gavilan in Mexico's wild Sierra Madre Mountains in 1937. What he found in these southern extensions of the Arizona and New Mexico mountains was live-oak country "coated with side-oats grama, pine clad mountains spangled with flowers . . . trout streams bubbling under great sycamores and cottonwoods . . . undisturbed virgin soils, great natural beauty and numerous deer co-existing with wolves in an unexploited environment."[5] Leopold contrasted this "picture of ecological health" with the sad condition of lands across the border in the United States, despite their management as forest reserves or national parks.

Leopold thought the Sierra Madres were in far better condition because they had been avoided by Mexican settlers, who feared and respected the resident Apaches. These Indigenous people had been driven out of the Chiricahua and other ranges in the United States in the late nineteenth century, opening them up to lumbering, cattle grazing, and other exploitive uses. In Mexico, the Apache had prevented such invasions and their damaging effects on forests, grasslands, soils, wildlife, and natural systems. Leopold found that the Sierra Madre burned every few years. Yet there were few ill effects. The pines were a little farther apart, regrowth was reduced, leaving less juniper and brush, but the watersheds were intact. In contrast, watersheds on the United States side had been "sedulously protected from fire," grazed much too hard, and were a "wreck."[6] Leopold consequently turned against fire control and questioned whether semi-arid lands could be grazed at all without harm.

Earlier, Leopold had not paid too much attention to Indigenous people and their ecological impacts, occasionally complaining while serving as a forester in New Mexico that they did not follow the rules, taking too much game and hunting out of season. His observations of the role of the Apache in Sierra Madre ecosystems led to the conclusion that most of the damage to United States national forests was a result of intense lumbering, grazing, and misguided management. His wilderness became a place in which predators, prey, fires, forests, grasslands, soils, watersheds, and relatively low populations of nomadic hunters, gatherers, and occasional growers of corn, beans, and squash all interacted to sustain healthy ecosystems. This inclusive view of wilderness and the role of Indigenous people is remarkably similar to the ecological integrity approach built into the 2009 expansion agreement for the Nahanni National Park Reserve.

A strong analogy can be drawn between Leopold's recognition of the key role of the Apache in protecting ecosystems of the Sierra Madre and the vital role that the Dehcho and other Indigenous groups have played and could play in the future of the Nahanni National Park Reserve. Leopold's wilderness view was developed through many years of insightful field observations. The conclusions in the 2009 Nahanni National Park Reserve agreement were built on intense and wide-ranging research, major advances in ecological or ecosystem thinking, great improvements in research technology, and long-term interactive and adaptive planning by major stakeholders. Their co-operative efforts and support made the result broadly acceptable to governments and citizens.

Despite the appeal of Leopold's wilderness ideas, they did not take a prominent place in the environmental movement of the 1960s and later years. The dominant view of wilderness continued to be the ideal model—remote lands undisturbed by human activity, Indigenous or otherwise. This model was strongly advocated by the Wilderness Society, the Sierra Club, and other conservation organizations. The continued use of the classical model by the United States National Parks Service, Parks Canada, and other organizations did, nevertheless, encounter growing resistance from long-time Indigenous and North American users who faced the loss of traditional activities or eviction through the establishment of ideal wilderness in national parks and other protected areas.

In 1977, the World Wilderness Congress was organized to promote "wild nature" in the classical or ideal sense and also seek reconciliations with the economic, social, cultural, and other arguments against ideal wilderness in many parts of the world. In 2001, David Rothenberg and Marta Ulvaeus edited *The World and the Wild*, a set of articles associated with the Fourth World Wilderness Congress held in Colorado in 1987. These articles reflect the state of play some ten years after the launching of the congress. The articles are international in scope, with presentations on the United States, Nepal, Africa, Borneo, Mexico, and other countries. They reveal multiple perspectives on wilderness and the cultural, socio-economic, land use, resource, and environmental issues associated with the idea. The great value of the papers and the congress itself is that interchange of experience and ideas helps build bridges globally, leading to greater understanding of cultural contexts and the need for research and co-operation into prospects for mutual benefits.

Several key articles from *The World and the Wild* can be used to illustrate the different viewpoints and challenges revolving around wilderness. The first is the Introduction by Rothenberg, which reveals a commitment to the ideal view of wilderness as remote, ineffable, and little disturbed by humans. But Rothenberg also recognizes that, in a global context, wilderness has to offer a place for long-time human users. He is uncertain how to do this and hopes for solutions from the congress participants.[7]

Two articles particularly highlight the fundamental nature of the challenge. These articles describe two different wildlands traditions and the historical and cultural contexts in which they developed. The traditions are the United States ideal wilderness model and the so-called social ecology model.[8] The United States, the major proponent of ideal wilderness, is a relatively young country, wealthy, highly industrialized, and committed to rapid growth despite its costs in terms of loss of biodiversity, air and water pollution, and other environmental and social consequences. As a counterweight, the United States sets large uninhabited wilderness areas aside from industrial development, except tourism, as a reservoir and hope for a return to a more natural world. India, a proponent of the alternative social ecology model, is a poor country, heavily populated, and still largely rural, with many lower-income farmers and a perspective on ideal wilderness as incompatible with the long history and needs of the people.

The consequences of the two traditions can be seen in the efforts to save the tiger and its wilderness habitat. Philip Cafaro and Monish Verma see Indigenous people as having borne too much of the cost of this program through loss of land and livelihood to tiger reserves, threats to human life, and the lack of alternative means to survive.[9] They call for more social justice, greater compensation, and more influence by local people in creating and operating tiger reserves. They advocate for cash and other payments for losses, including more employment, guiding, and other opportunities, as well as providing alternative land use options in surrounding areas.

Having called for changes in the planning and management approach for the tiger and its wild habitat, Cafaro and Verma support the tiger program in principle, saying that, contrary to the social ecologists' claim that the program lacks value to Indigenous people, the loss of the tiger would be a loss to them, India, and the world. They see the "goodness of the tiger itself, its beauty and its complexity, its ancient and unique history." If the tiger and the land are not preserved, "we close off important ties to the human past and possibilities for future human aesthetic, scientific and spiritual developments."[10]

This bold argument could strike a chord with some local people if expressed appropriately. But the idea of compensation and greater economic and social benefits would seem more important to gaining their support. Co-operation among interested organizations is essential to meet this and other challenges. Indian and other Third World people seem little different than North Americans such as California farmers who have been persuaded to change their agricultural practices to provide more water and wetland habitat for staging waterfowl and bird life during their migrations from wintering grounds in Central and South America to nesting habitat in northern Canada. This California project involves research and co-operation among "citizen scientists" who collect and report on bird occurrences and routes; analysts and mapping staff at New York's Cornell University Lab of Ornithology; the U.S. Nature Conservancy, which pays farmers to modify their practices; and the farmers themselves, who participate because of the economic benefits, seeing the birds as another crop.[11]

In light of this discussion, it is very apparent that the lengthy research and co-operative process leading to the expansion of the Nahanni National Park Reserve in 2009 was a remarkable achievement. It succeeded in bridging the gap between the views of relatively well-to-do mainstream Canadians on ideal wilderness and Canadian Indigenous views on homeland, which have some links to social ecology thinking in India. Other especially instructive examples of the value of co-operative projects have developed in recent years along the USA–Mexico border. An array of government agencies and NGOs exchange information, research, funds, staff, and other resources to conserve and restore wildlife habitat and wilderness areas across shared ecosystems on either side of the international boundary.[12] Among the most relevant initiatives are cross-border co-operation to reallocate water from the United States to Mexico to revitalize the desiccated wetlands of the Colorado River Delta;[13] restoring the Big Bend reach of the Rio Grande River;[14] reconciling conservation and security in two sister parks on either side of the Arizona–Mexico border;[15] and the transborder recovery program for the Mexican wolf between New Mexico and Arizona and the Mexican Republic.[16]

The Mexican wolf recovery program is particularly helpful in providing insights into the requirements for a successful research and co-operative approach. The recent reintroduction of the wolf is an exceedingly challenging effort, notably because of the large ranges needed to maintain this animal and the long-standing antipathy of many ranchers and residents, on both sides of the border, toward this predator. Cross-border research on the needs of co-operating restoration workers focused first on interviews with Mexican wolf recovery participants, and second on stakeholders working on other endangered species in the border area. The results (Table 9.1) are very useful to those involved in planning recovery programs everywhere.

Table 9.1 can be compared to the efforts involved in the Nahanni National Park Reserve expansion program. The comparison is a general one and does not correspond exactly with the criteria listed in the United States cross-border research. Some of the Nahanni criteria are my modifications of the United States–Mexico criteria. The modified criteria are emphasized and can be readily related to the criteria in Table 9.1.

We can begin with the issue of *resources*, which are a major challenge for stakeholders in the Nahanni. No data are known to have been published on the funds expended by Parks Canada, the Dehcho, the Canadian Parks and Wilderness Society, and other stakeholders in the forty-to-fifty-year effort. Millions of dollars were undoubtedly spent by the Canadian Wildlife Service and Parks Canada, as well as Energy, Mines and Resources on research, information, and communication. Additional *funding* was obtained through grants and other assistance for CPAWS, Wildlife Conservation Society Canada, and other nongovernmental organizations to participate. Cross-country *communication, education,* and *information exchange* by CPAWS involved costly workshops and national campaigns. The work of the Northwest Territories CPAWS chapter depended on grants. The work of Nahanni River Adventures was privately funded.

Table 9.1.

Results of Research and Co-operative Needs Assessment Program

Issue Cluster	Need
Resources	funding increase funding management information exchange new information skills training technology transfer
Coordinated Projects	project design project management project review balance of captive/field effort national autonomy
Organizations	coordination: federal institutional continuity balance of government and nongovernmental organizations formal procedures decentralization of decision making
Culture	exchange visits trust/reciprocity bilingual skills intercultural skills
People (interpersonal skills)	communication skills continuity of participants understanding diverse perspectives leadership skills personal interaction skills negotiation skills

Modified from Bernal Stoopen, Packard, and Reading (2009).

The costly work of *coordination, design, management,* and *review of research* was largely undertaken by Parks Canada, which generally shared the results with all of the stakeholders. *Organizational* issues were challenging for all the major stakeholders, including the Dehcho, with their bands scattered throughout the Nahanni region. Several key organizational devices were developed. For example, a joint consultative group, the Nah? ą Dehé Consensus Team, was established at the local level by the Dehcho and Parks Canada with the involvement of CPAWS. Another coordinating effort was the Parks Canada Dehcho First Nations Park Expansion Committee. A *workable balance of major stakeholders* thus seems to have been achieved. Much was decentralized to the local level, where the complexities and implications of land use compromises were most apparent. *Informal relationships* seem to have been very influential among the leaders of the Dehcho, Parks Canada, CPAWS, and Nahanni River Adventures.

Interpersonal relationships and *communication skills* were developed over a long period of time and were fundamental to achieving consensus among initially competing stakeholder objectives. CPAWS and Nahanni River Adventures were especially important in communicating information to the wider public in Canada and the United States. *Continuity* was important in maintaining co-operation and addressing evolving challenges with the passage of time. Some key leaders arose among the major stakeholders. They gained a good understanding of the various challenges and worked to *bridge the different cultural and other perspectives* involved in expanding the reserve through well-honed *interaction, negotiation, and adaptive skills.*

Unfortunately, as we saw earlier, much experience, skill, and mutual understanding may be lost because of budget and staff cuts, as well as the need for funding and resources by all major stakeholders. Strong government support has not been forthcoming for the co-operative process necessary to implement the 2009 reserve expansion effectively. Parks Canada and the Dehcho are dependent on government commitments for funding and staff to carry out such tasks as completing environmental and cultural inventories of the lands and waters added to the reserve in 2009, managing the expanded reserve, researching and monitoring environmental change, educating and involving the

Dehcho and other local people, addressing the challenges of Prairie Creek and other mining projects, undertaking important archaeological and historical research projects, and developing improved ways to communicate the value of distant northern wildlands to the greater Canadian public, particularly in Canada's growing metropolitan areas. Urban isolation limits the understanding of wildlands and their contributions to society as a whole. Much has been accomplished. The great challenge of effective implementation remains.

Another important analogy is the relationships between national parks and Indigenous peoples. This is a topic on which citizens are overwhelmingly uninformed, as indeed are many professionals and decision makers. Comparisons can be usefully made between the United States and Canada. Information on national park policy and practice for Indigenous people can be derived from Robert H. Keller and Michael F. Turek's 1998 comprehensive study of policy and practice in the United States and, to a much lesser extent, in Canada.[17]

Keller and Turek's research spanned a dozen years of field studies and interviews with national park spokespeople and Indigenous people. The study was nationwide, with the results described in selected case studies of Apostle Islands National Seashore, Lake Superior, Yosemite National Park in California, Glacier National Park in Montana, Yellowstone National Park in Wyoming, and Everglades National Park in Florida. The product is a series of chapters dealing with national park experiences with numerous different Indigenous groups such as the Chippewa, Zuni, Anasazi, Blackfeet, and Navajo, as well as east coast people such as the Seminole. An introduction and conclusion on "Parks and Indians in America" refers to experience with a number of other Indigenous people and summarizes the results.

This is not the place to make detailed comparisons between U.S. and Canadian policy and practice, largely because a careful study like Keller and Turek's has not been completed in Canada. Some of their major findings do, however, apply to both countries. Examples include the long-standing idea that national parks include wilderness originally devoid of Indigenous people. They point out that, to the contrary, long-term historic Indigenous presence was true for virtually all U.S. national parks, including Yellowstone and Yosemite, where Indigenous fires and cultivation contributed to the formation of savannah and grassland land-scapes. In many cases in the United States, the interests of Indigenous people were contorted or suppressed during negotiation for and man-agement of national parks. The same is true for numerous older Cana-dian national parks such as Banff, Glacier, and Prince Albert, although Keller and Turek recognize the adaptability of the Canadian national park program in the case of Wood Buffalo and, more recently, other northern national parks. In a recent book entitled *Spirits of the Rock-ies*, historian Courtney Mason describes the dislocation of the Nakoda people (Stoney Indians) from Banff National Park. He also mentions a series of relatively recent studies of the exclusion of Indigenous people and Metis from Canadian national parks such as Kluane National Park in Yukon, Riding Mountain National Park in Manitoba, Georgian Bay National Park in Ontario, and Jasper National Park in Alberta.[18]

In both the United States and Canada, legal commitment and pro-cess not uncommonly seem to have been overlooked or circumvented in the course of national park operations. An overt force in driving hard bargains with the Indigenous peoples was the widespread view that assimilation into mainline society was best for the Indigenous peoples, and this was in fact national park and government policy in both countries for many years. The potential for tourism benefits to Indigenous people through the establishment of national parks, although potentially significant, has been exaggerated in both coun-tries, with employment in staff and management positions often indef-initely delayed or evaded.

Along with other northern national parks, the establishment of the Nahanni National Park Reserve and the agreements for Indigenous hunting, foraging, and other rights within it represent major advances on past practice in Canada as well as the United States. Attempts have been made at co-management in Canyon de Chelly, Nez Perce, and other U.S. parks with less than ideal results. Nahanni National Park Reserve, therefore, stands as a potential model for a more mutually satisfactory way forward for national parks and Indigenous people. Continued federal government support and co-operation are neces-sary if a promising path forward to an uncertain but hopeful future is to be followed.

Two recent Supreme Court of Canada rulings strongly support findings on the importance of informed co-operation in projects like the Nahanni National Park Reserve. The first case involved an appeal by the Tsilhqot'in First Nation against British Columbia provincial approval of a logging licence without adequate consultation with the Indigenous people.[19] In this case, no previous treaty or other agreement had been reached with the Tsilhqot'in people involving Aboriginal title to the lands in question.

The Tsilhqot'in claimed that as hunters and gatherers they had used this land for centuries. The Supreme Court found that such continued use and control of the land gave the Tsilhqot'in title, in spite of government and other understandings that title depended on continuous settlement of the kind characteristic of an agricultural or industrial society. The Court went on to require that, in future, companies and governments should engage in close consultations with Indigenous peoples and secure their consent to mining, lumbering, park, or other development proposals.

Exceptions may be allowed for projects that are considered by government as necessary to the greater public interest, but careful consultation and co-operation are called for in these cases as well. The details on the Tsilhqot'in decision are not yet clear. It would seem that the long research and co-operative process carried out by Parks Canada, the Dehcho people, the Canadian Parks and Wilderness Society, and other groups parallels the general procedures backed by the Supreme Court. Ideally, this process should continue into the management phase of the Nahanni National Park Reserve.

Some pundits have reacted to the Tsilhqot'in ruling by saying that it will impede or even prevent development.[20] The ruling actually seems to require negotiation with Indigenous people to determine their wishes and offer an opportunity to share strongly in benefits, this often having been denied in the past. Broken treaties, land grabs, and other behaviour by the federal government are described in recent publications such as *The Inconvenient Indian* by Thomas King and *The Winter We Danced*, a record of the 2012–2013 Idle No More Movement edited by the Kino-nda-niimi Collective.[21] The Supreme Court also held that British Columbia retained ultimate authority in right of the Crown and, where close consultation and consent were not successful, could approve proposals considered vital to the greater public interest.

The second case involved the Grassy Narrows First Nation in north-western Ontario.[22] Here the province had approved a development initiative where, in the opinion of the Indigenous people, their views about the project had not been adequately heard. The Indigenous case hinged on their contention that approval of the federal government was also required because while the province had constitutional juris-diction over land use and resources, the government in Ottawa was responsible for the welfare of First Nations.

The Court found that, unlike the Tsilhqot´in First Nation case, an early treaty with the Grassy Narrows First Nation gave the provincial government the power to make decisions on development proposals for lands covered by the treaty. On these grounds, the Court found that the province had the authority to make the development decision in question. The Court was critical of the way the decision was made and, once again, ruled that the province had a duty to consult with Indig-enous people about such proposals and work to accommodate First Nations' interests beforehand.[23] The Supreme Court decisions in both these cases strongly support the co-operative approach underlying mutually beneficial decisions for the Nahanni National Park Reserve.

In contrast to the critical response of many pundits, particularly those with a deep interest in proposed pipelines across land claimed by Indigenous people, some observers generally welcomed the Supreme Court rulings. After the Supreme Court decision, members of the Tsil-hqot´in First Nation announced plans to establish Dasiqox Tribal Park, covering about 300,000 hectares of traditional wildlands in west cen-tral British Columbia.[24] One commentator, Chief Russell Myers Ross, reportedly said Tsilhqot´in thinking about a park is different than that of most Canadians. The boundaries of Dasiqox Tribal Park are intended to meet the needs of grizzly bears, moose, wolves, and other wildlife. But within the park area, room is available for some development as well. Another commentator, Chief Joe Alphonse, said the form of the park has not yet been decided. It could be a special management zone. Local residents, businesses, and local ranchers have been invited to pro-vide input. Other commentators said a tribal park is usually unilaterally declared by a First Nation to protect an area in its territory, with rules being laid down by that First Nation. In some cases, the First Nations work with federal or provincial governments to establish a more formal designation such as a provincial park. Other areas have been set aside by Indigenous people without any provincial or federal designation. Yet these areas have provided protection against logging and other activities. An example is Meares Island off the southern coast of British Columbia.[25] These varying responses by Indigenous people to the Tsilhqot'in ruling show that different people have different views of the implications. The overall Indigenous reaction will have to be worked out internally, as well as in the wider political arena.

Two potentially promising ways forward are resource revenue sharing and co-operatively proposed plans for traditional Indigenous land use areas. The resource revenue sharing idea was put forward in the March 15, 2015, report of the Working Group on National Resource Development established after a meeting between then Prime Minister Stephen Harper and former Assembly of First Nations (AFN) Chief Shawn Atleo.[26] The working group was co-chaired by AFN's regional chief in Alberta and a Toronto-based former deputy chair of TD Securities. The motives for establishing the working group seem to be mixed. The federal government and business were concerned about the blockage of development projects. Indigenous peoples were concerned about getting greater benefits from projects with as little impact on the environment as possible. They also wished to protect wildlands for traditional land uses such as trapping and hunting.[27] The orientation of the working group toward resource revenue sharing echoes a recent call by the newly elected AFN Chief Perry Bellegarde.[28] The path to revenue sharing is not likely to be easy or uniform because of opposition to it by some prominent leaders such as Premier Brad Wall of Saskatchewan.

A second way forward is offered by front-end project planning, which would build consultation and negotiation into the early stages of proposed projects. Differences can be more readily worked out than later, when a virtually completed plan may be presented to Indigenous users for their comments, more or less as a fait accompli. Useful examples of early First Nations' involvement in park establishment planning can be found in Ontario. At least four large northern areas have been protected under community-based land use plans. These involve co-operative planning by First Nations and Ontario. Of the four cases at hand, Whitefeather Forest has 36 per cent of the planning area in the dedicated protected category, with Cat Lake–Slate Falls at 34 per cent, Pauingassi at 79 per cent, and Little Grand Rapids at 100 per cent.

To illustrate the planning process, we can consider the *Little Grand Rapids Community Based Land Use Plan.* The road to the plan has been long and involved much interaction, negotiation, and adjudication on the part of the Little Grand Rapids Band and the Ontario Ministry of Natural Resources (OMNR) on behalf of the Province of Ontario. In 2004, terms of reference were signed for a three-year planning process for 188,738 hectares. Dialogue, preparation, and exchange of information occurred regularly, leading to a 2010 draft plan, essentially a strategic plan with goals, objectives, and principles set out by the band and Ontario. The community was consulted about the plan. It was also opened up to discussion by all interested people.[29] In July 2011, the plan was approved by the Little Grand Rapids First Nation and Ontario. It calls for the protection of traditional and existing land uses and the environment. Zoning supports the protection of lands and waters, traditional uses, and existing and new tourism opportunities.

Indigenous traditional activities are protected by Aboriginal and treaty rights, including hunting, trapping, fishing, and gathering. Other permitted uses to be continued through future management planning include motorized boat, snowmobile, all-terrain vehicles, or airplanes; sport fishing, hunting, research, and education; communal fur harvesting; communal fishing; communal tourism; and communal bait fishing. Among excluded uses are commercial forestry; mineral exploration; mining; power generation; new energy transmission and communication corridors; road building; and aggregate and peat extraction.

Overall, then, co-operation in Little Grand Rapids planning is generally comparable to Nahanni, but nongovernmental conservation organizations are not as involved, although CPAWS had a stronger role in a counterpart area in the bordering province of Manitoba. Even so, in Little Grand Rapids, forestry and other exploitive activities were seen as threats to habitat, traditional use, and protected area planning. A range of uses has been permitted or decisions delayed that have not been permitted in Nahanni or other national or provincial parks. The arrangements are a reflection of the views, to date, of the Little Grand Rapids people. Decisions may differ elsewhere.

The wide-ranging co-operative approach used in the Nahanni is in line with national and international declarations of principles and procedures considered applicable to mining, forestry, energy, national park, and other development projects, where Indigenous and local people's traditional access to land, human rights, freedom, and justice are to be respected. For example, in his book, *Redefining Human Rights in the Struggle for Peace and Development*, Terrence E. Paupp argues that a transition from top-down, focused, and exclusive decision making to a broad, inclusive, and more co-operative approach is fundamental to the protection and enhancement of culture, environment, heritage, and livelihood among Indigenous people, emerging economies, and societies.[30] Paupp makes his case primarily in the context of conflicts among groups dominated by the corporate or neo-liberal approach, with its demand for less regulation, lower taxes, standardization, and a relatively unbridled market.[31] He advances certain principles in support of co-operative efforts to achieve fairness and justice in these situations. These principles include recognizing the rights of Indigenous peoples, consulting with and inviting Indigenous participation in the use of resources, developing strategies to share benefits, increasing the transparency of environmental costs and benefits, building local capacity to participate, and encouraging research on successful methods of involving local people in projects. This book on protecting the magnificent Nahanni is an example of this last principle.

In *Fairness and Justice in Environmental Decision Making*, Catherine Gross defines *fairness* primarily in terms of interactions, processes, and procedures, while *justice* is the result of appropriate planning and management for development.[32] According to Gross, in the 1960s the focus was on justice in the sense of a generally acceptable distribution of the costs and benefits of projects. Experience in mining, lumbering, water, energy, and other development proposals in the 1970s and afterward showed, however, that affected people wanted to be informed, consulted, and, to a considerable degree, involved in project planning and development. In other words, they were as much, if not more, interested in fair interactions, processes, and procedures as in results. This is, once again, illustrated in the Nahanni.

Another relevant recent study is Andrea Olive's *Land, Stewardship, and Legitimacy: Endangered Species Policy in Canada and the United States.*[33] Olive points out some important differences in the approach to endangered species in the United States and Canada. In the United States, the focus is more on regulation and the role of government. In Canada, the spotlight is on the landowner. The U.S. regulatory approach has, however, given way with time and conflict. Both countries now ultimately rely on the understanding and co-operation of landowners and citizens in protecting endangered species. Olive found that while some landowners are strongly committed to the Lockean notion that they have the right to do as they wish with their land and any species upon it, many landowners will commit to species protection if they are properly informed and involved. As with the Dehcho and other Indigenous people, understanding, research, and co-operation are vital to success.

That the co-operative approach may still have a strong future is supported by the announcement by the federal government on July 29, 2015, that it is entering into an agreement with a First Nation and the Northwest Territories to create the new Thaidene Nëné National Park Reserve at the eastern end of Great Slave Lake. CPAWS has been working with the Lutsel K'e Denesoline First Nation on this proposal for four years. The original proposal for the reserve was put forward by Parks Canada about 1970. It was a top-down effort that was based on the ideal wilderness model and was strongly opposed by the Indigenous people. The new reserve will be co-managed by the Indigenous people and is said to provide for the Dene use of the land, as well as "their culture, language and world view." The new reserve will involve fourteen thousand square kilometres of forest and tundra abutting a territorial park of more than twelve thousand square kilometres, making for a large protected area "where caribou, moose, wolves and bears can range unimpeded by industrial development."[34]

Indigenous people will continue to hunt in the national park reserve. All Canadians with valid licences will be allowed to hunt in the lands protected by the Northwest Territories. The national park reserve will contain historic villages and gathering sites of Indigenous people, as well as old Fort Reliance. The reserve is expected to create seasonal and year-round employment for the people.[35] The new Thaidene Nëné National Park Reserve can be seen as taking a step beyond the processes used in the Nahanni. The Thaidene Nëné approach seems to mirror the 1960s shared planning model used widely in regional land use planning in British Columbia. Provincial research and professional staff worked with citizens' committees that had business, recreational, farming, forestry, and other cross-sectoral membership representative of the economy, social, and environmental makeup of the region involved.[36]

Calls for a less autocratic approach are growing in frequency and volume. Chief Justice Beverley McLachlin has called past actions of the federal government "cultural genocide."[37] The long-awaited report of the Truth and Reconciliation Commission of Canada calls for rec-onciliation efforts that involve both Aboriginals and non-Aboriginals.[38] Civic organizations such as the Circle on Philanthropy and Aboriginal Peoples in Canada call for a reconciliation process that involves "mul-tiple different voices on multiple different topics." This organization prepared a Declaration for the Truth and Reconciliation Commission that has been signed by the Laidlaw Foundation, Ontario Trillium Foundation, RBC Foundation, TD Bank Group, the Martin Aborigi-nal Education Initiative, and the Molson Foundation, among others.[39]

John Ralston Saul, Canada's pre-eminent civic scholar and critic, has drawn attention to the national resurgence of Indigenous people in his latest book, *The Comeback*.[40] He sees Indigenous people as growing in creativity and influence in Canada because of their strong sense of heritage and dedication to a more self-directed future. Saul argues that all Canadians should support this comeback. One very promising way forward is through national parks and other protected areas. They offer very workable and mutually beneficial opportunities for innovative co-operation among government, Indigenous people, business, con-servation, and other organizations, in the spirit of the path generally taken in the Nahanni National Park Reserve. It should not be assumed, however, that even with shared intentions and a co-operative attitude interaction between Parks Canada and Indigenous people will be read-ily workable. Indigenous nations—First Nations, Metis, and Inuit—are diverse and complex, frequently consisting of subgroups with different values, land use and conservation ideas, and objectives. In such circumstances, patience, commitment, mutual learning, intercultural skills, experience, and funding are essential if planning and management are to be fair, just, and generally effective.

A Note on Sources

T he *Magnificent Nahanni* is based on my own long involvement in national park and wildland conservation experience in the North, a rafting trip to the valley in August 2013, and discussions with knowledgeable people in Fort Simpson, Yellowknife, and Ottawa. Many of these people are acknowledged earlier in the book. Much of the information in this book is derived from publications, reports, and documents included in the list of references. Most of these provide evidence for the story of the river and the long struggle to protect it in a national park reserve. Other references are scientific and scholarly studies that provide the concepts, theory, approaches, and perspectives used to organize, analyze, and interpret the evidence.

The scientific and scholarly studies will now be reviewed briefly for the benefit of other researchers, as well as public officials, planners, students, and citizens interested in assessing this book and potentially applying it to their own research and practice. The studies are wide-ranging, derived predominantly from disciplines such as geography, anthropology, archaeology, history, biology, and geology, as well as other fields of study including ecology, conservation, and planning. These disciplines and fields of study have been brought together over time in broad schools of thought about landscapes and places and the ways in which they are shaped and changed by people. A number of these schools of thought, or lines of inquiry, have been especially influential in writing this book. I would like to outline them with references to relevant studies for follow-up by interested people. I should emphasize that the references are not intended to approach completeness. They are intended to be illustrative and are selected primarily through my own experience.

One line of inquiry that has had a significant influence on *The Magnificent Nahanni* is research on *land use history* and *landscape change*. This endeavour in itself has a long history, especially among geographers, anthropologists, and archaeologists intrigued by the ways in which changes in nature, human beliefs, goals, values, perceptions, technology, and learning, or culture, have influenced the character of places historically. Over the years, these scientists and scholars have used increasingly sophisticated field research, along with mapping, historic documents, excavation of artifacts, interviews, and technological and other methods to determine how hunting, agriculture, and other activities have affected people, plants, animals, soils, drainage, landscapes, and places around the world.

Examples of these are the classic *Man and Nature; Man's Role in Changing the Face of the Earth; The Highlands and Islands; The Early Spanish Main; Man's Impact on the Western Canadian Landscape; The Inuit Land Use and Occupancy Project; People of the Ice Whale; Land Use Changes in Europe;* and, more recently, *Places: Linking Nature and Culture for Understanding and Planning.*[1] These studies show how a central interest in land use history and landscape change has been advanced by improved theory, methods, and technology to address varying issues and concerns about people, landscapes, and places internationally. Excellent examples of how this is being addressed in widening cross-disciplinary research in archaeology are *The Archaeology of Global Change* and *Ancient Plants and People.*[2]

Land use history and landscape change studies tend to flow into other wide-ranging schools of thought such as environmental history. Until recently, this has been a neglected area among historians, a few of whom showed an early interest in it, mostly in dealing with concerns about economy, society, trade, and regional or national development. Early examples are *The Fur Trade in Canada* and *The North American*

Assault on the Canadian Forest.[3] Other studies, with a stronger ecological bent, include *North American Indian Ecology, The Ends of the Earth, Game in the Garden,* and *The Lessening Stream.*[4] A groundbreaking study, especially in the United States, is *Changes in the Land.*[5]

In more recent years, increasingly sophisticated approaches have been taken to environmental history, particularly from an historical ecological standpoint. These studies incorporate more science, theory, technical advances, analysis, and modelling. This produces remarkably wide-ranging cross-disciplinary research and promotes greater overall understanding and improved applications to planning. Three useful examples are *The Once and Future Great Lakes Country, Marine Historical Ecology in Conservation,* and *Human Ecodynamics in the North Atlantic.*[6]

Environmental history has increasingly become a worldwide enterprise but is still finding its way in terms of goals, foci, methods, approaches, and perspectives. The recent volume, *Nature's End,* reflects the diversity of this school of thought and its links with studies in land use history, landscape change, historical geography, environmental economics, and climate change.[7] Of special interest in *Nature's End* is Chapter 9: "54, 40 or Fight: Writing Within and Across Borders in North American Environmental History," written by two historical geographers, Matthew Evenden and Graeme Wynn.[8] The journal *Environmental History* demonstrates the scope and diversity of research in this growing line of inquiry.

Studies in land use history, landscape change, and environmental history also merge into the broad field of conservation history. Interest in this line of inquiry is long-standing and continues to evolve, particularly in the United States and Canada, with some focus on ideas of nature, wilderness, and planning and development of parks and protected areas. Examples are *The Conservation of the Wild Life in Canada, Nature and the American, Wilderness and the American Mind, Canadian Parks in Perspective, Working for Wildlife, National Parks, Parks and Protected Areas in Canada, Changing Parks,* and *A Century of Parks Canada, 1911–2011.*[9] Some biographical studies also constitute very useful examples of conservation history, for example, *J.B. Harkin* and *The Wilderness Warrior.*[10]

Broad ecological approaches to people and places have been undertaken for decades by biologists and students of natural history, as well
as geographers, geologists, and other researchers. Their contributions
are very wide-ranging and include detailed studies of plants, animals,
technology, and landscapes. Examples are *Prairie*; "Technological
Denudation"; *Future Environments of North America, Transformation
of a Continent*; *After the Ice Age*; and *The Ptarmigan's Dilemma*.[11]

Ultimately, all these schools of thought can be brought together
under the umbrella of human ecology, although this broad perspective
on knowledge has been defined in various ways. Karl Butzer, for example, puts much stress on natural systems in his models in *Archaeology as
Human Ecology*.[12] For others, the central idea is that nature and culture,
or ecosystems and humans, constantly change and interact with one
another over long time spans at various rates and scales. The natural
changes and interactions involve adjustments among natural processes
such as earthquakes, erosion, plant succession, animal migration, and
climate change. The natural processes also interact with and adjust to
human changes driven by differences in beliefs, values, perceptions,
technology, and other aspects of culture. All these natural and cultural
interactions work to explain the changing character of people, places,
and landscapes around the globe. Studies illustrating the foregoing
ideas include *Hunters of the Northern Ice, Prehistoric Maritime Adaptations of the Circumpolar Zone, The Buffalo People, The Complete Ice Age,
The World Until Yesterday*, and *First Migrants*.[13]

In his *Human Ecology: Following Nature's Lead*, the architect Frederick Steiner echoes the foregoing ideas and emphasizes the need for
greater stress on natural systems—or biological ecology—in design.[14]
He also points out that the architect needs to be very aware of how
ideas, approaches, and perceptions have changed fundamentally in
recent decades. Practising architects, landscape designers, and planners need to be up to date on these. In this respect, he writes, on the
one hand, of traditional ecology, and on the other, of the new ecology.

Traditional ecology, according to Steiner, relied on the assumption
that nature could achieve balance. Natural plant communities were
seen as succeeding, independent of humans, through several stages
to a climax, or last landscape, capable of persisting indefinitely—not

unlike the traditional American concept of wilderness discussed in this book.

As Steiner describes it, the new ecology stresses change, disequilibria, instability, and chaotic fluctuations in nature or ecosystems. "New ecologists" increasingly see humans and their cultures as part of these ecosystems. Steiner sees the overlay mapping of forests, soils, hydrology, bedrock types, and other natural variables, introduced and used by the Scottish landscape architect Ian McHarg in the 1960s to 1980s,[15] as an early manifestation of an increasingly dynamic human ecological approach in design and related fields.

The years from the 1960s to the 1980s also saw advances in other disciplines and fields of study that have changed the way we think about and plan for protected areas such as the Nahanni National Park Reserve. Anthropology, archaeology, and geography have all introduced or adopted new ideas, methods, and approaches, including the improved use of radiocarbon and other advanced dating techniques; more sophisticated analysis of pollen, beetles, and other plant and animal remains; DNA and other advances in genetics; and computer-based GIS and satellite image analysis.[16] Such advances made major contributions to the research and planning leading to the expanded Nahanni National Park Reserve in 2009.

Planning has changed considerably as well. It moved, in the 1980s, from emphasis on the top-down command and control approach of federal governments and corporations to a bottom-up, interactive, adaptive, and generally co-operative or shared approach.[17] In the struggle for the Nahanni National Park Reserve, major players including Parks Canada, First Nations, NGOs such as CPAWS, and ecotourism outfitters such as Nahanni River Adventures used this broad approach. Ultimately, the varied disciplines, fields of study, and schools of thought encompassed by human ecology were brought together and focused on the long struggle to protect the special qualities of the Nahanni within a watershed-scale national park reserve.

A Timeline for the Protection of the Nahanni

- *1920s and 1930s:* Gaining vivid impressions of the natural wonders of the Nahanni Valley through the experiences and writings of adventurers such as Raymond Patterson.

- *1945:* E.G. Oldham's call for research on a possible Nahanni National Park.

- *1951:* Raymond Patterson's warnings of heavy hunting and decline of Dall's sheep and other wildlife in the lower Nahanni Valley.

- *1940s and 1950s:* The journalist Pierre Berton's winter flight into the lower Nahanni and national press coverage of the wonders of the valley.

- *1959:* Establishment of a federal committee to study a possible Nahanni National Park.

- *1960s and 1970s:* Biological, ecological, and geomorphological research by George Scotter, Derek Ford, and others provides basic scientific understanding of the Nahanni ecosystem.

- *1960s and 1970s:* Proposals for mining in the Nahanni watershed, a big power dam at towering Virginia Falls, and rising concern about impacts on wildlife, water quality and quantity, and the ecosystem generally.

- *1960s, 1970s, and 1980s:* Indigenous opposition to a national park built on the then guiding concepts of ideal wilderness, devoid of the activities of humans, and top-down planning and control by the national parks agency and federal government.

- *1970s onwards:* The National and Provincial Parks Association of Canada (later the Canadian Parks and Wilderness Society) and other nongovernmental organizations campaign for a larger, watershed-scale Nahanni National Park Reserve.

- *1976:* Government establishment of a small initial Nahanni National Park Reserve around Virginia Falls and the lower valley, focusing on the wild and scenic Nahanni, its deep canyons, and limestone terrain.

- *1980s:* Adoption of the concept of a national park reserve, postponing the contentious issue of government land control until settlement of Indigenous claims more generally.

- *1980s onwards:* Introduction of innovative theory and the practice of biodiversity, landscape ecology, biological conservation, and other major advances in ecosystem thinking.

- *1980s onwards:* Shift from top-down planning by federal government to co-operative planning among major interest groups.

- *1988:* Introduction of new science-based mandate of ecological integrity into the Canadian National Parks Act.

- *1990s:* Historical and archaeological research and experience in Canada and other parts of the world support the move from the guiding concept of ideal to inhabited wilderness and the acceptance of Indigenous hunting and other traditional activities in national parks, including the Nahanni and others in the North.

- *1990s to 2000s:* Exceptionally vigorous national campaign led by the Canadian Parks and Wilderness Society, with the support of Nahanni River Adventures, Indigenous people, scientists, and others, to expand the Nahanni National Park Reserve.

- *Early 2000s:* Research, monitoring, and mapping using advances in DNA and ecosystem thought and practice, led by John Weaver of the Wildlife Conservation Society, demonstrate the dependence of Nahanni National Park Reserve caribou, grizzly, Dall's sheep, and other wildlife on extensive ranges outside the initial 1976 reserve.

- *1970s to early 2000s:* Study and mapping of globally unique cave and karst drainage systems in the lower valley demonstrate they depend upon systems extending beyond the initial national park reserve boundary.

- *1990s to 2000s:* Dehcho and other Indigenous people support an expanded Nahanni National Park Reserve based on the concept of ecological integrity, inhabited wilderness, acceptance of hunting and traditional activities, economic benefits, and shared management with Parks Canada.

- *2009:* Federal government makes decision to expand the Nahanni National Park Reserve to watershed scale at approximately thirty-five thousand square kilometres.

- **2009 onwards:** Outstanding issues include the risk of serious pollution and other environmental effects from mining within enclaves in the expanded Nahanni National Park Reserve, the need for more archaeological and historical research on early Indigenous land use and conservation activities, meeting financial and other obligations to Indigenous people, addressing ecologically inappropriate boundaries of the Nááts'ihch'oh National Park Reserve on Sahtu and Metis lands in the northern Nahanni watershed, and developing a workable and acceptable shared management regime.

- **2000s onwards:** Current goals include considering the Nahanni National Park Reserve as a model for other protected areas, learning from analogous experience in other parts of the world, and planning for a greater contribution of national parks and other conservation areas to the well-being of Indigenous people in the spirit of the recent Canadian Truth and Reconciliation Commission report.

A List of Traditional Place Names in the Dene Language (*Dehcho Dene Zhatie*)

Ala Tthe Zhíhgojʔa (First Canyon): first hole in the mountain

Chitú (Yohin Lake): Duck Lake

Dahaehtth'į (Deadmen Valley): the spread-out river or flat area along the shore of the river

Deh Cho (Mackenzie River): big river or sacred river

Dexahtu Ehdaá (Swan Point): where the swans go

Ehdzoo ítálíh (second bend in the river past the Little Butte): the tongue in the trap

Eht'ąįlį: back current or reversing river

Endaro Dehé (Clausen Creek): muddy creek

Gahnįhthah Mįe (Rabbitkettle Lake): Rabbitkettle Lake or pot lake

Kandajoh (Twisted Mountain): something big pushing up, emerging

Lįįdlįį Kų́ę́ (Fort Simpson): meeting of the water

Medzih Dehé (Caribou River): Caribou River

Náįlįcho (Virginia Falls): big falls

Nácháh Dehé (Liard River): swift river

Nahʔą Dehé (South Nahanni River): river of the land of Nahʔą people—"Nahʔą" means people who live in the mountains

Nahʔą Dehé Ts'ę́ Tu Zhánįlį (South Nahanni River Watershed): waters that flow to the South Nahanni River

Ndutah (the Splits): lots of islands

Nintsí Daheda (Sand Blowouts): live wind

Tł'ogotsho (Tlogotsho): grassy meadow

Tło Dehé (Prairie Creek): grassy river, referring to the grassy tundra of the headwaters

Tthéht'eah (Blackstone River): burnt rock

Tthedalǫh (Base of Twisted Mountain): the place at the end of the stone wall

Tthenáágó (the Butte): mountain sloping down

Tthetaehtłą́h (the Gate): the mountains that pass (refers to the appearance that one mountain is passing in front of the other as you move upstream)

Tu Kádeegai (White Spray Spring): white water spray

Tu Naka Dé (Flat River): interpreted by Charles Yohin to mean boiling water river, referring to its rapids—Gus Kraus translated the name to mean white water river, referring to the silty white colour

Tułetsę̀ę (Kraus Hot Springs): smelly water

Nááts'ihch'oh National Park Reserve: "Nááts'ihch'oh" is the Shúhtagot'ine language description of this mountain and it refers to its unique shape, which is sharp and pointed on the top like a porcupine quill[1]

Notes

Acknowledgements

1   Charles Blyth, *Nahanni Nah? ̨ Dehé: A Selection of Photographic Images of the South Nahanni Watershed (2007–2010)* (n.p.: Creative Publishing Service, 2011).

Chapter 1: Envisioning the Magnificent Nahanni

1   Raymond Murray Patterson, "The Nahany Lands," *The Beaver* (Summer 1961): 40–47.

2   Nahanni Butte Band, *Nahe Nahodhe is who we are and where we come from* (Nahanni Butte, NT: Nahanni Butte Band, n.d.).

3   R. Neil Hartling, *Nahanni: River of Gold . . . River of Dreams* (Merrickville, ON: Canadian Recreational Canoeing Association, 1998); Peter Jowett, *Nahanni: The River Guide* (Calgary: Rocky Mountain Books, 1998); Pat Keough and Rosemarie Keough, *The Nahanni Portfolio*, 2 vols. (Don Mills, ON: Stoddard/Nahanni Production, 1988); Richard C. Davis, ed., *Nahanni Journals: R.M. Patterson's 1927–1929 Journals* (Edmonton: University of Alberta Press, 2008); Blyth, *Nahanni Nah? ̨ Dehé*.

4   Raymond Murray Patterson, *The Dangerous River: Adventures on the Nahanni* (Erin, ON: Boston Mills Press, 1999), 3.

5   Davis, *Nahanni Journals*; Patterson, *Dangerous River*, 4.

6   Davis, *Nahanni Journals*.

7   David Finch, *R.M. Patterson: A Life of Great Adventure* (Calgary: Rocky Mountain Books, 2000).

8   Also called Deadman's Valley.

9   Davis, *Nahanni Journals*, 29.

10   Ibid., 34.

11   Ibid., xxxvi.

12   Ibid., 30.

13   Ibid., 32.

14   Ibid., 32–33.

15   John L. Weaver, *Big Animals and Small Parks, Implications of Wildlife Distribution and Movements for Expansion of Nahanni National Park Reserve*. Conservation Report No. 1 (Toronto: Wildlife Conservation Society Canada, 2006); Nahanni Expansion Working Group, *Greater Nahanni Ecosystem Atlas* (Ottawa: Parks Canada, 2007).

16   Pierre Berton, *Klondike: The Last Great Gold Rush* (Toronto: Anchor Canada, 2001).

17   J.G. MacGregor, *The Klondike Rush through Edmonton, 1897–1898* (Toronto: McClelland & Stewart, 1970); Joan Wein, *Back Door to the Klondike* (Erin, ON: Boston Mills Press, 1988).

18   Fenley Hunter, *That Summer on the Nahanni 1928: The Journals of Fenley Hunter* (Ottawa: McGahern Stewart Publishing, 2015).

19   Ibid., 142.

20   Ibid., 145.

21   Hans Huth, *Nature and the American: Three Centuries of Changing Attitudes* (Berkeley: University of California Press, 1957); Roderick Frazier Nash, *Wilderness and the American Mind* (New Haven: Yale University Press, 1967).

22   Maxine E. McCloskey and James P. Gilligan, eds., *Wilderness and the Quality of Life* (San Francisco: Sierra Club, 1969); William Schwartz, ed., *Voices for the Wilderness* (New York: Ballantine Books, 1969).

23   J.G. Nelson and R.C. Scace, eds., *The Canadian National Parks: Today and Tomorrow*. 2 vols. (Calgary: The National and Provincial Parks Association of Canada and the University of Calgary, 1969); Ian McTaggart Cowan, "The Role of Ecology in the National Parks," in *The Canadian National Parks: Today and Tomorrow*, ed. J.G. Nelson and R.C. Scace (Calgary: The National and Provincial Parks Association of Canada and the University of Calgary, 1969), 931–940.

24   William O. Douglas, *A Wilderness Bill of Rights* (Boston: Little, Brown and Company, 1965), 28–29.

25   Ibid.

26   J.G. Nelson and A.R. Byrne, "Man as an Instrument of Landscape Change: Fire, Floods and National Parks in the Bow Valley, Alberta." *Geographical*

Review LVI, no. 2 (1966): 226–238; J.G. Nelson, "Man and Landscape Change in Banff National Park: A National Park Problem in Perspective," in *The Canadian National Parks: Today and Tomorrow*, ed. J.G. Nelson and R.C. Scace (Calgary: The National and Provincial Parks Association of Canada and the University of Calgary, 1969), 111–150; J.G. Nelson, "Man and Landscape Change in Banff National Park: A National Park Problem in Perspective," in *Canadian Parks in Perspective*, ed. J.G. Nelson, with R.C. Scace (Montreal: Harvest House, 1973), 63–97; and J.G. Nelson, *Man's Impact on the Western Canadian Landscape*, the Carleton Library, no. 90 (Toronto: McClelland & Stewart, 1976).

27   Donald J. Hughes, *North American Indian Ecology* (El Paso: Texas Western Press, 1996); Leslie B. Davis and Brian O.K. Reeves, eds., *Hunters of the Recent Past* (London: Unwin Hyman, 1990).

28   William Cronon, ed., *Uncommon Ground: Toward Reinventing Nature* (New York: Norton, 1995); Simon Schama, *Landscape and Memory* (New York: Knopf, 1995).

29   Charles Zerner, ed., *Culture and the Question of Rights: Forests, Coasts, and Seas in Southeast Asia* (Durham, NC: Duke University Press, 2003), 7.

30   Stephanie Gorson Fried, "Writing for Their Lives: Bentian Dayak Authors and Indonesian Development Discourse," in *Culture and the Question of Rights: Forests, Coasts, and Seas in Southeast Asia*, ed. Charles Zerner (Durham, NC: Duke University Press, 2003), 142–183.

31   Zerner, *Culture and the Question of Rights*, 8.

32   Nancy Lee Peluso, "Fruit Trees and Family Trees in an Anthropogenic Forest: Property Zones, Resource Access, and Environment Change in Indonesia," in *Culture and the Question of Rights: Forests, Coasts, and Seas in Southeast Asia*, ed. Charles Zerner (Durham, NC: Duke University Press, 2003), 184–218.

33   A.A. den Otter, *Civilizing the Wilderness: Culture and Nature in Pre-Confederation Canada and Rupert's Land* (Edmonton: University of Alberta Press, 2012), 142–183.

Chapter 2: Creating the Initial Nahanni National Park Reserve

1   E.G. Oldham to R.A. Gibson, Deputy Minister of Mines and Resources, Ottawa, February 6, 1948 (courtesy of George Scotter).

2   Ibid.

3   Finch, *R.M. Patterson*.

4   Pierre Berton, *The Mysterious North* (New York: Alfred A. Knopf, Inc., 1961).

5   Finch, *R.M. Patterson*.

6   Thomas R. Berger, *Northern Frontier, Northern Homeland: The Report of the Mackenzie Valley Pipeline Inquiry*, 2 vols. (Ottawa: Minister of Supply and Services Canada, 1977).

7   Thomas R. Berger, *A Long and Terrible Shadow: White Values, Native Rights in the Americas, 1492–1992* (Vancouver: Douglas & McIntyre, 1991).

8   M. Taghi Farvar and John P. Milton, eds., *The Careless Technology: Ecology and International Development* (Garden City, NY: The Natural History Press, 1972).

9   G.W. Scotter et al., "Ecology of the South Nahanni and Flat River Areas" (Edmonton: Canadian Wildlife Service, 1971).

10   Not all of the many reports ensuing from this research could be consulted for this book, with some remaining unpublished. However, for the record, they include G.W. Scotter, "Distribution of Pine (*Pinus* spp.) in the South Nahanni and Flat Rivers Region, Northwest Territories," *Canadian Journal of Forest Research* 4, no. 4 (1974): 555–557; G.W. Scotter, "White-tailed Deer and Mule Deer Observations in Southwestern District of Mackenzie, Northwest Territories," *Canadian Field-Naturalist* 88 (1974): 487–489; Scotter et al., "Ecology of the South Nahanni"; G.W. Scotter and N.M. Simmons, "Park or Power?" *Park News* 8, no. 1 (1972): 8–12; G.W. Scotter and N.M. Simmons, "Mortality of Dall's sheep (*Ovis dalli*) within a cave, Nahanni National Park, Northwest Territories," *Journal of Mammalogy* 57, no. 2 (1976): 387–389; A.H. Marsh and G.W. Scotter, *Vegetation Survey and Development Recommendations for the Rabbitkettle Area, Nahanni National Park* (Edmonton: Canadian Wildlife Service, 1976); G.W. Scotter and J.D. Henry, *Vegetation, Wildlife and Recreational Assessment of Deadmen Valley. Nahanni National Park* (Edmonton: Canadian Wildlife Service, 1977); G.W. Scotter and H.M. Kershaw, *Vegetation of Deadmen Valley, Nahanni National Park* (Edmonton: Canadian Wildlife Service, 1978); G.W. Scotter et al., "Birds of Nahanni National Park, Northwest Territories," Special Publications No. 15 (Regina: Saskatchewan Natural History Society, 1985).

11   Scotter and Henry, *Vegetation, Wildlife and Recreational Assessment*; A.L. Cairns, J.D. Henry, and G.W. Scotter, "Vegetation, Wildlife, and Recreation Assessment of the Flat—South Nahanni Rivers Confluence Area, Nahanni National Park" (Edmonton: Canadian Wildlife Service, 1978).

12   Parks Canada, *Nahanni National Park Reserve Resource Description and Analysis*, Natural Resource Conservation Section, Parks Canada Prairie Region (Winnipeg: Parks Canada, 1984).

13   Ibid., 875.

14   George Scotter, personal communication, September 30, 2013.

15   G.W. Scotter et al., "Birds of Nahanni."

16   Parks Canada, *Resource Description and Analysis*.

17   Canadian Wildlife Service, "NWT—Nunavut Bird Checklist Survey Form" (Yellowknife: Canadian Wildlife Service, 2009).

18   Parks Canada, *Resource Description and Analysis.*

19   Jean Poirel, *Nahanni: La Vallée des Hommes Sans Tête* (Montreal: Stanké, 1980).

20   D.C. Ford, "Evidences of multiple glaciation in South Nahanni National Park, Mackenzie Mountains, Northwest Territories," *Canadian Journal of Earth Sciences* 13, no. 10 (1976): 1433–1445; Derek Ford, "Antecedent Canyons of the South Nahanni River, Mackenzie Mountains, N.W.T.," *The Canadian Geographer* 35, no. 4 (1991): 426–431; Russell S. Harmon, Derek C. Ford, and Henry P. Schwarcz, "Interglacial chronology of the Rocky and MacKenzie Mountains based upon ^{230}Th-^{234}U dating of calcite speleothems," *Canadian Journal of Earth Sciences* 14, no. 11 (1977): 2543–2552; J. Schroeder, "Les formes de glaces des grottes de la Nahanni, Territoires du Nord-Ouest, Canada," *Canadian Journal of Earth Sciences* 14, no. 5 (1977): 1179–1185; G.A. Brook and D.C. Ford, "The origin of labyrinth and tower karst and the climatic conditions necessary for their development," *Nature* 275 (1978): 493–496.; Derek Ford, "Expanding South Nahanni National Park, Northwest Territories, Canada, to Include and Manage Some Remarkable Sub-Arctic/Arctic Karst terrains," in *Karst Management*, ed. Philip E. van Beynen (Dordrecht: Springer Science and Business Media, 2001), 415–437.

21   Ford, "Antecedent Canyons," 426.

22   Ibid.

23   Ibid., 430.

24   Ibid.

25   Ibid., 430–431.

26   Ibid., 426–431.

27   Ibid.

28   Parks Canada, *Resource Description and Analysis*, 1–3, 4.

29   Ibid., 1–4, 5.

30   Ibid., para. 11.5.

31   Ibid.

32   Nahanni National Park Reserve of Canada, *Nah ? ą Dehé: Report on Research and Monitoring* (Ottawa: Parks Canada, 2004–2005).

33   Parks Canada, "Glaciers," in *Nahanni National Park Reserve of Canada: Nah ? ą Dehé State of the Park Report, 2009* (Ottawa: Parks Canada, 2009), 37–40.

34   Michael N. Demuth, *Secular Change in the Glacier Cover Contributing Flow to a World Heritage River—Ragged Ranges, South Nahanni River*, Northwest Territories Research Database, 2007, http://data.nwtresearch.com/scientific/14229.

35   Anne Casselman, "The Big One," *Canadian Geographic*, June 2015, 48–58.

36　Bob Weber, "Scientist says lake falling off cliff is not a unique situation," *The Globe and Mail*, July 13, 2015, A11.

37　Finch, *R.M. Patterson*.

38　R.M. Patterson, *Those Earlier Hills: Reminiscences 1928 to 1961* (Surrey, BC: Touchwood Editions, 2008). See especially Chapter 1, "River of Deadmen Valley"; Chapter 2, "The Nahany Lands"; and Chapter 3, "South Nahanni Revisited."

Chapter 3: The Struggle for Expansion

1　E.O. Wilson and F.M. Peter, eds., *Biodiversity* (Washington, DC: National Academy Press, 1988); Richard T.T. Forman and Michel Godron, *Landscape Ecology* (New York: John Wiley and Sons, 1986); M.E. Soulé and B.A. Wilcox, *Conservation Biology: An Evolutionary–Ecological Perspective* (Sunderland, MA: Sinauer Associates, 1980).

2　Weaver, *Big Animals and Small Parks*; John Weaver, *Conserving Caribou Landscapes in the Nahanni Trans-Border Region: Using Fidelity to Seasonal Ranges and Migration Routes*. Wildlife Conservation Report No. 4 (Toronto: Wildlife Conservation Society Canada, 2008).

3　Weaver, *Big Animals and Small Parks*.

4　Stephen Woodley, James Kay, and George Francis, eds., *Ecological Integrity and the Management of Ecosystems* (Delray Beach, FL: St. Lucie Press, 1993); James Porter and J. Gordon Nelson, eds., "Ecological Integrity and Protected Areas," in *Parks Research Forum of Ontario (PRFO)* (Waterloo, ON: Heritage Resources Centre, University of Waterloo, 2001); Harvey Locke and Philip Dearden, "Rethinking protected areas categories and the new paradigm," *Environmental Conservation* 32, no. 1 (2005): 1–10.

5　Cristina Eisenberg, *The Carnivore Way: Coexisting with and Conserving North America's Predators* (Washington, DC: Island Press, 2014).

6　Parks Canada Agency, "'Unimpaired for Future Generations?' Protecting Ecological Integrity with Canada's National Parks," in *Report of the Panel on Ecological Integrity of Canada's National Parks* (Ottawa: Parks Canada, 2000).

7　Parks Canada, *Proposed Expansion of Nahanni National Park Reserve: Boundary Options* (Ottawa: Parks Canada, 2006); Parks Canada, *Nahanni National Park Reserve of Canada: Nah ? ą Dehé Management Plan* (Ottawa: Parks Canada, 2010).

8　Parks Canada, *Nahanni National Park Reserve of Canada: Nah ? ą Dehé State of the Parks Report, 2009* (Ottawa: Parks Canada, 2009).

9　Catharine McClellan, *Part of the Land, Part of the Water: A History of the Yukon Indians* (Vancouver: Douglas & McIntyre, 1987).

10 Peter Bellwood, *First Migrants: Ancient Migration in Global Perspective* (Chichester, UK: Wiley Blackwell, 2013).

11 E.C. Pielou, *After the Ice Age: The Return of Life to Glaciated North America* (Chicago: University of Chicago Press, 1992); William J. Burroughs, *Climate Change in Prehistory: The End of the Reign of Chaos* (Cambridge, UK: Cambridge University Press, 2005); Brian Fagan, ed., *The Complete Ice Age: How Climate Change Shaped the World* (London: Thames & Hudson, 2009).

12 Michael Vincent McGinnis, ed., *Bioregionalism* (London: Routledge, 1999).

13 Barry Sadler, ed., *Involvement and Environment* (Edmonton: Environmental Council of Alberta, 1977); Len Gertler, Karl Bennett, and Kari Levitt, eds., "Planning with People: Human Ecology and Development in Canada and the Caribbean," *Environments* 16, no. 3 (1984): 1–186; J.G. Nelson and D.W. Hoffman, eds., "Sharing Heritage Management," *Environments* 17, no. 3 (1985): 1–145; G.S. Stains, "Collaborative Park Planning in a Municipal Landscape: The Rouge Park in Ontario," in *Managing Protected Areas in a Changing World: Proceedings of the Fourth International Conference on Science and Management of Protected Areas, 14–19 May 2000*, ed. S. Bondrup-Nielson, N.W.P. Munro, G. Nelson, J.H.M. Willison, T.B. Herman, and P. Eagles (Wolfville, NS: Science and Management of Protected Areas Association, 2002), 790–802.

14 C.S. Holling, ed., *Adaptive Environmental Assessment and Management* (New York: John Wiley and Sons, 1978); Carl Walters, *Adaptive Management of Renewable Resources* (New York: Macmillan, 1986); Lance H. Gunderson, C.S. Holling, and Stephen S. Light, eds., *Barriers and Bridges to the Renewal of Ecosystems and Institutions* (New York: Columbia University Press, 1995).

15 Parks Canada, *Nahanni National Park Reserve Management Plan* (Ottawa: Environment Canada, 1987).

16 Blyth, *Nahanni Nahʔ ą Dehé*.

17 Neil Hartling, personal communication, August 20, 2013.

18 Nahanni River Adventures, *Northern Currents* (Whitehorse, YT: Nahanni River Adventures, various years), see especially nos. 21–43, from 2000 to 2009. See also www.Nahanni.com.

19 Parks Canada, *Nahanni National Park Ecological Statement* (Ottawa: Parks Canada, 2001), 13.

20 Parks Canada and Deh Cho First Nations, *Memorandum of Understanding between Parks Canada and Deh Cho First Nations: Respecting the Expansion of Nahanni National Park Reserve of Canada* (Ottawa: Parks Canada, 2003).

21 Parks Canada, *Ecological Statement*.

22 Claude Mondor, *Areas of High Conservation Value Adjacent to Nahanni National Park Reserve* (Ottawa: Parks Canada, Park Establishment Branch, National Parks Directorate, 2001); Parks Canada and Deh Cho First Nations, *Memorandum of Understanding*; Parks Canada, *Taking Care of Naha Dehé: A*

Proposal to Expand Nahanni National Park Reserve of Canada (Ottawa: Parks Canada, 2006); Parks Canada, *Boundary Options*; Parks Canada, *Nah? ą Dehé Management Plan* (2010); Parks Canada, *Proposed Establishment of Nááts'ihch'oh National Park Reserve* (Yellowknife: Parks Canada, 2010).

23 Parks Canada and Deh Cho First Nations, *Memorandum of Understanding*; Parks Canada, *Nahanni National Park Reserve of Canada: Nah? ą Dehé Interim Park Management Arrangement* (Ottawa: Parks Canada, 2003).

24 Parks Canada, *Interim Park Management Arrangement*.

25 Nahanni Butte Band, *Nahe Nahodhe*.

26 A complete list of the protocols is available from the Nahanni Butte Band offices. See also Nahanni Butte Band, *Nah? ą Dehé: Traditional Harvesting Protocols—Nah? ą Dehé Keodi: taking care of Nah? ą Dehé* (Nahani Butte, NT: Nahanni Butte Band, n.d.).

Chapter 4: The Nineteenth-Century Fur Trade: The Early Years

1 Alan Cooke and Clive Holland, eds., *The Exploration of Northern Canada 500 to 1920: A Chronology* (Toronto: Arctic History Press, 1978).

2 Ibid.

3 Lloyd Keith, ed., *North of Athabasca: Slave Lake and Mackenzie River Documents of the North West Company, 1800–1821* (Montreal: McGill-Queen's University Press, 2001).

4 Ibid.

5 Barry Gough, *The Elusive Mr. Pond: The Soldier, Fur Trader and Explorer Who Opened the Northwest* (Madeira Park, BC: Douglas & McIntyre, 2014).

6 Ibid., 93–118.

7 Ibid., 105–106.

8 James Daschuk, *Clearing the Plains: Disease, Politics of Starvation, and the Loss of Aboriginal Life* (Regina: University of Regina Press, 2013).

9 Gough, *The Elusive Mr. Pond*, 110.

10 Arthur J. Ray, "Smallpox: The Epidemic of 1837–38," *The Beaver* (Autumn 1975): 7–13.

11 Gough, *The Elusive Mr. Pond*, 110.

12 Shepard Krech III, *The Ecological Indian: Myth and History* (New York: W.W. Norton & Company, 1999), 79.

13 Ibid., 86–89.

14 Daschuk, *Clearing the Plains*, 5.

15 Ibid., 53.

16 Keith, *North of Athabasca*.

17 Ibid., 288–364.

18 Ibid., 303.

19 Ibid., 293.

20 Ibid., 303.

21 Ibid., 351–364.

22 Ibid., 351.

23 Ibid., 351.

24 Ibid., 360.

25 Ibid., 350–361.

26 John K. Stager, "Fur Trading Posts in the Mackenzie Region up to 1850," in *Canada's Changing North*, ed. William C. Wonders (Toronto: McClelland & Stewart, 1971), 50–58.

27 James Raffan, *Emperor of the North: Sir George Simpson and the Remarkable Story of the Hudson's Bay Company* (Toronto: HarperCollins, 2007).

28 Cooke and Holland, *The Exploration of Northern Canada.*

29 Ibid.

30 Ibid.

31 Parks Canada, *Resource Description and Analysis*; Clifford Wilson, *Campbell of the Yukon* (Toronto: Macmillan, 1970).

32 E.E. Rich, ed., *A Journal of a Voyage from Rocky Mountain Portage in Peace River to the Sources of Finlay's Branch and North West Ward in Summer 1824* (London: Hudson's Bay Record Society, 1955).

33 Ibid., see R.M. Patterson's Introduction.

34 Ibid., see R.M. Patterson's Introduction.

35 Ibid., xiii–xiv.

36 Ibid.

37 Cooke and Holland, *The Exploration of Northern Canada.*

38 Rich, *A Journal of a Voyage*, 53.

39 Ibid., 205.

40 Ibid., 98.

41 Ibid., 40–41.

42 Ibid., 11–12.

43 Davis and Reeves, *Hunters of the Recent Past.*

44 Joel C. Janetski, *Indians in Yellowstone National Park* (Salt Lake City: University of Utah Press, 2002).

45 Ibid.

46 Janetski, *Indians in Yellowstone National Park*; Elizabeth A. Morris, "Prehistoric Game Drive Systems in the Rocky Mountains and High Plains Areas of Colorado," in *Hunters of the Recent Past*, ed. Leslie B. Davis and Brian O.K. Reeves, (London: Unwin Hyman, 1990), 195–203.

47 Rich, *A Journal of a Voyage*, 153.

48 Hughes, *North American Indian Ecology.*

49 Ibid., 28.

50 Steve Nicholls, *Paradise Found: Nature in America at the Time of Discovery* (Chicago: Chicago University Press, 2009), 347–350.

51 Richard K. Nelson, *Make Prayers to the Raven: A Koyukon View of the Northern Forest* (Chicago: University of Chicago Press, 1983).

52 Rich, *A Journal of a Voyage*, 110–111.

53 Natalie B. Stoddard, "Some Ethnological Aspects of the Russian Fur Trade," in *People and Pelts: Selected Papers of the Second North American Fur Trade Conference*, ed. Malvina Bolus (Winnipeg: Peguis Publishers, 1972), 39–58.

54 Rich, *A Journal of a Voyage*, 118.

55 Alfred W. Crosby, *Ecological Imperialism: The Biological Expansion of Europe, 900–1900* (Cambridge: Cambridge University Press, 2004), 38.

56 Stoddard, "Some Ethnological Aspects of the Russian Fur Trade," 55.

57 Paul Chrysler Phillips, *The Fur Trade*, vol. 2 (Norman, OK: University of Oklahoma Press, 1961), 52–53.

58 Nahanni Expansion Working Group, *Greater Nahanni Ecosystem Atlas*.

59 Rich, *A Journal of a Voyage*, 187.

60 Ibid., 88.

61 P.M. Bothwell et al., "Fire Regimes in Nahanni National Park and the Mackenzie Bison Sanctuary, Northwest Territories, Canada," in *Proceedings of the 22nd Tall Timbers Fire Ecology Conference: Fire in Temperate, Boreal, and Montane Ecosystems*, ed. R.T. Engstrom, K.E.M. Galley, and W.J. de Groot (Tallahassee, FL: Tall Timbers Research Station, 2004), 43–54.

62 Patterson, *Those Earlier Hills*. See especially Chapter 1, "River of Deadmen Valley"; Chapter 2, "The Nahany Lands"; and Chapter 3, "South Nahanni Revisited."

63 C. Parnell, "Campbell of the Yukon: Part I," *The Beaver* (June 1942): 4–6.

64 HBC, Fort Simpson journals, July 10, 1823, HBCA.

65 Ibid.

66 HBC, Fort Simpson journals, July 12, 1823, HBCA.

67 Ibid.

Chapter 5: The Nineteenth-Century Fur Trade: The Later Years

1 Patterson, "The Nahany Lands," 46.

2 Ibid., 46–47.

3 Ibid., 44.

4 HBC, Fort Simpson journals, 1822–1823, 1833–1834, 1843–1844, and 1863–1864, HBCA, specifically July 12, 1823.

5 Ibid., specifically November 26, 1832.

6 D.W. Moodie, "Gardening on Hudson's Bay: The First Century," *The Beaver* (Summer 1978): 54–59.

7 Wilson, *Campbell of the Yukon.*

8 Parnell, "Campbell of the Yukon."

9 Ibid.

10 Owen Matthews, *Glorious Misadventures: Nikolai Rezanov and the Dream of a Russian America* (New York: Bloomsbury, 2013).

11 Roger Bartlett, *A History of Russia* (New York: Palgrave Macmillan, 2005).

12 Ibid.

13 Basil Dmytryshyn, *A History of Russia* (Englewood Cliffs, NJ: Prentice Hall, 1977), 191.

14 James R. Gibson, *Feeding the Russian Fur Trade: Provisionment of the Okhotsk Seaboard and the Kamchatka Peninsula, 1639–1856* (Madison: University of Wisconsin Press, 1969).

15 Ibid., 24.

16 Ibid., 17.

17 Ibid., 28.

18 Richard Somerset Mackie, *Trading beyond the Mountains: The British Fur Trade on the Pacific, 1793–1843* (Vancouver: UBC Press, 1997), ch. 6.

19 Debra Komar, *The Bastard of Fort Stikine: The Hudson's Bay Company and the Murder of John McLoughlin Jr.* (Fredericton, NB: Goose Lane Editions, 2015).

20 Parnell, "Campbell of the Yukon."

21 See Patterson, *Dangerous River*, 3.

22 Parnell, "Campbell of the Yukon."

23 McClellan, *Part of the Land.*

24 Ibid., 160.

Chapter 6: Mining and a Mixed Economy

1 Berton, *Klondike*, ch. 1.

2 Ibid., 4–5.

3 Ibid.

4 Berton, *Klondike*, 218; MacGregor, *The Klondike Rush*, 235, 245.

5 Berton, *Klondike*, 189.

6 Dick Turner, *Nahanni* (Saanich, BC: Hancock House Publishers, 1975).

7 Ibid., 108–109.

8 Ibid., 109.

9 Patterson, *Those Earlier Hills*, 56. See especially Chapter 1, "River of Deadmen Valley"; Chapter 2, "The Nahany Lands"; and Chapter 3, "South Nahanni Revisited."

10 Turner, *Nahanni*, 109.

11 Scotter and Simmons, "Park or Power?"; Hartling, *Nahanni.*

12　Parks Canada, *Resource Description and Analysis*, para. 11.4.

13　Turner, *Nahanni*, 15.

14　Ibid., 40.

15　Ibid., 119.

16　Ibid., 163.

17　E.G. Oldham to R.A. Gibson (courtesy of George Scotter).

18　Turner, *Nahanni*, 224–225.

19　Patterson, *Those Earlier Hills*. See especially Chapter 1, "River of Deadmen Valley"; Chapter 2, "The Nahany Lands"; and Chapter 3, "South Nahanni Revisited."

20　Ibid., 60. See especially Chapter 1, "River of Deadmen Valley"; Chapter 2, "The Nahany Lands"; and Chapter 3, "South Nahanni Revisited."

21　Poirel, *Nahanni*, 183.

22　Ibid., 205–219.

23　Ibid., 216.

24　Joanne Ronan Moore, *Nahanni Trailhead: A Year in the Northern Wilderness*. Surrey, BC: Hancock House Publishers, 2000.

25　Ibid.

26　Neil Hartling, personal communication, August 23, 2013.

Chapter 7: Conserving the Ecological Integrity of the Nahanni

1　Constance Hunt, "The Development and Decline of Northern Conservation Reserves," *Contact* 8, no. 4 (1976): 30–75.

2　H.F. Lambert, Mines and Geology Branch, Department of Mines and Resources, to Austin L. Cumming, Esq., Superintendent Mackenzie district, Lands, Parks and Forests Branch, Ottawa, ON, RG85, Northern Affairs Program, Series C-1-a, Volume 876, Reel T-13366, File: 8861, Access Code 90: File title: Patrols, reports, etc. South Nahanni River and Flat River areas—also proposed game reserve C map and photos: outside Dates: 1936–1938, Finding Aid number 85-44, November 16, 1937; Harry Snyder to R.A. Gibson, Deputy Commissioner, Department of Northwest Territories, RG 85, Northern Affairs Program, Series C-1-a, Volume 905, Reel T-13919, File: 10377, File title S.P. Peterson—Northwest Game Act—big game hunting, Nahanni river Area Outside Dates: 1939, Finding Aid number: 85-44, October 10, 1939.

3　R.M. Anderson, Chief, Division of Biology, National Museum of Canada, Department of Mines and Resources, to R.A. Gibson, Deputy Commissioner, administration of the Northwest Territories, Ottawa, ON, R 985, Northern Affairs Program, Series C-1-a, Volume 876, Reel T-13366, File 8861, File Title: P. Peterson, Northwest Game Act—big game hunting, Nahanni River area Outside Dates: 1939, Finding Aid number 85-44, November 17, 1937.

4 Ibid.

5 Harry Snyder to R.A. Gibson.

6 Ibid.

7 John Sandlos, *Hunters at the Margin: Native People and Wildlife Conservation in the Northwest Territories* (Vancouver: UBC Press, 2007).

8 Hunt, "The Development and Decline of Northern Conservation Reserves."

9 Sandlos, *Hunters at the Margin*.

10 Ibid.

11 Patterson, *Those Earlier Hills*. See especially Chapter 1, "River of Deadmen Valley"; Chapter 2, "The Nahany Lands"; and Chapter 3, "South Nahanni Revisited."

12 McClellan, *Part of the Land*.

13 Thomas D. Andrews and Glen MacKay, "The Archaeology and Paleoecology of Alpine Ice Patches: A Global Perspective," *Arctic* 65, Supplement 1 (2012): iii–vi.

14 Berton, *The Mysterious North*.

15 Hugh Brody, *The Other Side of Eden: Hunters, Farmers and the Shaping of the World* (New York: North Point Press, 2000).

16 Ibid.

17 Nelson, *Make Prayers to the Raven*; Richard C. Foltz, ed., *Worldviews, Religion, and the Environment: A Global Anthology* (Belmont, CA: Thomson Wadsworth, 2003).

18 The summary is from Nelson, *Make Prayers to the Raven*, Chapter 11, "Ecological Patterns and Conservation Practices," especially pages 218–224.

19 Nelson, *Make Prayers to the Raven*, 220.

Chapter 8: Challenges and Opportunities

1 D.F. Wright, D. Lemkow, and J.R. Harris, eds., *Mineral and Energy Resource Assessment of the Greater Nahanni Ecosystem Under Consideration for the Expansion of the Nahanni National Park Reserve, Northwest Territories* (Ottawa: Natural Resources Canada, 2007).

2 Kevin Menicoche, MLA (Member of the Legislative Assembly) Nahendeh, Development and Operation of the Canadian Zinc Prairie Creek Mine, to Mackenzie Valley Land and Water Board, Yellowknife, NT, August 6, 2008.

3 Meagan Wohlberg, "Mining holds empty promises for Northerners," *Northern Journal*, April 15, 2013, https://norj.ca/2013/04/mining-holds-empty-promises-for-northerners/.

4 Claire Singer, Environmental Regulatory Analyst, Environment and Natural Resources, Northwest Territories, Canadian Zinc Corp, MV2008 T0012,

MV2008 T0063, MV2008 D0014, MV2008 L2-0002, Land Use Permit and Water License Application—Prairie Creek Mine and Liard and Tetcela Transfer Facilities, to Tyre Mullaney, Regulatory Office, Mackenzie Valley Land and Water Board, Yellowknife, NT, Attachment: ENR comments, August 8, 2008.

5   Sam Gargan, Grand Chief Dehcho First Nations, Fort Simpson, NT, Re: Canadian Zinc, Prairie Creek Mine Environmental Assessment Report and Reasons for Decision released by the Mackenzie Valley Environmental Impact Review Board, to Honourable John Duncan, Aboriginal Affairs and Northern Development Canada, Gatineau, QC, December 13, 2011.

6   Ibid.

7   Derek Ford, "Re: A very serious mining threat to the integrity of Nahanni National Park Reserve, Mackenzie Mountains, Northwest Territories, Canada," *Northern Currents* 5, no. 9 (Fall 2005).

8   Alison Woodley, Manager, National Protected Area Programs, Canadian Parks and Wilderness Society, Re: Canadian Zinc Corporation Water License and Land Use Permit Applications for Prairie Creek Mine, to Valerie Meeves, Regulatory Office, Mackenzie Valley Land and Water Board, Yellowknife, NT, August 15, 2008.

9   The information and quotes in this and the preceding paragraph are from Kris Brekke, Executive Director, Canadian Parks and Wilderness Society, Northwest Territories Chapter, Yellowknife, NT, Re: Mackenzie Valley Environmental Impact Review Board, EAO 809-002, Canadian Zinc Corporation, Prairie Creek Mine, to Honourable John Duncan, December 15, 2011.

10 Eric Hebert-Daly, National Executive Director, Canadian Parks and Wilderness Society, Re: EA0809-02—Canadian Zinc Corporation, Prairie Creek Mine Environmental Assessment Impact Review Board (MVEIRB) Report of Environmental Assessment and Reasons for Decision, to Honourable John Duncan, Minister of Aboriginal Affairs and Northern Development, Ottawa, ON, December 19, 2011.

11 Bern Will Brown, *End-of-Earth People: The Arctic Sahtu Dene* (Toronto: Dundurn, 2014).

12 Derek Ford and Alison Woodley, personal communication, July 2012.

13 Stephen Trimble, *The People: Indians of the American Southwest* (Santa Fe, NM: School of American Research Press, 1993), 130–131.

14 See J. Keele, "A Reconnaissance across the Mackenzie Mountains on the Pelly, Ross and Gravel Rivers, Yukon and Northwest Territories," *Geological Survey of Canada, Report 1097*, Ottawa, 1910, which is referred to in Scotter et al., "Ecology of the South Nahanni" but was not directly available for this study.

15 Hartling, *Nahanni*, 120–121.

16 Parks Canada, *Nah? ą Dehé: South Nahanni River Touring Guide*, Nah? ą Dehé Consensus Team (Ottawa: Parks Canada, 2011).

17 Beryl C. Gillespie, "Nahani," in *Handbook of North American Indians*, Volume 6: Subarctic, ed. June Helm (Washington, DC: Smithsonian Foundation, 1981), 451–453.

18 McClellan, *Part of the Land*.

19 Paul S. Martin and Christine Szuter, "Revising the 'Wild' West: Big Game Meets the Ultimate Keystone Species," in *The Archaeology of Global Change: The Impact of Humans on Their Environment*, ed. Charles L. Redman et al. (Washington, DC: Smithsonian Books, 2004), 63–89, see especially 77–82.

20 George Colpitts, "Peace, War, and Climate Change on the Northern Plains: Bison Hunting in the Neutral Hills during the Mild Winters of 1830–34," *Canadian Journal of History* 50, no. 3 (2015): 420–441.

21 Andrews and MacKay, "Archaeology and Paleoecology"; Thomas D. Andrews, Glen MacKay, and Leon Andrew, "Archaeological Investigations of Alpine Ice Patches in the Selwyn Mountains, Northwest Territories, Canada," *Arctic* 65, Supplement 1 (2012): 1–21.

22 Andrews, MacKay, and Andrew, "Alpine Ice Patches."

23 Charles L. Redman et al., eds., *The Archaeology of Global Change: The Impact of Humans on Their Environment* (Washington, DC: Smithsonian Books, 2004).

24 Janetski, *Indians in Yellowstone National Park*; Dennis J. Stanford and Jane Stevenson Day, eds., *Ice Age Hunters of the Rockies* (Denver: Denver Museum of Natural History and University Press of Colorado, 1992); Leslie B. Davis and Sally T. Greiser, "Indian Creek Paleoindians: Early Occupation of the Elkhorn Mountains' Southeast Flank, West-Central Montana," in *Ice Age Hunters of the Rockies*, ed. Dennis J. Stanford and Jane Stevenson Day (Denver: Denver Museum of Natural History and University Press of Colorado, 1992), 225–283; George C. Frison, "The Foothills-Mountains and the Open Plains: The Dichotomy in Paleoindian Subsistence Strategies between Two Ecosystems," in *Ice Age Hunters of the Rockies*, ed. Dennis J. Stanford and Jane Stevenson Day (Denver: Denver Museum of Natural History and University Press of Colorado, 1992), 323–342; James B. Benedict, "Along the Great Divide: Paleoindian Archaeology of the High Colorado Front Range," in *Ice Age Hunters of the Rockies*, ed. Dennis J. Stanford and Jane Stevenson Day (Denver: Denver Museum of Natural History and University Press of Colorado, 1992), 343–360; Davis and Reeves, *Hunters of the Recent Past*; Morris, "Prehistoric Game Drive Systems"; George C. Frison, Charles A. Reher, and Danny N. Walker, "Prehistoric Mountain Sheep Hunting in the Central Rocky Mountains of North America," in *Hunters of the Recent Past*, ed. Leslie B. Davis and Brian O.K. Reeves (London: Unwin Hyman, 1990), 208–240.

25 Brian O.K. Reeves, "Communal bison hunters of the Northern Plains," In *Hunters of the Recent Past*, ed. Leslie B. Davis and Brian O.K. Reeves (London: Unwin Hyman, 1990), 168–194.

26 Willa Campbell, "Megaproject no quick fix for Native issues, says Rae," *Toronto Star*, October 6, 2013, A12.

27 Peter Kulchyski, *Aboriginal Rights Are Not Human Rights: In Defence of Indigenous Struggles* (Winnipeg: ARP Books, 2013); Peter Kulchyski, "Getting Aboriginal Rights Right, Related Letters and Responses," *Literary Review of Canada* 21, no. 9 (2013): 32.

28 Berger, *A Long and Terrible Shadow*.

29 Vicki Cummings, *The Anthropology of Hunter-Gatherers: Key Themes for Archaeologists* (London: Bloomsbury, 2013).

30 Brent Jang, "B.C. First Nations Group unanimously opposes LNG Venture," *The Globe and Mail*, May 9, 2015, B1; Brent Jang, "Allied tribes likely to reject Petronas project," *The Globe and Mail*, May 12, 2015, B8; Brent Jang, "Petronas exploring options to salvage LNG terminal plan," *The Globe and Mail*, May 14, 2015, A1.

31 Chris Turner, *The War on Science: Muzzled Scientists and Wilful Blindness in Stephen Harper's Canada* (Vancouver: Greystone Books, 2013).

32 Office of the Auditor General of Canada, *Fall Report of the Commissioner of the Environment and Sustainable Development*, Ottawa, 2013, http://www.oag-bvg.gc.ca/internet/English/parl_cesd_201311_e_38658.html.

33 J.G. Nelson, "Research in Human Ecology and Planning: An Interactive, Adaptive Approach," *Canadian Geographer* 35, no. 2 (1991): 114–127.

34 Terry Fenge and Tony Penikett, "Paper Promises: By Avoiding Treaty Obligations, Canada Undermines Its Own Legal Basis," *Literary Review of Canada* 22, no. 6 (2014): 7–9.

35 Ibid., 8.

Chapter 9: Analogies with Experience Elsewhere

1 Aldo Leopold, *A Sand County Almanac: And Sketches Here and There* (New York: Oxford, 1949); David E. Brown and Neil B. Carmony, eds., *Aldo Leopold's Southwest* (Albuquerque: University of New Mexico Press, 1995).

2 Nathan Miller, *Theodore Roosevelt: A Life* (New York: William Morrow, 1992).

3 Brown and Carmony, *Aldo Leopold's Southwest*.

4 Ibid., 148–151.

5 Ibid., 201–203.

6 Ibid., 203.

7   David Rothenberg, "Introduction," in *The World and the Wild*, ed. David Rothenberg and Marta Ulvaeus (Tucson: The University of Arizona Press, 2001), xi.

8   Sahotra Sarkar, "Restoring wilderness or reclaiming forests?" in *The World and the Wild*, ed. David Rothenberg and Marta Ulvaeus (Tucson: University of Arizona Press, 2001), 38–55; Philip Cafaro and Monish Verma, "For Indian Wilderness," in *The World and the Wild*, ed. David Rothenberg and Marta Ulvaeus (Tucson: University of Arizona Press, 2001), 57–64.

9   Cafaro and Verma, "For Indian Wilderness," 57–65.

10   Ibid., 62.

11   Jim Robbins, "Paying Farmers to Welcome Birds," *New York Times*, April 14, 2014, http://www.nytimes.com/2014/04/15/science/paying-farmers-to-welcome-birds.html.

12   Laura López-Hoffman et al., eds., *Conservation of Shared Environments: Learning from the United States and Mexico* (Tucson: The University of Arizona Press, 2009).

13   Luis E. Calderon-Aguilera and Karl W. Flessa, "Just Add Water? Transboundary Colorado River Flow and Ecosystem Services in the Upper Gulf of California," in *Conservation of Shared Environments: Learning from the United States and Mexico*, ed. Laura López-Hoffman et al. (Tucson: University of Arizona Press, 2009), 154–169; Francisco Zamora-Arroyo and Karl W. Flessa, "Nature's Fair Share: Finding and Allocating Water for the Colorado River Delta," in *Conservation of Shared Environments: Learning from the United States and Mexico*, ed. Laura López-Hoffman et al. (Tucson: University of Arizona Press, 2009), 23–38.

14   Mark Briggs et al., "Restoring a Desert Lifeline: The Big Bend Reach of the Rio Grande," in *Conservation of Shared Environments: Learning from the United States and Mexico*, ed. Laura López-Hoffman et al. (Tucson: University of Arizona Press, 2009), 39–53.

15   Jessica Piekielek, "Cooperative Conservation, Unilateral Security: The Story of Two Sister Parks on the U.S.–Mexico Border," in *Conservation of Shared Environments: Learning from the United States and Mexico*, ed. Laura López-Hoffman et al. (Tucson: University of Arizona Press, 2009), 213–225.

16   José F. Bernal Stoopen, Jane M. Packard, and Richard Reading, "Mexican Wolf Recovery: Insights from Transboundary Stakeholders," in *Conservation of Shared Environments: Learning from the United States and Mexico*, ed. Laura López-Hoffman et al. (Tucson: University of Arizona Press, 2009), 115–132.

17   Robert H. Keller and Michael F. Turek, *American Indians and National Parks* (Tucson: University of Arizona Press, 1999).

18 Courtney W. Mason, *Spirits of the Rockies: Reasserting an Indigenous Presence in Banff National Park* (Toronto: University of Toronto Press, 2014).

19 *Tsilhqot'in Nation v British Columbia*, 2014 SCC 44, [2014] 2 SCR 257.

20 Brian Hutchinson, "Staggering implications for energy projects as top court grants B.C. First Nation land title," *The National Post*, June 27, 2014, A1.

21 Thomas King, *The Inconvenient Indian: A Curious Account of Native People in North America* (Toronto: Anchor Canada, 2013); Kino-nda-niimi Collective, ed., *The Winter We Danced: Voices from the Past, the Future, and the Idle No More Movement* (Winnipeg: ARP Books, 2014), 22–26, 51–64.

22 *Grassy Narrows First Nation v Ontario (Natural Resources)*, 2014 SCC 48, [2014] 2 SCR 447.

23 Ibid., para 52.

24 Mark Hume, "First Nations chiefs seek to develop new tribal park in B.C.," *The Globe and Mail*, October 6, 2014, A4.

25 Ibid.

26 Shawn McCarty, "Share revenue with aboriginal communities, report suggests," *The Globe and Mail*, March 4, 2015, B4.

27 Ibid.

28 Perry Bellegarde, "This is just the beginning," *The Globe and Mail*, June 1, 2015, A12.

29 Little Grand Rapids First Nation and Ontario Ministry of Natural Resources, *Little Grand Rapids Community Based Land Use Plan* (Little Grand Rapids–Ontario Planning Area, Red Lake District: Ministry of Natural Resources and Little Grand Rapids, 2011).

30 Terrence E. Paupp, *Redefining Human Rights in the Struggle for Peace and Development* (New York: Cambridge University Press, 2014).

31 Ibid., 129.

32 Catherine Gross, *Fairness and Justice in Environmental Decision Making: Water under the Bridge* (London: Routledge Press, 2014).

33 Andrea Olive, *Land, Stewardship, and Legitimacy: Endangered Species Policy in Canada and the United States* (Toronto: University of Toronto Press, 2014).

34 Gloria Galloway, "First Nation to help manage 14,000-square-kilometre national park reserve in NWT," *The Globe and Mail*, July 29, 2015, A3–4.

35 Ibid.

36 Peter W. Williams, J.C. Day, and Thomas I. Gunton, "Land and Water Planning in British Columbia in the 1990s: Lessons on More Inclusive Approaches," *Environments: A Journal of Interdisciplinary Studies* 25, nos. 2 and 3 (1998): 1–7.

37 Sean Fine, "Chief Justice says Canada attempted 'cultural genocide' on aboriginals," *The Globe and Mail*, May 28, 2015, http://www.theglobeandmail.com/news/national/chief-justice-says-canada-attempted-cultural-genocide-on-aboriginals/article24688854/.

38 Joanna Smith, "A need to engage non-aboriginals in healing process," *The Toronto Star*, May 31, 2015, A6.

39 Marco Chown Oved, "To last, reconciliation must involve 'multiple voices,'" *The Toronto Star*, May 31, 2015, A6; John Ibbotson, "A Challenge for Canada," *The Globe and Mail*, June 6, 2015, A12–13.

40 John Ralston Saul, *The Comeback: How Aboriginals Are Reclaiming Power and Influence* (Toronto: Penguin Books, 2014).

A Note on Sources

1   George Perkins Marsh, *Man and Nature; Or, Physical Geography as Modified by Human Action*, 1864, reprint ed. David Lowenthal (Cambridge, MA: Harvard University Press, 1965); William L. Thomas, Jr., ed., *Man's Role in Changing the Face of the Earth* (Chicago: University of Chicago Press, 1956); F. Fraser Darling and J. Morton Boyd, *The Highlands and Islands* (Glasgow, Scotland: Collins, 1964); Carl Ortwin Sauer, *The Early Spanish Main* (London: Cambridge University Press, 1966); Nelson, *Man's Impact*; Milton Freeman Research Limited, *The Inuit Land Use and Occupancy Project*, vol. 1 (Ottawa: Minister of Supply and Services Canada, 1976); David Boeri, *People of the Ice Whale: Eskimos, White Men, and the Whale* (New York: E.P. Dutton, 1983); F.M. Brouwer, A.J. Thomas, and M.J. Chadwick, eds., *Land Use Changes in Europe: Processes of Change, Environmental Transformations and Future Patterns* (Dordrecht, Netherlands: Kluwer Academic Publishers, 1991); J. Gordon Nelson and Patrick L. Lawrence, *Places: Linking Nature and Culture for Understanding and Planning* (Calgary: University of Calgary Press, 2009).

2   Redman et al., *Archaeology of Global Change*; Marco Madella, Carla Lancelotti, and Manon Savard, eds., *Ancient Plants and People: Contemporary Trends in Archaeobotany* (Tucson: University of Arizona Press, 2014).

3   Harold A. Innis, *The Fur Trade in Canada: An Introduction to Canadian Economic History* (Toronto: University of Toronto Press, 1930); A.R.M. Lower, *The North American Assault on the Canadian Forest: A History of the Lumber Trade between Canada and the United States* (Toronto: Ryerson Press, 1938).

4   Hughes, *North American Indian Ecology*; Donald Worster, *The Ends of the Earth: Perspectives on Modern Environmental History* (Cambridge: Cambridge University Press, 1988); George Colpitts, *Game in the Garden: A Human History of Wildlife in Western Canada to 1940* (Vancouver: UBC Press, 2002); Michael F. Logan, *The Lessening Stream: An Environmental History of the Santa Cruz River* (Tucson: The University of Arizona Press, 2002).

5   William Cronon, *Changes in the Land: Indians, Colonists, and the Ecology of New England* (New York: Hill and Wang, 1983).

6   John L. Riley, *The Once and Future Great Lakes Country: An Ecological History* (Montreal: McGill-Queen's University Press, 2014); John N. Kittinger et al., eds., *Marine Historical Ecology in Conservation: Applying the Past to Manage for the Future* (Berkeley: University of California Press, 2015); Ramona Harrison and Ruth A. Maher, eds., *Human Ecodynamics in the North Atlantic: A Collaborative Model of Humans and Nature through Space and Time* (Lanham, MD: Lexington Books, 2014).

7   Sverker Sörlin and Paul Warde, eds., *Nature's End: History and the Environment* (New York: Palgrave Macmillan, 2011).

8   Matthew Evenden and Graeme Wynn, "54, 40 or Fight: Writing Within and Across Borders in North American Environmental History," in *Nature's End: History and the Environment*, ed. Sverker Sörlin and Paul Warde (New York: Palgrave Macmillan, 2011), 215–246.

9   C. Gordon Hewitt, *The Conservation of the Wild Life in Canada* (New York: Charles Scribner's Sons, 1921); Huth, *Nature and the American*; Nash, *Wilderness and the American Mind*; J.G. Nelson with R.C. Scace, eds., *Canadian Parks in Perspective* (Montreal: Harvest House, 1970); Janet Foster, *Working for Wildlife: The Beginning of Preservation in Canada* (Toronto: University of Toronto Press, 1978); Alfred Runte, *National Parks: The American Experience*, 2nd ed. revised (Lincoln: University of Nebraska Press, 1987); Philip Dearden and Rick Rollins, eds., *Parks and Protected Areas in Canada: Planning and Management*, 3rd ed. (Toronto: Oxford University Press, 2009); John S. Marsh and Bruce W. Hodgins, eds., *Changing Parks: The History, Future and Cultural Context of Parks and Heritage Landscapes* (Toronto: Natural Heritage/Natural History Inc., 1998); Claire Elizabeth Campbell, ed., *A Century of Parks Canada, 1911–2011* (Calgary: University of Calgary Press, 2011).

10 E.J. Hart, *J.B. Harkin: Father of Canada's National Parks* (Edmonton: University of Alberta Press, 2010); Douglas Brinkley, *The Wilderness Warrior: Theodore Roosevelt and the Crusade for America* (New York: HarperCollins, 2009).

11 Candace Savage, *Prairie: A Natural History*, 2nd ed. (Vancouver: Greystone Books, 2011); Harrison Brown, "Technological Denudation," in *Man's Role in Changing the Face of the Earth*, ed. William L. Thomas, Jr. (Chicago: University of Chicago Press, 1956), 1023–1032; F. Fraser Darling and John P. Milton, eds., *Future Environments of North America, Transformation of a Continent* (Garden City, NY: The Natural History Press, 1966); Pielou, *After the Ice Age*; John Theberge and Mary Theberge, *The Ptarmigan's Dilemma: An Exploration into How Life Organizes and Supports Itself* (Toronto: McClelland & Stewart, 2010).

12 Karl W. Butzer, *Archaeology as Human Ecology: Method and Theory for a Contextual Approach* (Cambridge: Cambridge University Press, 1982).

13   Richard K. Nelson, *Hunters of the Northern Ice* (Chicago: University of Chicago Press, 1969); William Fitzhugh, ed., *Prehistoric Maritime Adaptations of the Circumpolar Zone* (The Hague and Chicago: Mouton and Co. and Aldine Publishing, 1975); Liz Bryan, *The Buffalo People: Pre-contact Archaeology on the Canadian Plains* (Surrey, BC: Heritage House, 2005); Fagan, *The Complete Ice Age*; Jared Diamond, *The World Until Yesterday: What Can We Learn from Traditional Societies?* (New York: Viking, 2012); Bellwood, *First Migrants*.

14   Frederick Steiner, *Human Ecology: Following Nature's Lead* (Washington, DC: Island Press, 2002).

15   Ian L. McHarg, *Design with Nature* (Philadelphia: Falcon Press, 1971).

16   Burroughs, *Climate Change in Prehistory*; Bellwood, *First Migrants*.

17   Holling, *Adaptive Environmental Assessment and Management*; Gertler, Bennett, and Levitt, "Planning with People"; Nelson and Hoffman, "Sharing Heritage Management"; Nelson, "Research in Human Ecology and Planning"; Gerald Hodge, *Planning Canadian Communities: An Introduction to the Principles, Practice and Participants*, 4th ed. (Toronto: Nelson Thomson Learning, 2001); Stains, "Collaborative Park Planning"; Dearden and Rollins, *Parks and Protected Areas*; Williams, Day, and Gunton, "Land and Water Planning."

Appendix B

1   The source for this list is information obtained from Parks Canada offices at Fort Simpson and Fort Smith.

References

Anderson, R.M. Chief, Division of Biology, National Museum of Canada, Department of Mines and Resources, November 17, 1937. Letter to R.A. Gibson, Deputy Commissioner, administration of the Northwest Territories, Ottawa, R 985, Northern Affairs Program, Series C-1-a. Volume 876. Reel T-13366, File 8861. File Title: P. Peterson, Northwest Game Act—big game hunting, Nahanni River area Outside Dates: 1939. Finding Aid number 85-44.

Andrews, Thomas D., and Glen MacKay. "The Archaeology and Paleoecology of Alpine Ice Patches: A Global Perspective." *Arctic* 65, Supplement 1 (2012): iii–vi.

Andrews, Thomas D., Glen MacKay, and Leon Andrew. "Archaeological Investigations of Alpine Ice Patches in the Selwyn Mountains, Northwest Territories, Canada." *Arctic* 65, Supplement 1 (2012): 1–21.

Bartlett, Roger. *A History of Russia*. New York: Palgrave Macmillan, 2005.

Bellegarde, Perry. "This is just the beginning." *The Globe and Mail*, June 1, 2015. A12.

Bellwood, Peter. *First Migrants: Ancient Migration in Global Perspective*. Chichester, UK: Wiley Blackwell, 2013.

Benedict, James B. "Along the Great Divide: Paleoindian Archaeology of the High Colorado Front Range." In *Ice Age Hunters of the Rockies*, edited by Dennis J. Stanford and Jane Stevenson Day, 343–360. Denver: Denver Museum of Natural History and University Press of Colorado, 1992.

Berger, Thomas R. *A Long and Terrible Shadow: White Values, Native Rights in the Americas, 1492–1992*. Vancouver: Douglas & McIntyre, 1991.

———. *Northern Frontier, Northern Homeland: The Report of the Mackenzie Valley Pipeline Inquiry*. 2 vols. Ottawa: Minister of Supply and Services Canada, 1977.

Bernal Stoopen, José F., Jane M. Packard, and Richard Reading. "Mexican Wolf Recovery: Insights from Transboundary Stakeholders." In *Conservation of Shared Environments: Learning from the United States and Mexico*, edited by Laura López-Hoffman, Emily D. McGovern, Robert G. Varady, and Karl W. Flessa, 115–132. Tucson: University of Arizona Press, 2009.

Berton, Pierre. *Klondike: The Last Great Gold Rush*. Toronto: Anchor Canada, 2001.

——. *The Mysterious North*. New York: Alfred A. Knopf, Inc., 1961.

Blyth, Charles. *Nahanni Nah? ą Dehé: A Selection of Photographic Images of the South Nahanni Watershed (2007–2010)*. N.p.: Creative Publishing Service, 2011.

Boeri, David. *People of the Ice Whale: Eskimos, White Men, and the Whale*. New York: E.P. Dutton, 1983.

Bolus, Malvina, ed. *People and Pelts: Selected Papers of the Second North American Fur Trade Conference*. Winnipeg: Peguis Publishers, 1972.

Bothwell, P.M., W.J. de Groot, D.E. Dubé, T. Chowns, D.H. Carlsson, and C.N. Stefner. "Fire Regimes in Nahanni National Park and the Mackenzie Bison Sanctuary, Northwest Territories, Canada." In *Proceedings of the 22nd Tall Timbers Fire Ecology Conference: Fire in Temperate, Boreal, and Montane Ecosystems*, edited by R.T. Engstrom, K.E.M. Galley, and W.J. de Groot, 43–54. Tallahassee, FL: Tall Timbers Research Station, 2004.

Briggs, Mark, Carlos Sifuentes, Joe Sirotnak, and Mark Lockwood. "Restoring a Desert Lifeline: The Big Bend Reach of the Rio Grande." In *Conservation of Shared Environments: Learning from the United States and Mexico*, edited by Laura López-Hoffman, Emily D. McGovern, Robert G. Varady, and Karl W. Flessa, 39–53. Tucson: University of Arizona Press, 2009.

Brinkley, Douglas. *The Wilderness Warrior: Theodore Roosevelt and the Crusade for America*. New York: HarperCollins, 2009.

Brody, Hugh. *The Other Side of Eden: Hunters, Farmers and the Shaping of the World*. New York: North Point Press, 2000.

Brook, G.A., and D.C. Ford. "The origin of labyrinth and tower karst and the climatic conditions necessary for their development." *Nature* 275 (1978): 493–496.

Brouwer, F.M., A.J. Thomas, and M.J. Chadwick, eds. *Land Use Changes in Europe: Processes of Change, Environmental Transformations and Future Patterns*. Dordrecht, Netherlands: Kluwer Academic Publishers, 1991.

Brown, Bern Will. *End-of-Earth People: The Arctic Sahtu Dene*. Toronto: Dundurn, 2014.

Brown, David E., and Neil B. Carmony, eds. *Aldo Leopold's Southwest*. Albuquerque: University of New Mexico Press, 1995.

Brown, Harrison. "Technological Denudation." In *Man's Role in Changing the Face of the Earth*, edited by William L. Thomas, Jr., 1023–1032. Chicago: University of Chicago Press, 1956.

Bryan, Liz. *The Buffalo People: Pre-contact Archaeology on the Canadian Plains.* Surrey, BC: Heritage House, 2005.

Burroughs, William J. *Climate Change in Prehistory: The End of the Reign of Chaos.* Cambridge, UK: Cambridge University Press, 2005.

Butzer, Karl W. *Archaeology as Human Ecology: Method and Theory for a Contextual Approach.* Cambridge: Cambridge University Press, 1982.

Cafaro, Philip, and Monish Verma. "For Indian Wilderness." In *The World and the Wild,* edited by David Rothenberg and Marta Ulvaeus, 57–64. Tucson: University of Arizona Press: 2001.

Cairns, A.L., J.D. Henry, and G.W. Scotter. "Vegetation, Wildlife, and Recreation Assessment of the Flat–South Nahanni Rivers Confluence Area, Nahanni National Park." Edmonton: Canadian Wildlife Service, 1978.

Calderon-Aguilera, Luis E., and Karl W. Flessa. "Just Add Water? Transboundary Colorado River Flow and Ecosystem Services in the Upper Gulf of California." In *Conservation of Shared Environments: Learning from the United States and Mexico,* edited by Laura López-Hoffman, Emily D. McGovern, Robert G. Varady, and Karl W. Flessa, 154–169. Tucson: University of Arizona Press, 2009.

Campbell, Claire Elizabeth, ed. *A Century of Parks Canada, 1911–2011.* Calgary: University of Calgary Press, 2011.

Campbell, Willa. "Megaproject no quick fix for Native issues, says Rae." *Toronto Star,* October 6, 2013. A12.

Canadian Wildlife Service. "NWT—Nunavut Bird Checklist Survey Form." Yellowknife: Canadian Wildlife Service, 2009.

Casselman, Anne. "The Big One." *Canadian Geographic,* June 2015, 48–58.

Colpitts, George. *Game in the Garden: A Human History of Wildlife in Western Canada to 1940.* Vancouver: UBC Press, 2002.

——. "Peace, War, and Climate Change on the Northern Plains: Bison Hunting in the Neutral Hills during the Mild Winters of 1830–34." *Canadian Journal of History* 50, no. 3 (2015): 420–441.

Cooke, Alan, and Clive Holland, eds. *The Exploration of Northern Canada 500 to 1920: A Chronology.* Toronto: Arctic History Press, 1978.

Cowan, Ian McTaggart. "The Role of Ecology in the National Parks." In *The Canadian National Parks: Today and Tomorrow,* edited by J.G. Nelson and R.C. Scace, 931–940. Calgary: The National and Provincial Parks Association of Canada and the University of Calgary, 1969.

Cronon, William. *Changes in the Land: Indians, Colonists, and the Ecology of New England.* New York: Hill and Wang, 1983.

——, ed. *Uncommon Ground: Toward Reinventing Nature.* New York: Norton, 1995.

Crosby, Alfred W. *Ecological Imperialism: The Biological Expansion of Europe, 900–1900.* Cambridge: Cambridge University Press, 2004.

Cummings, Vicki. *The Anthropology of Hunter-Gatherers: Key Themes for Archaeologists*. London: Bloomsbury, 2013.

Darling, F. Fraser, and J. Morton Boyd. *The Highlands and Islands*. Glasgow, Scotland: Collins, 1964.

Darling, F. Fraser, and John P. Milton, eds. *Future Environments of North America, Transformation of a Continent*. Garden City, NY: The Natural History Press, 1966.

Daschuk, James. *Clearing the Plains: Disease, Politics of Starvation, and the Loss of Aboriginal Life*. Regina: University of Regina Press, 2013.

Davis, Leslie B., and Brian O.K. Reeves, eds. *Hunters of the Recent Past*. London: Unwin Hyman, 1990.

Davis, Leslie B., and Sally T. Greiser. "Indian Creek Paleoindians: Early Occupation of the Elkhorn Mountains' Southeast Flank, West-Central Montana." In *Ice Age Hunters of the Rockies*, edited by Dennis J. Stanford and Jane Stevenson Day, 225–283. Denver: Denver Museum of Natural History and University Press of Colorado, 1992.

Davis, Richard C., ed. *Nahanni Journals: R.M. Patterson's 1927–1929 Journals*. Edmonton: University of Alberta Press, 2008.

Dearden, Philip, and Rick Rollins, eds. *Parks and Protected Areas in Canada: Planning and Management*. 3rd Edition. Toronto: Oxford University Press, 2009.

Demuth, Michael N. *Secular Change in the Glacier Cover Contributing Flow to a World Heritage River—Ragged Ranges, South Nahanni River*. Northwest Territories Research Database, 2007. http://data.nwtresearch.com/scientific/14229.

den Otter, A.A. *Civilizing the Wilderness: Culture and Nature in Pre-Confederation Canada and Rupert's Land*. Edmonton: University of Alberta Press, 2012.

Diamond, Jared. *The World Until Yesterday: What Can We Learn from Traditional Societies?* New York: Viking, 2012.

Dmytryshyn, Basil. *A History of Russia*. Englewood Cliffs, NJ: Prentice Hall, 1977.

Douglas, William O. *A Wilderness Bill of Rights*. Boston: Little, Brown and Company, 1965.

Eisenberg, Cristina. *The Carnivore Way: Coexisting with and Conserving North America's Predators*. Washington, DC: Island Press, 2014.

Evenden, Matthew, and Graeme Wynn. "54, 40 or Fight: Writing Within and Across Borders in North American Environmental History." In *Nature's End: History and the Environment*, edited by Sverker Sörlin and Paul Warde, 215–246. New York: Palgrave Macmillan, 2011.

Fagan, Brian, ed. *The Complete Ice Age: How Climate Change Shaped the World*. London: Thames & Hudson, 2009.

Farvar, M. Taghi, and John P. Milton, eds. *The Careless Technology: Ecology and International Development*. Garden City, NY: The Natural History Press, 1972.

Fenge, Terry, and Tony Penikett. "Paper Promises: By Avoiding Treaty Obligations, Canada Undermines Its Own Legal Basis." *Literary Review of Canada* 22, no. 6 (2014): 7–9.

Finch, David. *R.M. Patterson: A Life of Great Adventure.* Calgary: Rocky Mountain Books, 2000.

Fine, Sean. "Chief Justice says Canada attempted 'cultural genocide' on aboriginals." *The Globe and Mail*, May 28, 2015. http://www.theglobeandmail.com/news/national/chief-justice-says-canada-attempted-cultural-genocide-on-aboriginals/article24688854/.

Fitzhugh, William, ed. *Prehistoric Maritime Adaptations of the Circumpolar Zone.* The Hague and Chicago: Mouton and Co. and Aldine Publishing, 1975.

Foltz, Richard C., ed. *Worldviews, Religion, and the Environment: A Global Anthology.* Belmont, CA: Thomson Wadsworth, 2003.

Ford, D.C. "Evidences of multiple glaciation in South Nahanni National Park, Mackenzie Mountains, Northwest Territories." *Canadian Journal of Earth Sciences* 13, no. 10 (1976): 1433–1445.

Ford, Derek. "Antecedent Canyons of the South Nahanni River, Mackenzie Mountains, N.W.T." *The Canadian Geographer* 35, no. 4 (1991): 426–431.

——. "Expanding South Nahanni National Park, Northwest Territories, Canada, to Include and Manage Some Remarkable Sub-Arctic/Arctic Karst Terrains." In *Karst Management*, edited by Philip E. van Beynen, 415–437. Dordrecht: Springer Science and Business Media, 2001.

——. "Re: A very serious mining threat to the integrity of Nahanni National Park Reserve, Mackenzie Mountains, Northwest Territories, Canada." *Northern Currents* 5, no. 9 (Fall 2005).

Forman, Richard T.T., and Michel Godron. *Landscape Ecology.* New York: John Wiley and Sons, 1986.

Foster, Janet. *Working for Wildlife: The Beginning of Preservation in Canada.* Toronto: University of Toronto Press, 1978.

Fried, Stephanie Gorson. "Writing for Their Lives: Bentian Dayak Authors and Indonesian Development Discourse." In *Culture and the Question of Rights: Forests, Coasts, and Seas in Southeast Asia*, edited by Charles Zerner, 142–183. Durham, NC: Duke University Press, 2003.

Frison, George C. "The Foothills-Mountains and the Open Plains: The Dichotomy in Paleoindian Subsistence Strategies between Two Ecosystems." In *Ice Age Hunters of the Rockies*, edited by Dennis J. Stanford and Jane Stevenson Day, 323–342. Denver: Denver Museum of Natural History and University Press of Colorado, 1992.

Frison, George C., Charles A. Reher, and Danny N. Walker. "Prehistoric Mountain Sheep Hunting in the Central Rocky Mountains of North America." In *Hunters of the Recent Past*, edited by Leslie B. Davis and Brian O.K. Reeves, 208–240. London: Unwin Hyman, 1990.

Galloway, Gloria. "First Nation to help manage 14,000-square-kilometre national park reserve in NWT." *The Globe and Mail*, July 29, 2015. A3–4.

Gertler, Len, Karl Bennett, and Kari Levitt, eds. "Planning with People: Human Ecology and Development in Canada and the Caribbean." *Environments* 16, no. 3 (1984): 1–186.

Gibson, James R. *Feeding the Russian Fur Trade: Provisionment of the Okhotsk Seaboard and the Kamchatka Peninsula, 1639–1856*. Madison: University of Wisconsin Press, 1969.

Gillespie, Beryl C. "Nahani." In *Handbook of North American Indians*, Volume 6: Subarctic, edited by June Helm, 451–453. Washington, DC: Smithsonian Foundation, 1981.

Gough, Barry. *The Elusive Mr. Pond: The Soldier, Fur Trader and Explorer Who Opened the Northwest*. Madeira Park, BC: Douglas & McIntyre, 2014.

Grassy Narrows First Nation v Ontario (Natural Resources), 2014 SCC 48, [2014] 2 SCR 447.

Gross, Catherine. *Fairness and Justice in Environmental Decision Making: Water under the Bridge*. London: Routledge Press, 2014.

Gunderson, Lance H., C.S. Holling, and Stephen S. Light, eds. *Barriers and Bridges to the Renewal of Ecosystems and Institutions*. New York: Columbia University Press, 1995.

Harmon, Russell S., Derek C. Ford, and Henry P. Schwarcz. "Interglacial chronology of the Rocky and Mackenzie Mountains based upon ^{230}Th-^{234}U dating of calcite speleothems." *Canadian Journal of Earth Sciences* 14, no. 11 (1977): 2543–2552.

Harrison, Ramona, and Ruth A. Maher, eds. *Human Ecodynamics in the North Atlantic: A Collaborative Model of Humans and Nature through Space and Time*. Lanham, MD: Lexington Books, 2014.

Hart, E.J. J.B. *Harkin: Father of Canada's National Parks*. Edmonton: University of Alberta Press, 2010.

Hartling, R. Neil. *Nahanni: River of Gold ... River of Dreams*. Merrickville, ON: Canadian Recreational Canoeing Association, 1998.

Hewitt, C. Gordon. *The Conservation of the Wild Life in Canada*. New York: Charles Scribner's Sons, 1921.

Hodge, Gerald. *Planning Canadian Communities: An Introduction to the Principles, Practice and Participants*. 4th Edition. Toronto: Nelson Thomson Learning, 2001.

Holling, C.S., ed. *Adaptive Environmental Assessment and Management*. New York: John Wiley and Sons, 1978.

Hudson's Bay Company. Fort Simpson Journals, 1822–1823, 1833–1834, 1843–1844, and 1863–1864. Hudson's Bay Company Archives, Winnipeg.

Hughes, J. Donald. *North American Indian Ecology*. El Paso: Texas Western Press, 1996.

Hume, Mark. "First Nations chiefs seek to develop new tribal park in B.C." *The Globe and Mail*, October 6, 2014. A4.

Hunt, Constance. "The Development and Decline of Northern Conservation Reserves." *Contact* 8, no. 4 (1976): 30–75.

Hunter, Fenley. *That Summer on the Nahanni 1928: The Journals of Fenley Hunter*. Ottawa: McGahern Stewart Publishing, 2015.

Hutchinson, Brian. "Staggering implications for energy projects as top court grants B.C. First Nation land title." *The National Post*, June 27, 2014. A1.

Huth, Hans. *Nature and the American: Three Centuries of Changing Attitudes*. Berkeley: University of California Press, 1957.

Ibbotson, John. "A Challenge for Canada." *The Globe and Mail*, June 6, 2015. A12–13.

Innis, Harold A. *The Fur Trade in Canada: An Introduction to Canadian Economic History*. Toronto: University of Toronto Press, 1930.

Janetski, Joel C. *Indians in Yellowstone National Park*. Salt Lake City: University of Utah Press, 2002.

Jang, Brent. "Allied tribes likely to reject Petronas project." *The Globe and Mail*, May 12, 2015. B8.

——. "B.C. First Nations Group unanimously opposes LNG Venture." *The Globe and Mail*, May 9, 2015. B1.

——. "Petronas exploring options to salvage LNG terminal plan." *The Globe and Mail*, May 14, 2015. A1.

Jowett, Peter. *Nahanni: The River Guide*. Calgary: Rocky Mountain Books, 1998.

Keith, Lloyd, ed. *North of Athabasca: Slave Lake and Mackenzie River Documents of the North West Company, 1800–1821*. Montreal: McGill-Queen's University Press, 2001.

Keller, Robert H., and Michael F. Turek. *American Indians and National Parks*. Tucson: University of Arizona Press, 1999.

Keough, Pat, and Rosemarie Keough. *The Nahanni Portfolio*. 2 vols. Don Mills, ON: Stoddart/ Nahanni Production, 1988.

King, Thomas. *The Inconvenient Indian: A Curious Account of Native People in North America*. Toronto: Anchor Canada, 2013.

Kino-nda-niimi Collective, ed. *The Winter We Danced: Voices from the Past, the Future, and the Idle No More Movement*. Winnipeg: ARP Books, 2014.

Kittinger, John N., Loren McClenachan, Keryn B. Gedan, and Louise K. Blight, eds. *Marine Historical Ecology in Conservation: Applying the Past to Manage for the Future*. Berkeley: University of California Press, 2015.

Komar, Debra. *The Bastard of Fort Stikine: The Hudson's Bay Company and the Murder of John McLoughlin Jr.* Fredericton, NB: Goose Lane Editions, 2015.

Krech III, Shepard. *The Ecological Indian: Myth and History.* New York: W.W. Norton & Company, 1999.

Kulchyski, Peter. *Aboriginal Rights Are Not Human Rights: In Defence of Indigenous Struggles.* Winnipeg: ARP Books, 2013.

——. "Getting Aboriginal Rights Right, Related Letters and Responses." *Literary Review of Canada* 21, no. 9 (2013): 32.

Lambert, H.F. Mines and Geology Branch, Department of Mines and Resources. Letter to Austin L. Cumming, Esq., Superintendent Mackenzie district, Lands, Parks and Forests Branch, Ottawa, RG85, Northern Affairs Program, Series C-1-a, Volume 876, Reel T-13366, File: 8861, Access Code 90: File title: Patrols, reports, etc. South Nahanni River and Flat River areas—also proposed game reserve C map and photos: outside Dates: 1936–1938. Finding Aid number 85-44, November 16, 1937.

Leopold, Aldo. *A Sand County Almanac: And Sketches Here and There.* New York: Oxford, 1949.

Little Grand Rapids First Nation and Ontario Ministry of Natural Resources. *Little Grand Rapids Community Based Land Use Plan.* Little Grand Rapids–Ontario Planning Area, Red Lake District: Ministry of Natural Resources and Little Grand Rapids, 2011.

Locke, Harvey, and Philip Dearden. "Rethinking protected areas categories and the new paradigm." *Environmental Conservation* 32, no. 1 (2005): 1–10.

Logan, Michael F. *The Lessening Stream: An Environmental History of the Santa Cruz River.* Tucson: The University of Arizona Press, 2002.

López-Hoffman, Laura, Emily D. McGovern, Robert G. Varady, and Karl W. Flessa, eds. *Conservation of Shared Environments: Learning from the United States and Mexico.* Tucson: The University of Arizona Press, 2009.

Lower, A.R.M. *The North American Assault on the Canadian Forest: A History of the Lumber Trade between Canada and the United States.* Toronto: Ryerson Press, 1938.

MacGregor, J.G. *The Klondike Rush through Edmonton, 1897–1898.* Toronto: McClelland & Stewart, 1970.

Mackie, Richard Somerset. *Trading beyond the Mountains: The British Fur Trade on the Pacific, 1793–1843.* Vancouver: UBC Press, 1997.

Madella, Marco, Carla Lancelotti, and Manon Savard, eds. *Ancient Plants and People: Contemporary Trends in Archaeobotany.* Tucson: University of Arizona Press, 2014.

Marsh, A.H., and G.W. Scotter. *Vegetation Survey and Development Recommendations for the Rabbitkettle Area, Nahanni National Park.* Edmonton: Canadian Wildlife Service, 1976.

Marsh, George Perkins. *Man and Nature; Or, Physical Geography as Modified by Human Action*. 1864. Reprint, edited by David Lowenthal. Cambridge, MA: Harvard University Press, 1965.

Marsh, John S., and Bruce W. Hodgins, eds. *Changing Parks: The History, Future and Cultural Context of Parks and Heritage Landscapes*. Toronto: Natural Heritage/Natural History Inc., 1998.

Martin, Paul S., and Christine Szuter. "Revising the 'Wild' West: Big Game Meets the Ultimate Keystone Species." In *The Archaeology of Global Change: The Impact of Humans on Their Environment*, edited by Charles L. Redman, Steven R. James, Paul R. Fish, and J. Daniel Rogers, 63–89. Washington, DC: Smithsonian Books, 2004.

Mason, Courtney W. *Spirits of the Rockies: Reasserting an Indigenous Presence in Banff National Park*. Toronto: University of Toronto Press, 2014.

Matthews, Owen. *Glorious Misadventures: Nikolai Rezanov and the Dream of a Russian America*. New York: Bloomsbury, 2013.

McCarty, Shawn. "Share revenue with aboriginal communities, report suggests." *The Globe and Mail*, March 4, 2015. B4.

McClellan, Catharine. *Part of the Land, Part of the Water: A History of the Yukon Indians*. Vancouver: Douglas & McIntyre, 1987.

McCloskey, Maxine E., and James P. Gilligan, eds. *Wilderness and the Quality of Life*. San Francisco: Sierra Club, 1969.

McGinnis, Michael Vincent, ed. *Bioregionalism*. London: Routledge, 1999.

McHarg, Ian L. *Design with Nature*. Philadelphia: Falcon Press, 1971.

Miller, Nathan. *Theodore Roosevelt: A Life*. New York: William Morrow, 1992.

Milton Freeman Research Limited. *The Inuit Land Use and Occupancy Project*. Vol. 1. Ottawa: Minister of Supply and Services Canada, 1976.

Mondor, Claude. *Areas of High Conservation Value Adjacent to Nahanni National Park Reserve*. Ottawa: Parks Canada, Park Establishment Branch, National Parks Directorate, 2001.

Moodie, D.W. "Gardening on Hudson's Bay: The First Century." *The Beaver* (Summer 1978): 54–59.

Moore, Joanne Ronan. *Nahanni Trailhead: A Year in the Northern Wilderness*. Surrey, BC: Hancock House Publishers, 2000.

Morris, Elizabeth A. "Prehistoric Game Drive Systems in the Rocky Mountains and High Plains Areas of Colorado." In *Hunters of the Recent Past*, edited by Leslie B. Davis and Brian O.K. Reeves, 195–203. London: Unwin Hyman, 1990.

Nahanni Butte Band. *Nah? ą Dehé: Traditional Harvesting Protocols—Nah? ą Dehé Keodi: taking care of Nah? ą Dehé*. Nahani Butte, NT: Nahanni Butte Band, n.d.

——. *Nahe Nahodhe is who we are and where we come from*. Nahanni Butte, NT: Nahanni Butte Band, n.d.

Nahanni Expansion Working Group. *Greater Nahanni Ecosystem Atlas.* Ottawa: Parks Canada, 2007.

Nahanni National Park Reserve of Canada. *Nah? ą Dehé: Report on Research and Monitoring.* Ottawa: Parks Canada, 2004–2005.

Nash, Roderick Frazier. *Wilderness and the American Mind.* New Haven: Yale University Press, 1967.

Nelson, J. G., ed. Inuit Tapirisat of Canada Renewable Resources Project. 12 vols. London and Waterloo: Universities of Western Ontario and Waterloo, 1975.

——. "Man and Landscape Change in Banff National Park: A National Park Problem in Perspective." In *The Canadian National Parks: Today and Tomorrow,* edited by J.G. Nelson and R.C. Scace, 111–150. Calgary: The National and Provincial Parks Association of Canada and the University of Calgary, 1969.

——. "Man and Landscape Change in Banff National Park: A National Park Problem in Perspective." In *Canadian Parks in Perspective,* edited by J.G. Nelson, with R.C. Scace, 63–97. Montreal: Harvest House, 1973.

——. *Man's Impact on the Western Canadian Landscape.* The Carleton Library. No. 90. Toronto: McClelland & Stewart, 1976.

——. "Research in Human Ecology and Planning: An Interactive, Adaptive Approach." *Canadian Geographer* 35, no. 2 (1991): 114–127.

Nelson, J.G., and A.R. Byrne. "Man as an Instrument of Landscape Change: Fire, Floods and National Parks in the Bow Valley, Alberta." *Geographical Review* LVI, no. 2 (1966): 226–238.

Nelson, J.G., and D.W. Hoffman, eds. "Sharing Heritage Management." *Environments* 17, no. 3 (1985): 1–145.

Nelson, J.G., and R.C. Scace, eds. *The Canadian National Parks: Today and Tomorrow.* 2 vols. Calgary: The National and Provincial Parks Association of Canada and the University of Calgary, 1969.

Nelson, J.G., with R.C. Scace, eds. *Canadian Parks in Perspective.* Montreal: Harvest House, 1970.

Nelson, J. Gordon, and Patrick L. Lawrence. *Places: Linking Nature and Culture for Understanding and Planning.* Calgary: University of Calgary Press, 2009.

Nelson, Richard K. *Hunters of the Northern Ice.* Chicago: University of Chicago Press, 1969.

——. *Make Prayers to the Raven: A Koyukon View of the Northern Forest.* Chicago: University of Chicago Press, 1983.

Nicholls, Steve. *Paradise Found: Nature in America at the Time of Discovery.* Chicago: Chicago University Press, 2009.

Office of the Auditor General of Canada. *Fall Report of the Commissioner of the Environment and Sustainable Development.* Ottawa, 2013. http://www.oag-bvg. gc.ca/internet/English/parl_cesd_201311_e_38658.html.

Olive, Andrea. *Land, Stewardship, and Legitimacy: Endangered Species Policy in Canada and the United States.* Toronto: University of Toronto Press, 2014.

Oved, Marco Chown. "To last, reconciliation must involve 'multiple voices.'" *The Toronto Star*, May 31, 2015. A6.

Parks Canada. "Glaciers." In *Nahanni National Park Reserve of Canada: Nah? ą Dehé State of the Park Report, 2009*, 37–40. Ottawa: Parks Canada, 2009.

——. *Nahanni National Park Ecological Statement.* Ottawa: Parks Canada, 2001.

——. *Nahanni National Park Reserve Management Plan.* Ottawa: Environment Canada, 1987.

——. *Nahanni National Park Reserve of Canada: Nah? ą Dehé Interim Park Management Arrangement.* Ottawa: Parks Canada, 2003.

——. *Nahanni National Park Reserve of Canada: Nah? ą Dehé Management Plan.* Ottawa: Parks Canada, 2004.

——. *Nahanni National Park Reserve of Canada: Nah? ą Dehé Management Plan.* Ottawa: Parks Canada, 2010a.

——. *Nahanni National Park Reserve of Canada: Nah? ą Dehé State of the Parks Report, 2009.* Ottawa: Parks Canada, 2009.

——. *Nahanni National Park Reserve Resource Description and Analysis.* Natural Resource Conservation Section. Parks Canada Prairie Region. Winnipeg: Parks Canada, 1984.

——. *Nah? ą Dehé: South Nahanni River Touring Guide. Nah? ą Dehé* Consensus Team. Ottawa: Parks Canada, 2011.

——. *Proposed Establishment of Nááts´ihch´oh National Park Reserve.* Yellowknife: Parks Canada, 2010b.

——. *Proposed Expansion of Nahanni National Park Reserve: Boundary Options.* Ottawa: Parks Canada, 2006.

——. *Taking Care of Nah? ą Dehé: A Proposal to Expand Nahanni National Park Reserve of Canada.* Ottawa: Parks Canada, 2006.

Parks Canada Agency. "'Unimpaired for Future Generations?' Protecting Ecological Integrity with Canada's National Parks." In *Report of the Panel on Ecological Integrity of Canada's National Parks.* Ottawa: Parks Canada, 2000.

Parks Canada and Deh Cho First Nations. *Memorandum of Understanding between Parks Canada and Deh Cho First Nations: Respecting the Expansion of Nahanni National Park Reserve of Canada.* Ottawa: Parks Canada, 2003.

Parnell, C. "Campbell of the Yukon: Part I." *The Beaver* (June 1942): 4–6.

Patterson, Raymond Murray. *The Dangerous River: Adventures on the Nahanni.* Erin, ON: Boston Mills Press, 1999).

Patterson, Raymond Murray. "The Nahany Lands." *The Beaver* (Summer 1961): 40–47.

Patterson, R.M. *Those Earlier Hills: Reminiscences 1928 to 1961.* Surrey, BC: TouchWood Editions, 2008.

Paupp, Terrence E. *Redefining Human Rights in the Struggle for Peace and Development*. New York: Cambridge University Press, 2014.

Peluso, Nancy Lee. "Fruit Trees and Family Trees in an Anthropogenic Forest: Property Zones, Resource Access, and Environmental Change in Indonesia." In *Culture and the Question of Rights: Forests, Coasts, and Seas in Southeast Asia*, edited by Charles Zerner, 184–218. Durham, NC: Duke University Press, 2003.

Phillips, Paul Chrysler. *The Fur Trade*. Vol. 2. Norman, OK: University of Oklahoma Press, 1961.

Piekielek, Jessica. "Cooperative Conservation, Unilateral Security: The Story of Two Sister Parks on the U.S.–Mexico Border." In *Conservation of Shared Environments: Learning from the United States and Mexico*, edited by Laura López-Hoffman, Emily D. McGovern, Robert G. Varady, and Karl W. Flessa, 213–225. Tucson: University of Arizona Press, 2009.

Pielou, E.C. *After the Ice Age: The Return of Life to Glaciated North America*. Chicago: University of Chicago Press, 1992.

Poirel, Jean. *Nahanni: La Vallée des Hommes Sans Tête*. Montreal: Stanké, 1980.

Porter, James, and J. Gordon Nelson, eds. "Ecological Integrity and Protected Areas." In *Parks Research Forum of Ontario (PRFO)*. Waterloo, ON: Heritage Resources Centre, University of Waterloo, 2001.

Raffan, James. *Emperor of the North: Sir George Simpson and the Remarkable Story of the Hudson's Bay Company*. Toronto: HarperCollins, 2007.

Ray, Arthur J. "Smallpox: The Epidemic of 1837–38." *The Beaver* (Autumn 1975): 7–13.

Redman, Charles L., Steven R. James, Paul R. Fish, and J. Daniel Rogers, eds. *The Archaeology of Global Change: The Impact of Humans on Their Environment*. Washington, DC: Smithsonian Books, 2004.

Reeves, Brian O.K. "Communal bison hunters of the Northern Plains." In *Hunters of the Recent Past*, edited by Leslie B. Davis and Brian O.K. Reeves, 168–194. London: Unwin Hyman, 1990.

Rich, E.E., ed. *A Journal of a Voyage from Rocky Mountain Portage in Peace River to the Sources of Finlay's Branch and North West Ward in Summer 1824*. London: Hudson's Bay Record Society, 1955.

Riley, John L. *The Once and Future Great Lakes Country: An Ecological History*. Montreal: McGill-Queen's University Press, 2014.

Robbins, Jim. "Paying Farmers to Welcome Birds." *New York Times*, April 14, 2014. http://www.nytimes.com/2014/04/15/science/paying-farmers-to-welcome-birds.html.

Rothenberg, David. "Introduction." In *The World and the Wild*, edited by David Rothenberg and Marta Ulvaeus, xi–xxiii. Tucson: The University of Arizona Press, 2001.

Runte, Alfred. *National Parks: The American Experience.* 2nd Edition Revised. Lincoln: University of Nebraska Press, 1987.

Sadler, Barry, ed. *Involvement and Environment.* Edmonton: Environmental Council of Alberta, 1977.

Sandlos, John. *Hunters at the Margin: Native People and Wildlife Conservation in the Northwest Territories.* Vancouver: UBC Press, 2007.

Sarkar, Sahotra. "Restoring wilderness or reclaiming forests?" In *The World and the Wild,* edited by David Rothenberg and Marta Ulvaeus, 38–55. Tucson: University of Arizona Press, 2001.

Sauer, Carl Ortwin. *The Early Spanish Main.* London: Cambridge University Press, 1966.

Saul, John Ralston. *The Comeback: How Aboriginals Are Reclaiming Power and Influence.* Toronto: Penguin Books, 2014.

Savage, Candace. *Prairie: A Natural History.* 2nd Edition. Vancouver: Greystone Books, 2011.

Scace, Robert. *Exploration, Settlement and Land Use Activities in Northern Canada: Historical Review.* Inuit Tapirisat of Canada Renewable Resources Project, edited by J. G. Nelson, Volume 1. London and Waterloo: Universities of Western Ontario and Waterloo, 1975.

Schama, Simon. *Landscape and Memory.* New York: Knopf, 1995.

Schroeder, J. "Les formes de glaces des grottes de la Nahanni, Territoires du Nord-Ouest, Canada." *Canadian Journal of Earth Sciences* 14, no. 5 (1977): 1179–1185.

Schwartz, William, ed. *Voices for the Wilderness.* New York: Ballantine Books, 1969.

Scotter, G.W. "Distribution of Pine (*Pinus* spp.) in the South Nahanni and Flat Rivers Region, Northwest Territories." *Canadian Journal of Forest Research* 4, no. 4 (1974): 555–557.

——. "White-tailed Deer and Mule Deer Observations in Southwestern District of Mackenzie, Northwest Territories." *Canadian Field-Naturalist* 88 (1974): 487–489.

Scotter, G.W., L.N. Carbyn, W.P. Neily, and J.D. Henry. "Birds of Nahanni National Park, Northwest Territories," Special Publications No. 15. Regina: Saskatchewan Natural History Society, 1985.

Scotter, G.W., and J.D. Henry, *Vegetation, Wildlife and Recreational Assessment of Deadmen Valley. Nahanni National Park.* Edmonton: Canadian Wildlife Service, 1977.

Scotter, G.W., and H.M. Kershaw. *Vegetation of Deadmen Valley, Nahanni National Park.* Edmonton: Canadian Wildlife Service, 1978.

Scotter, G.W., and N.M. Simmons. "Mortality of Dall's sheep (*Ovis dalli*) within a cave, Nahanni National Park, Northwest Territories." *Journal of Mammalogy* 57, no. 2 (1976): 387–389.

Scotter, G.W., and N.M. Simmons. "Park or Power?" *Parks News* 8, no. 1 (1972): 8–12.

Scotter, G.W., N.M. Simmons, H.L. Simmons, and S.C. Zoltai. "Ecology of the South Nahanni and Flat River Areas." Unpublished report. Edmonton: Canadian Wildlife Service, 1971.

Smith, Joanna. "A need to engage non-aboriginals in healing process." *The Toronto Star*, May 31, 2015. A6.

Snyder, Harry. Letter to R.A. Gibson, Deputy Commissioner, Department of Northwest Territories, RG 85, Northern Affairs Program, Series C-1-a, Volume 905, Reel T-13919, File: 10377. File title S.P. Peterson—Northwest Game Act—big game hunting, Nahanni river Area Outside Dates: 1939. Finding Aid number: 85-44, October 10, 1939.

Sörlin, Sverker, and Paul Warde, eds. *Nature's End: History and the Environment.* New York: Palgrave Macmillan, 2011.

Soulé, M.E., and B.A. Wilcox. *Conservation Biology: An Evolutionary–Ecological Perspective.* Sunderland, MA: Sinauer Associates, 1980.

Stager, John K. "Fur Trading Posts in the Mackenzie Region up to 1850." In *Canada's Changing North*, edited by William C. Wonders, 50–58. Toronto: McClelland & Stewart, 1971.

Stains, G.S. "Collaborative Park Planning in a Municipal Landscape: The Rouge Park in Ontario." In *Managing Protected Areas in a Changing World: Proceedings of the Fourth International Conference on Science and Management of Protected Areas, 14–19 May 2000*, edited by S. Bondrup-Nielson, N.W.P. Munro, G. Nelson, J.H.M. Willison, T.B. Herman, and P. Eagles, 790–802. Wolfville, NS: Science and Management of Protected Areas Association, 2002.

Stanford, Dennis J., and Jane Stevenson Day, eds. *Ice Age Hunters of the Rockies.* Denver: Denver Museum of Natural History and University Press of Colorado, 1992.

Steiner, Frederick. *Human Ecology: Following Nature's Lead.* Washington, DC: Island Press, 2002.

Stoddard, Natalie B. "Some Ethnological Aspects of the Russian Fur Trade." In *People and Pelts: Selected Papers of the Second North American Fur Trade Conference*, edited by Malvina Bolus, 39–58. Winnipeg: Peguis Publishers, 1972.

Theberge, John, and Mary Theberge. *The Ptarmigan's Dilemma: An Exploration into How Life Organizes and Supports Itself.* Toronto: McClelland & Stewart, 2010.

Thomas, Jr., William L., ed. *Man's Role in Changing the Face of the Earth.* Chicago: University of Chicago Press, 1956.

Trimble, Stephen. *The People: Indians of the American Southwest.* Santa Fe, NM: School of American Research Press, 1993.

Tsilhqot´in Nation v British Columbia, 2014 SCC 44, [2014] 2 SCR 257.

Turner, Chris. *The War on Science: Muzzled Scientists and Wilful Blindness in Stephen Harper's Canada.* Vancouver: Greystone Books, 2013.

Turner, Dick. *Nahanni.* Saanich, BC: Hancock House Publishers, 1975.

Walters, Carl. *Adaptive Management of Renewable Resources.* New York: Macmillan, 1986.

Weaver, John L. *Big Animals and Small Parks: Implications of Wildlife Distribution and Movements for Expansion of Nahanni National Park Reserve.* Conservation Report No. 1. Toronto: Wildlife Conservation Society Canada, 2006.

——. *Conserving Caribou Landscapes in the Nahanni Trans-Border Region: Using Fidelity to Seasonal Ranges and Migration Routes.* Wildlife Conservation Report No. 4. Toronto: Wildlife Conservation Society Canada, 2008.

Weber, Bob. "Scientist says lake falling off cliff is not a unique situation." *The Globe and Mail*, July 13, 2015. A11.

Wein, Joan. *Back Door to the Klondike.* Erin, ON: Boston Mills Press, 1988.

Williams, Peter W., J.C. Day, and Thomas I. Gunton. "Land and Water Planning in British Columbia in the 1990s: Lessons on More Inclusive Approaches." *Environments: A Journal of Interdisciplinary Studies* 25, nos. 2 and 3 (1998): 1–7.

Wilson, Clifford. *Campbell of the Yukon.* Toronto: Macmillan, 1970.

Wilson, E.O., and F.M. Peter, eds. *Biodiversity.* Washington, DC: National Academy Press, 1988.

Wohlberg, Meagan. "Mining holds empty promises for Northerners." *Northern Journal*, April 15, 2013. https://norj.ca/2013/04/mining-holds-empty-promises-for-northerners/.

Woodley, Stephen, James Kay, and George Francis, eds. *Ecological Integrity and the Management of Ecosystems.* Delray Beach, FL: St. Lucie Press, 1993.

Worster, Donald. *The Ends of the Earth: Perspectives on Modern Environmental History.* Cambridge: Cambridge University Press, 1988.

Wright, D.F., D. Lemkow, and J.R. Harris, eds. *Mineral and Energy Resource Assessment of the Greater Nahanni Ecosystem Under Consideration for the Expansion of the Nahanni National Park Reserve, Northwest Territories.* Ottawa: Natural Resources Canada, 2007.

Zamora-Arroyo, Francisco, and Karl W. Flessa. "Nature's Fair Share: Finding and Allocating Water for the Colorado River Delta." In *Conservation of Shared Environments: Learning from the United States and Mexico*, edited by Laura López-Hoffman, Emily D. McGovern, Robert G. Varady, and Karl W. Flessa, 23–38. Tucson: University of Arizona Press, 2009.

Zerner, Charles, ed. *Culture and the Question of Rights: Forests, Coasts, and Seas in Southeast Asia.* Durham, NC: Duke University Press, 2003.

Permissions Acknowledgements

Thanks to Parks Canada and individual photographers—Bill Caulfeild-Browne, Derek Ford, Wendy Francis, Harvey Locke, Fritz Mueller, George Scotter, Norman Simmons, Dorothy Stearns, and Alison Woodley—for granting permission to use their images. Photo credits are included in the captions in the full-colour insert.

Figure 1.1 is adapted from John L. Weaver, *Big Animals and Small Parks: Implications of Wildlife Distribution and Movements for Expansion of Nahanni National Park Reserve*, Conservation Report No. 1 (Toronto: Wildlife Conservation Society Canada, 2006); **Figure 3.1** is adapted from Weaver, *Big Animals and Small Parks* (2006) and John L. Weaver, *Conserving Caribou Landscapes in the Nahanni Trans-Border Region: Using Fidelity to Seasonal Ranges and Migration Routes*, Wildlife Conservation Report No. 4 (Toronto: Wildlife Conservation Society Canada, 2008). Used with the permission of John L. Weaver.

Figures 1.3 and **1.4** are adapted from Fenley Hunter, *That Summer on the Nahanni 1928: The Journals of Fenley Hunter* (Ottawa: McGahern Stewart Publishing, 2015). Used with the permission of McGahern Stewart Publishing.

Figures 2.1, 2.5, and **2.6** are adapted from *Nahanni National Park Reserve Resource Description and Analysis*, Natural Resource

Conservation Section, Parks Canada Prairie Region (Winnipeg: Parks Canada, 1984); **Figure 2.7** is adapted from *Nah?ą Dehe: South Nahanni River Touring Guide. Nah?ą* Dehe Consensus Team (Ottawa: Parks Canada, 2011); **Figure 3.2** is adapted from *Nahanni National Park Reserve of Canada: Nah?ą Dehe State of the Parks Report, 2009* (Ottawa: Parks Canada, 2009); and **Figure 8.1** and **Table 8.1** are adapted from *Proposed Establishment of Naats´ihch´oh National Park Reserve* (Yellowknife: Parks Canada, 2010). All are used with the permission of Parks Canada.

Figures 2.2 and **2.3** are adapted from maps by Derek Ford in R. Neil Hartling, *Nahanni: River of Gold ... River of Dreams* (Merrickville, ON: Canadian Recreational Canoeing Association, 1998). **Figure 2.4** is adapted from Derek Ford, "Antecedent Canyons of the South Nahanni River, Mackenzie Mountains, N.W.T.," *The Canadian Geographer* 35, no. 4 (1991): 426–431. Used with the permission of Derek Ford.

Figure 4.1 is adapted from John K. Stager, "Fur Trading Posts in the Mackenzie Region up to 1850," in *Canada's Changing North*, edited by William C. Wonders, 50–58 (Toronto: McClelland & Stewart, 1971. Used with the permission of John Stager.

Figure 4.2 is adapted from Raymond Murray Patterson, "The Nahany Lands," *The Beaver* (Summer 1961): 40–47. Used with the permission of *The Beaver* magazine (now *Canada's History*).

Figure 7.1 is adapted from the map originally researched and prepared by Robert C. Scace and published in Robert C. Scace, *Exploration, Settlement and Land Use Activities in Northern Canada: Historical Review,* Inuit Tapirisat of Canada Renewable Resources Project, Volume 1 (London and Waterloo: Universities of Western Ontario and Waterloo, 1975); and in Constance Hunt, "The Development and Decline of Northern Conservation Reserves," *Contact* 8, no. 4 (1976), 30-75. Used with the permission of R.C. Scace.

Table 9.1 is adapted from Jose F. Bernal Stoopen, Jane M. Packard, and Richard Reading, "Mexican Wolf Recovery: Insights from Transboundary Stakeholders, " in *Conservation of Shared Environments: Learning from the United States and Mexico*, edited by Laura Lopez-Hoffman, Emily D. McGovern, Robert G. Varady, and Karl W. Flessa, 115–132 (Tucson: University of Arizona Press, 2009). Used with permission.

Index

Page references in *italic* indicate figures; page references in **bold** indicate tables.

prospects, 76; on Indigenous hunting, 77; journals of, 75, 76; personality, 75; reports on "Nahanni people," 80–81; on wild fires, 82–83

Blyth, Chuck, 5, 52, 53

Brody, Hugh, xxii, 126

Brower, David, 17

Butzer, Karl, 180

C

Cadillac Explorations, 132

Cafaro, Philip, 161

California co-operative conservation project, 162

California gold rush, 101

Campbell, Robert: building of Fort Selkirk, 102; encounters with Russians, 98; expeditions, 13, 94, 97; meetings with Nahanni, 94, 98, 143; references to, 85

Canadian National Heritage River, 41

Canadian Parks and Wilderness Society (CPAWS): big wilderness approach, 53; campaign for Nahanni Reserve, 41, 184; concerns of mining impact, 134, 136–37; funding, 163; national tour, 54; public communications, 23, 165

Canadian Tungsten Mining Corporation, 106

Canadian Wildlife Service (CWS), 24, 26–28, 163

Canadian Zinc Inc., 132–35

Canadian Zinc's mine on the Prairie Creek, plate 30

caribou: Kaska hunting of, 99; Patterson's observations of, 10; photograph, plate 23; population, 125; research on, 44–46; seasonal distribution and movements, 45; tracking methods, 45

Carnivore Way, The (Eisenberg), 47

Cat Lake–Slate Falls, 171

caves, 31, 144

Chow, Olivia, 54

Circle on Philanthropy and Aboriginal Peoples, 174

Clearing the Plains (Daschuk), 69, 70

climate change, 39–40, 147–48

Colpitts, George, 144

Comeback, The (Saul), 174

conservation biology, 44

conservation history, 179

Cook, James, 81

Cooke, Alan, 74

co-operative projects along USA–Mexico border, 162–63

Cossacks, 95

Crosby, Alfred, 81

"cultural genocide," 174

Cummings, Vicki, 152

D

Dall's sheep: habitat, 132; photographs, plates 21–22, plate 24; population, 125; remains of, plate 25; studies of, 46; as trophy animals, 110

Dangerous River, The (Patterson), xix, 7, 14, 17

Daschuk, James, 69, 70, 71

Dasiqox Tribal Park, 169

Davis, Richard, 5, 7

Deadmen Valley, 15, 38, 108, 114, plate 15, plate 17

Dehcho First Nations: collaboration with Park Canada, 56, 58, 165; CPAWS' relationship with, 53; habitat, 50; harvesting protocols, 60–62; mining project and, 135; organization of students' tours, 56; research projects, 166; vision for traditional lands, 57

G

game regulations, 124, 125
geology and land forms, 33–38
Gibson, James R., 96
Gibson, R. A., 22, 122
Gila National Forest, 158
Gillespie, Beryl, 142, 143
glaciation, 32–33
gold discovery and exploration, 105–6, 108–9
Gough, Barry, 68
Graham, Bill, 5
Grassy Narrows First Nation v. Ontario, 169
grizzly bear study, 44
Gross, Catherine, 172
Grotte Valerie, plate 25
Gwaii Haanas National Park Reserve, 153

H

Handbook of North American Indians (Gillespie), 142
Harper, Stephen, 54, 170
Harrison, Mount, plate 2
Hartling, Neil, 4, 52, 53, 141
Hayes, Andrew, 103
Headless Creek, 38
Headless Range (Second Canyon), 37–38
Henderson, Gavin, 27
Hetch Hetchy Dam, 17
Holland, Clive, 74
Hudson's Bay Company (HBC): amalgamation with Northwesters, 74; archives, 84–85; board of governors, 102; conservation policies, 119; encounters with Indigenous people, 94; expeditions to Nahanni country, 74, 90–91; exploration of fur grounds, 102; forts, xxi; fur trade, xx–xxi, 66; growth of competition, 73; negotiations with the Russians, 97–98; opposition to mining, 101; profit, 79
Hughes, J. Donald, 79
human ecology, 180–81
Human Ecology: Following Nature's Lead (Steiner), 180
Hunter, Fenley: hunting and fishing, 15; journal of Nahanni trip, 14–15, 17; map of Nahanni River, 16, 37; meeting with Patterson, 13; observations of wildlife, xxi, 15; travel routes, 13–14, 14
Hunters at the Margin (Sandlos), 124

I

Inconvenient Indian, The (King), 168
Indigenous people: archaeological sites, 146; assimilation policy, 167; attitude toward animals, 79, 80; buffer zones, 143–44; calls for reconciliation with, 19, 174; concept of unilinear development, 152; conflicts between, 143–44; conservation ethic of, 126, 128; control of wildlife, 125–26; cooperation between, 144; diseases and outbreaks, 69–70, 71–72, 82; diversity of, 174–75; early trade of, 95; ecological integrity and, 50, 138, 141; economic changes and, 108; game regulations and, 124; hunting, 31, 77, 78, 82, 145–46; identity of, 138, 141–43; interaction with nature, 144; land claims settlements, 56; lifestyle, 151–52; migration, 147–48; mining and industrial projects and, 151, 152; mountain people, 141–42; Nahanni Reserve expansion and, 185; newcomers and, 10; North

American ecosystem and, 18; nutrition, 82; oral histories, 99; reconciliation process, 19; relations with national parks, 150, 166; resource revenue sharing, 170; separations among, 98; territories inhabited by, 18; tourism benefits for, 167; trade with Russians, 94; Traditional Ecological Knowledge (TEK) of, 51; treaties with Canadian government, 154–55; in the United States, 159, 167. *See also* Dehcho First Nations; Dene people; Finlay River people; Koyukon people; Nahanni people; Sheepeaters

intact wildlands / ecosystems, 47

interactive planning, 51–52

Interim Park Management Arrangement (2003), 59–60

Inuvialuit Agreement (1984), 56

J

Jorgenson, Martin, 105

Journal of Forestry, 158

Jowett, Peter, 5

justice in environmental decision-making, 172–73

K

Karst terrain, 21–22, *plate 26, plate 28*

Kaska people, 99, 125, 143

Keele, J., 105

Keele's report on reconnaissance across Mackenzie Mountains, 141

Keller, Robert H., 166, 167

Keough, Rosemarie, 5

King, Thomas, 168

Klondike gold rush, 103, 104–5

Klondike: The Last Great Gold Rush (Berton), 11

Koyukon ecosystem, 127–28

Koyukon people, 80, 126

Kraus, Gus, 38, 105, 113, *plate 19*

Kraus, Mary, 113, *plate 19*

Krech, Shepard, 69, 70

L

Land, Stewardship, and Legitimacy (Olive), 173

Land Claims Agreements Coalition, 155

landscape ecology, 43

landscape studies, 178–79

Lax Kw'alaams: opposition to LNG terminal construction, 152

Layton, Jack, 54

Leopold, Aldo, xxiii, 157, 158–60

Liard lowlands, *plate 20*

Liard River fur trade posts, 66

life zones, 28–29, 48

Literary Review of Canada (Fenge and Penikett), 154

Little Grand Rapids Community Based Land Use Plan, 171

Little Grand Rapids planning, 171

Little Ice Age, 65, 70

Locke, Harvey, xii, 52, 54

Long and Terrible Shadow, A (Berger), 151

M

MacBrien, Mount, *plate 5*

MacGregor, J.G., 103

Mackenzie, Alexander, 66, 68, 69

Mackenzie Mountains Game Preserve, 121, 123, 124

Mackenzie River, 72

Trudeau's trip to, 40–41; public communications, **23**; public opinion poll on protection of, 136; recommendations to establish, 22, 24; as research centre, 149–50; research methodology, 181; research on wildlife, 44–46, 185; simplified ecosystem model, 56, 57; sources of research, 177–81; tourism control, 116; UNESCO recommendations on, 135–36; value of, 148, 149; wilderness protection, 48–49

Nahanni National Park Reserve Resource Description and Analysis, 28

Nahanni people: clothing, 80; descriptions of, 6–7; fur traders and, 73; history of, 141–43; meeting with McLeod's group, 86–88, 87; origin of name, 143; trade activities, 74, 81, 87, 91, 94. *See also* Kaska people

Nahanni Plateau (First Canyon), 37, 38, *plate 18*

Nahanni River: Braided channels or Splits, *plate 20*; discharge, 34, 38, 39; ecosystem, xix–xx; expeditions, 121–22; glaciers, 33, 33–34, 39; natural wonders, xvii–xviii, xviii–xix, 3; photographs of, *plate 4, plate 9, plate 13, plate 18*; raft and canoe expeditions, 39; research agenda, xviii–xxiii

Nahanni River Adventures: collaboration with CPAWS, 54; expansion activities, 54, **55**; expeditions, 52; funding, 163; protection of Nahanni River, 53; public communications, 54, **55**, 165

Nahanni: River of Gold ... River of Dreams (Hartling), 141

Nahanni River Outfitters Association, 52

Nahanni Trailhead (Moore), 116

Nahanni Valley: biological surveys, 24, 31; bird population, 30; camp sites, 114–15; Canadian Wildlife Service's report on, 26–27; comparative perspective, xxiii; descriptions, 5–6, 9–10, 115–16; earth tremors and quakes, 40; ecological integrity, 117–18, 125, 137–38, 141; economic activities, 99; effects of human activity, 28, 125; elevations, 36; environmental concerns, 24, 111–12; exploration and mapping, 105; extend of wild fires, 83, 111; fauna, 30–31; food shortage, 118; fur trade, xxi, 117; geology, 36; geomorphic wealth, 33–34; gold discovery and mining, xxi–xxi, 103–4, 105–6; history, xviii; human activities, 115–16; hunting, xxii, 119, 120; impact of Yukon gold rush on, 118; Indigenous groups in, 148; journeys into, 110; maps, 16, 32, 36; mineral exploration, 119, 184; Moore's observations of, 115; moose population, 49–50; photograph of camping site, *plate 16*; plant diversity, 30; prospects of archaeological research, 147; publications on, 4–5, 22–24; research on caves and karst, 31–32; sources of research, 177–81; tales and legends of, 10; topography, xvii, 3–4, 5–6, 32, 118; wildlife protection, 22, 122–23

"Nahany Lands, The" (Patterson), 84

Nahʔą Dehé Consensus Team, 57, 165

National and Provincial Parks Association, 25

National Park Act, 47

national park reserve concept, 184

national parks: assessment of ecological integrity, 153–54; as centres of learning, 149; co-operative planning and management, 41, 167; federal policies, 25, 153; Indigenous people and, 150, 153, 166–67

nature-culture interactions, 180

Nature's End, 179

About the Author

J AMES GORDON NELSON is a distinguished professor emeritus at the University of Waterloo. He has done research and applied work on planning, conservation, and national parks since the mid-1960s. His active interest in the Nahanni River and the North extends back to the early 1970s. He has published numerous papers, reports, and books in the broad fields of land use, environment, and planning. He is especially interested in the historical interactions between humans and the environment. He has published over two hundred scholarly papers and articles. His books include *Man's Impact on the Western Canadian Landscape* (1976), *National Parks and Protected Areas: Keystones to Conservation and Sustainable Development* (1997), *Protected Areas and the Regional Planning Imperative in North America* (2003), *Places: Linking Nature and Culture for Understanding and Planning* (2009), and *Beyond the Global City: Understanding and Planning for the Diversity of Ontario* (2012).

The Magnificent Nahanni is based on close to fifty years of research, education, and practice in the interrelated fields of national parks and protected areas, conservation, land use, environmental history, and planning. This work began with the launching of national park master planning in the 1960s and a series of new national parks in Canada in the early 1970s, including the Nahanni, which he has followed ever since. He has continued to do research and educational work up to the present, serving as a board member for academic organizations such as the Canadian Association of Geographers and the Association of Canadian Universities for Northern Studies, as well as a board member, consultant, and contributor to government and nongovernmental organizations such as the Heritage Canada Foundation, the Canadian Parks and Wilderness Society, the Public Advisory Committee of Bruce National Park, the Bruce Sources of Knowledge Forum, the Carolinian Canada Coalition, and the Ontario Parks Board of Directors. He has done considerable work in the North, notably in the 1970s and 1980s, for example serving as a renewable resource consultant for the Inuit Tapirisat of Canada in its first land claim. He has field experience in the United States, England, Eastern Europe, Indonesia, New Zealand, and other countries. His work has been recognized by a number of organizations, including the Canadian Association of Geographers (Award for Scholarly Distinction in Geography), the Royal Canadian Geographical Society (Massey Medal), the federal government (Natural Heritage Award), and the Canadian Parks and Wilderness Society (Harkin Medal). He has degrees from McMaster University, University of Colorado, and Johns Hopkins University. He has been a faculty member at University of Calgary, University of Western Ontario, and University of Waterloo.